PRINCIPLES OF DATA MANAGEMENT

BCS, THE CHARTERED INSTITUTE FOR IT

BCS, The Chartered Institute for IT champions the global IT profession and the interests of individuals engaged in that profession for the benefit of all. We promote wider social and economic progress through the advancement of information technology science and practice. We bring together industry, academics, practitioners and government to share knowledge, promote new thinking, inform the design of new curricula, shape public policy and inform the public.

Our vision is to be a world-class organisation for IT. Our 70,000 strong membership includes practitioners, businesses, academics and students in the UK and internationally. We deliver a range of professional development tools for practitioners and employees. A leading IT qualification body, we offer a range of widely recognised qualifications.

Further Information
BCS, The Chartered Institute for IT,
First Floor, Block D,
North Star House, North Star Avenue,
Swindon, SN2 1FA, United Kingdom.
T +44 (0) 1793 417 424
F +44 (0) 1793 417 444
www.bcs.org/contact

PRINCIPLES OF DATA MANAGEMENT
FACILITATING INFORMATION SHARING
Second edition

Keith Gordon

bcs
The Chartered
Institute
for IT

Published by BCS Learning and Development Ltd, a wholly owned subsidiary of BCS, The Chartered Institute for IT, First Floor, Block D, North Star House, North Star Avenue, Swindon, SN2 1FA, UK.
www.bcs.org

Paperback ISBN: 978-1-78017-184-5
PDF ISBN: 978-1-78017-185-2
ePUB ISBN: 978-1-78017-186-9
Kindle ISBN: 978-1-78017-187-6

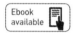
Ebook available

British Cataloguing in Publication Data.
A CIP catalogue record for this book is available at the British Library.

Typeset by Lapiz Digital Services, Chennai, India.
Printed by Hobbs the Printers Ltd, Totton, Hampshire SO40 3WX.

There is nothing more difficult to take in hand, more perilous to conduct, or more uncertain in its success, than to take the lead in the introduction of a new order of things.

Niccolo Machiavelli (1469–1527)

The beginning of wisdom is the definition of terms.

Socrates (470–399 BC)

Data analysis is a very useful tool for efficient database design. It is much less useful as a means of identifying information requirements (especially where these are 'fuzzy' and unstructured), or in allowing different viewpoints to be taken into consideration. Too often based on an analysis of current situations, data analysis – in the extreme case – is a great way of encapsulating organisational ineffectiveness in the resultant database!

Professor Robert Galliers (1947–)

CONTENTS

List of figures and tables	xi
Author	xiv
Foreword to the first edition	xv
Glossary	xvii
Preface	xxii
Introduction	xxv

PART 1: PRELIMINARIES · 1

1.	**DATA AND THE ENTERPRISE**	3
	Information is a key business resource	3
	The relationship between information and data	4
	The importance of the quality of data	6
	The common problems with data	7
	An enterprise-wide view of data	9
	Managing data is a business issue	10
	Summary	11

2.	**DATABASE DEVELOPMENT**	12
	The database architecture of an information system	12
	An overview of the database development process	17
	Conceptual data modelling (from a project-level perspective)	22
	Relational data analysis	39
	The roles of a data model	51
	Physical database design	52
	Summary	55

3.	**WHAT IS DATA MANAGEMENT?**	57
	The problems encountered without data management	57
	Data management responsibilities	59
	Data management activities	60
	Roles within data management	63
	The benefits of data management	64
	The relationship between data management and enterprise architecture	65
	Summary	66

PART 2: DATA ADMINISTRATION   **67**

4.   **CORPORATE DATA MODELLING**   **69**
       Why develop a corporate data model?   69
       The nature of a corporate data model   70
       How to develop a corporate data model   72
       Corporate data model principles   74
       Summary   78

5.   **DATA DEFINITION AND NAMING**   **80**
       The elements of a data definition   80
       Data naming conventions   84
       Summary   86

6.   **METADATA**   **87**
       What is metadata?   87
       Metadata for data management   87
       Metadata for content management   88
       Metadata for describing data values   89
       Summary   90

7.   **DATA QUALITY**   **91**
       What is data quality?   91
       Issues associated with poor data quality   91
       The causes of poor data quality   92
       The dimensions of data quality   93
       Data model quality   94
       Improving data quality   95
       Summary   98

8.   **DATA ACCESSIBILITY**   **99**
       Data security   99
       Data integrity   104
       Data recovery   106
       Summary   108

9.   **MASTER DATA MANAGEMENT**   **109**
       What is master data?   109
       How do problems with master data occur?   112
       How do we manage master data?   112
       Summary   114

PART 3: DATABASE AND REPOSITORY ADMINISTRATION   **115**

10.   **DATABASE ADMINISTRATION**   **117**
       Database administration responsibilities   117
       Performance monitoring and tuning   119
       Summary   120

11.	REPOSITORY ADMINISTRATION	**121**
	Repositories, data dictionaries, encyclopaedias, catalogs and directories	121
	Repository features	124
	The repository as a centralised source of information	126
	Metadata models	127
	Summary	127

| | PART 4: THE DATA MANAGEMENT ENVIRONMENT | **129** |

12.	THE USE OF PACKAGED APPLICATION SOFTWARE	**131**
	What are application software packages?	131
	The impact on data management	131
	Summary	133

13.	DISTRIBUTED DATA AND DATABASES	**134**
	The rationale for distributing data	134
	The perfect distributed database system?	135
	Top-down fragmentation and partitioning	136
	Bottom-up integration	137
	The management of replication	139
	Summary	140

14.	BUSINESS INTELLIGENCE	**141**
	Data warehousing	141
	The multidimensional model of data	143
	Standard reporting tools	144
	Online analytical processing (OLAP)	144
	Data mining	145
	A relational schema for a data warehouse	146
	Summary	148

15.	OBJECT ORIENTATION	**149**
	What is object orientation?	149
	The fundamental concepts of object orientation	150
	Object oriented databases	151
	Object-relational databases	153
	Summary	156

16.	MULTIMEDIA	**158**
	What is multimedia?	158
	Storing multimedia outside a database	158
	Storing multimedia inside a database	159
	Storing multimedia using special packages	160
	Summary	160

17.	WEB TECHNOLOGY	**161**
	The internet and the web	161
	The architecture of the web	162
	XML and databases	163
	Other ways to link databases into web technology	164

Dealing with the large quantities of data generated over the web   165
The semantic web   167
Summary   169

APPENDICES   **171**

APPENDIX A COMPARISON OF DATA MODELLING NOTATIONS   **173**

APPENDIX B HIERARCHICAL AND NETWORK DATABASES   **183**

APPENDIX C GENERIC DATA MODELS   **191**

APPENDIX D AN EXAMPLE OF A DATA NAMING CONVENTION   **195**

APPENDIX E METADATA MODELS   **206**

APPENDIX F A DATA MINING EXAMPLE   **212**

APPENDIX G HTML AND XML   **218**

APPENDIX H XML AND RELATIONAL DATABASES   **225**

APPENDIX I TECHNIQUES AND SKILLS FOR DATA MANAGEMENT   **233**

APPENDIX J INTERNATIONAL STANDARDS FOR DATA MANAGEMENT   **236**

APPENDIX K BIBLIOGRAPHY   **239**

Index   243

LIST OF FIGURES AND TABLES

Figure 1.1	The relationship between data and information	6
Figure 2.1	A model of a database system	13
Figure 2.2	The three-level schema architecture	16
Figure 2.3	A simplified view of the database development process	18
Figure 2.4	A conceptual data model diagram	20
Figure 2.5	A portion of an SQL create script	21
Figure 2.6	The EMPLOYEE entity type	23
Figure 2.7	The attributes of the EMPLOYEE entity type	23
Figure 2.8	The PROPERTY entity type	24
Figure 2.9	The 'resident at' relationship	25
Figure 2.10	Splitting the EMPLOYEE entity type	27
Figure 2.11	The QUALIFICATION and PERSON QUALIFICATION entity types	28
Figure 2.12	The GRADE and EMPLOYEE GRADE entity types	29
Figure 2.13	The DEPARTMENT and ASSIGNMENT entity types	30
Figure 2.14	The one-to-one 'managed by' relationship	31
Figure 2.15	The many-to-many 'managed by' relationship	32
Figure 2.16	The resolution of the many-to-many 'managed by' relationship	33
Figure 2.17	Adding entity subtypes	34
Figure 2.18	Adding an exclusive arc	36
Figure 2.19	The PERSON NEXT OF KIN entity type	38
Figure 2.20	A relation shown as a table	40
Figure 2.21	The human resources paper record	42
Figure 2.22	The 'data items' identified from the human resources paper record	43
Figure 2.23	The first normal form relations	44
Figure 2.24	The second normal form relations	47
Figure 2.25	The third normal form relations	48
Figure 2.26	The employee interview relation	49
Figure 2.27	The equivalent Boyce–Codd normal form relations	50
Figure 3.1	Data management activities	61
Figure 3.2	Data management deliverables	62
Figure 3.3	The relationship between data management and information management	63
Figure 4.1	The 'supply chain' model	75
Figure 4.2	The improved 'supply chain' model	76
Figure 4.3	More than one type of support?	76
Figure 4.4	The combined support model	77

Figure 4.5	The generic 'unit' model	77
Figure 5.1	A data definition with validation criteria and valid operations	83
Figure 5.2	A data definition with valid values	83
Figure 5.3	An entity type definition	84
Figure 7.1	The dimensions of data quality	94
Figure 7.2	The five dimensions of data model quality	95
Figure 7.3	Total Quality data Management methodology	96
Figure 7.4	The TEN STEPS process	97
Figure 8.1	Table privilege statements	100
Figure 8.2	A function privilege statement	101
Figure 8.3	A database object privilege statement	101
Figure 8.4	A view statement and an associated table privilege statement	101
Figure 8.5	A user-specific view statement and an associated table privilege statement	102
Figure 9.1	The six data layers	110
Figure 9.2	Different data categories	110
Figure 9.3	The three master data layers	111
Figure 9.4	The relationship between business processes and master data	111
Figure 9.5	The MDM Hub	113
Figure 11.1	The role of directories or catalogs	122
Figure 11.2	The relationship between a CASE tool and its encyclopaedia or data dictionary	123
Figure 11.3	The architecture of a repository	124
Figure 11.4	The scope of a repository	125
Figure 11.5	A repository as a centralised source of information	126
Figure 13.1	An example of vertical fragmentation	136
Figure 13.2	An example of hybrid fragmentation	138
Figure 14.1	A typical data warehouse architecture	142
Figure 14.2	A multidimensional data model	143
Figure 14.3	A typical relational schema for a data warehouse	146
Figure 14.4	A snowflake schema	147
Figure 14.5	A galaxy schema	148
Figure 15.1	A partial conceptual data model	151
Figure 15.2	The ODL schema definitions for the partial conceptual data model	152
Figure 15.3	Structured type declarations	154
Figure 15.4	Table declarations using structured types and collections	154
Figure 15.5	Revised partial conceptual data model with entity subtypes	155
Figure 15.6	Creating structured types	156
Figure 15.7	Creating tables based on the structured types	157
Figure 17.1	The two-tier architecture	162
Figure 17.2	The three-tier architecture	163
Figure 17.3	Example of a JSON document	167
Figure 17.4	Conceptual view of an extensible record store	168
Figure A.1	A data model in Ellis–Barker notation	174
Figure A.2	Ellis–Barker data model with attribute annotation and unique identifiers	175
Figure A.3	A data model in Chen notation	176

Figure A.4	A data model in Information Engineering notation	177
Figure A.5	A data model in IDEF1X notation	178
Figure A.6	A UML class diagram	180
Figure A.7	Comparison of the relationship notations	181
Figure A.8	Comparison of the overall data model notations	182
Figure B.1	Conceptual data model used in comparison	184
Figure B.2	Relational database occurrences	184
Figure B.3	Hierarchical database schema	185
Figure B.4	Data definition statements for a hierarchical database	186
Figure B.5	Hierarchical database occurrences	187
Figure B.6	Hierarchical database records in sequence	187
Figure B.7	Network database schema	188
Figure B.8	Data definition statements for a network database	189
Figure B.9	Network database occurrences	190
Figure C.1	The generic to specific continuum	192
Figure C.2	The cost-balance of flexible design	194
Figure E.1	A metadata model describing conceptual data model concepts	207
Figure E.2	A conceptual data model snippet	208
Figure E.3	A metadata model describing physical SQL database concepts	209
Figure E.4	A metadata model showing mapping between elements	210
Figure E.5	The ICL Data Dictionary System	211
Figure G.1	An example of an HTML document	219
Figure G.2	The HTML document rendered in Mozilla Firefox	220
Figure G.3	An example of an XML document	221
Figure G.4	The tree structure of the XML document	222
Figure H.1	Specimen data for XML representation examples	225
Figure H.2	The employee table represented as a valid XML document	226
Figure H.3	The employee table represented as XML without a root element	227
Figure H.4	An example SQL query to create an XML document	228
Figure H.5	An example of an XML document	229
Figure H.6	An edge table created by shredding an XML document	231
Figure H.7	A query on an XML document	232
Figure H.8	The result of the query on an XML document	232
Figure I.1	The data administration skill set	233
Table D.1	Restricted terms used in the naming of entity types	202
Table D.2	Restricted terms used in the naming of domains	202
Table D.3	Restricted terms used in the naming of attributes	203
Table D.4	Restricted terms used in the naming of relationships	203
Table D.5	Examples of formal attribute names	205
Table F.1	A-priori algorithm: Step 1 results	212
Table F.2	A-priori algorithm: Step 2 results	213
Table F.3	A-priori algorithm: Step 3 results	214
Table F.4	A-priori algorithm: Step 4 results	215
Table F.5	A-priori algorithm: Step 5 results	216
Table F.6	A-priori algorithm: Step 6 results	217

AUTHOR

Keith Gordon was a professional soldier for 38 years, joining the army straight from school at 16 and retiring on his 55th birthday. During his service he had a number of technical, educational and managerial appointments and gained a Higher National Certificate in Electrical and Electronic Engineering, a Certificate in Education from the Institute of Education of the University of London, a BA from the Open University and an MSc from Cranfield Institute of Technology. From 1992 until his retirement in 1998, he was first a member of and then head of the army's data management team.

He is now an independent consultant and lecturer specialising in data management and business analysis. As well as developing and teaching commercial courses he was for a number of years a tutor for the Open University.

He is a Chartered Member of BCS, The Chartered Institute for IT, a Member of the Chartered Institute of Personnel and Development and a Fellow of the Institution for Engineering and Technology.

He holds the Diploma in Business Systems Development specialising in Data Management from BCS – formerly the Information Systems Examination Board (ISEB) – and he is now a member of their Business Systems Development Examination and Audit and Accreditation Panels.

He represents the UK within the international standards development community by being nominated by BSI to ISO/IEC JTC1 SC32 WG2 (Information Technology – Data management and interchange – Metadata).

For a number of years he was the secretary of the BCS Data Management Specialist Group and, as a founder member, was a committee member of the UK chapter of DAMA International, the worldwide association of data management professionals.

FOREWORD TO THE FIRST EDITION

The author of this book is a soldier through and through – but he also has a comprehensive understanding of the principles of data management and is a highly skilled professional educator. This rather unusual blend of experience makes this book very special.

Data management can be seen as a chore best left to people with no imagination, but Keith Gordon taught me that it can be a matter of life and death.

We all know that any collective enterprise must have records that are both reasonably accurate and readily accessible. In a commercial operation, failures in data management can lead to bankruptcy. In a public service it can put the lives of thousands of people at risk and waste public money on a grand scale. For a soldier in the heat of battle, any weakness in the availability, quality or timeliness of information can lead to a poor decision that may result in disaster.

So what has this to do with the 'principles of data management'? It serves as a reminder that a computer application is only as good as the data on which it depends.

It is common for the development of computer systems to start from the desired facilities and work backwards to identify the objects involved and so to the data by which these objects are described. One bad result of this approach is that the data resource gets skewed by the design of specific facilities that it is required to support.

When the business decides that these facilities have to be changed, the data resource must be modified. Does this matter? Some people would say 'Oh, it's easy enough to add another column to a table – no problem.' But these are the same people who get bogged down in the soul-destroying tasks of data fill and the mapping of one database onto another.

There is another way. We don't have to treat data design as a minor detail understood only by the programmers of a single system. An enterprise can choose to treat its data as a vital corporate asset and take appropriate steps to ensure that it is fit for purpose. To do this it must draw on the body of practical wisdom that has been built up by those large organisations that have already taken this message to heart. The British Army is one such organisation and it was Keith Gordon that made this happen.

The big issue here is how to ensure that the records on which an enterprise depends remain valid and useful beyond the life of individual systems and facilities. This requires good design resting on sound principles validated through extensive practical experience. We live in a changing world where new demands for information are arising all the time. Whether this is due to new technology, new social problems or the pressures of competition, these new demands cannot be met by creating yet more stove-pipe systems.

The goal we should aim at is for all data to be captured in digital form once only, as close as possible to the time and place of the observations, decisions and results that it is required to reflect. Once captured it should then be stored and distributed in such a manner that it can be made readily available to any person or system with a legitimate 'need to know' while remaining safe from loss, damage or theft.

The tricks of the trade through which the best practitioners contrive to bring this about are well documented in this book. I commend it to all people who seek to understand what is involved as well as those who aspire to develop the necessary skills.

Harry Ellis FBCS CITP
Independent consultant and member of W3C
Little Twitchen
Devon, UK

GLOSSARY

Access control   The ability to manage which users or groups of users have the privilege to create, read, update or delete data that is held in a database.

Attribute   Any detail that serves to qualify, identify, classify, quantify or express the state of a relation or an entity type.

Boyce–Codd normal form (BCNF)   In relational data analysis, a relation is in Boyce–Codd normal form if every determinant is a candidate key.

CASE   Acronym for Computer-Aided Software Engineering – a combination of software tools that assist computer development staff to engineer and maintain software systems, normally within the framework of a structured method.

Column   The logical structure within a table of a relational database management system (RDBMS) that corresponds to the attribute in the relational model of data.

Conceptual data model   A detailed model that captures the overall structure of organisational data while being independent of any database management system or other implementation consideration – it is normally represented using entities, relationships and attributes with additional business rules and constraints that define how the data is to be used.

Corporate data model   A conceptual data model whose scope extends beyond one application system.

Data   A re-interpretable representation of information in a formalised manner suitable for communication, interpretation or processing.

Data administration   A role in data management concerned with mechanisms for the definition, quality control and accessibility of an organisation's data.

Data dictionary   Software in which metadata is stored, manipulated and defined – a data dictionary is normally associated with a tool used to support software engineering.

Data governance   The formal orchestration of people, process and technology to enable an organisation to leverage data as an enterprise asset.

Data management   A corporate service which helps with the provision of information services by controlling or co-ordinating the definitions and usage of reliable and relevant data.

Data mining   The process of finding significant, previously unknown and potentially valuable knowledge hidden in data.

Data model   (1) An abstract, self-contained logical definition of the data structures and associated operators that make up the abstract machine with which users interact (such as the relational model of data). (2) A model of the persistent data of an enterprise (such as an entity-relationship model of data required to support the human resources department of Jameson Wholesale Limited – the example used in Chapter 2).

Data modelling   The task of developing a data model that represents the persistent data of an enterprise.

Data owner   (1) The owner of a data definition is the person in the organisation who has the authority to say that this data should be held and that this definition is the appropriate definition for the data. (2) The owner of a data value is the person or organisation that has authority to change that value.

Data profiling   A set of techniques for searching through data looking for potential errors and anomalies, such as similar data with different spellings, data outside boundaries and missing values.

Data quality   The state of completeness, validity, consistency, timeliness and accuracy that makes data appropriate for a specific use.

Data recovery   Restoring a database to a state that is known to be correct after a failure.

Data security   Protecting the database against unauthorised users.

Data steward   The person who maintains a data definition on behalf of the owner of the data definition.

Data warehouse   A specialised database containing consolidated historical data drawn from a number of existing databases to support strategic decision making.

Database   (1) An organised way of keeping records in a computer system. (2) A collection of data files under the control of a database management system.

Database administration   A role in data management concerned with the management and control of the software used to access physical data.

Database management system (DBMS)   A software application that is used to create, maintain and provide controlled access to databases.

Datatype   A constraint on a data value that specifies its intrinsic nature, such as numeric, alphanumeric, date.

Discretionary access control (DAC)   Access control where the users who are granted access rights are allowed to propagate those rights to other users.

Domain   A named pool of values from which an attribute must take its value – a domain provides a set of business validation rules, format constraints and other properties for one or more attributes that may exist as a list of specific values, as a range of values, as a set of qualifications or any combination of these.

Enterprise architecture   A process of understanding the different elements that make up the enterprise, such as the people, the information, the processes and the communications, and how those elements interrelate.

Enterprise resource planning (ERP) software   A software package that provides a single integrated database that is planned to meet an organisation's entire data needs for the management of its resources.

Entity   A named thing of significance about which information needs to be held in support of business operations.

Entity type   An element of a data model that represents a set of entities that all conform to the same template.

First normal form (1NF)   In relational data analysis, a relation is in first normal form if all the values taken by the attributes of that relation are atomic or scalar values – the attributes are single-valued or, alternatively, there are no repeating groups of attributes.

Foreign key   One or more attributes in a relation (or columns in a table) that implement a many-to-one relationship that the relation (or table) has with another relation (or table) or with itself.

HTML   Acronym for HyperText Markup Language – the markup language used to convey the way that a document is presented by a web browser.

IEC   Acronym for the International Electrotechnical Commission – collaborates with ISO in the development of international standards for information systems.

Information   (1) Something communicated to a person. (2) Knowledge concerning objects, such as facts, events, things, processes or ideas, including concepts, that have a particular meaning within a certain context.

Information management   The function of managing information as an enterprise resource, including planning, organising and staffing, and leading, directing and controlling information.

Information resource management   The concept that information is a major corporate resource and must be managed using the same basic principles used to manage other assets.

Information system   A collection of manual and automated components that manages a specific information resource.

ISO   Acronym for the International Organization for Standardization – collaborates with IEC in the development of international standards for information systems.

Mandatory access control (MAC)   Access control where access rights cannot be changed by the users.

Master data management   The authoritative, reliable foundation for data used across many applications and constituencies with the goal to provide a single version of the truth.

Metadata   Data about data – that is, data describing the structure, content or use of some other data.

Multilevel security   The ability of a computer system to process information with different security levels, to permit access by users with different security clearances and to prevent users from obtaining access to information for which they do not have authorised access.

Multimedia data   Data representing documents, audio (sound), still images (pictures) and moving images (video).

Normal form   A state of a relation that can be determined by applying simple rules regarding dependencies to that relation.

Normalisation   Another name for relational data analysis.

Object orientation   A software development strategy based on the concept that systems should be built from a collection of reusable components called objects that encompass both data and functionality.

ODMG   Acronym for the Object Data Management Group – a body that has produced a specification for object oriented databases.

OLAP   Acronym for online analytical processing – a set of techniques that can be applied to data to support strategic decision making.

OLTP   Acronym for online transactional processing – data processing that supports operational procedures.

Primary key   The set of mandatory attributes in a relation (or mandatory columns in a table) that is used to enforce uniqueness of tuples (or rows).

RDBMS   Acronym for relational database management system – a database management system whose logical constructs are derived from the relational model of data. Most relational database management systems available are based on the SQL database language and have the table as their principal logical construct.

Relation   The basic structure in the relational model of data – formally a set of tuples, but informally visualised as a table with rows and columns.

Relational data analysis   A technique of transforming complex data structures into simple, stable data structures that obey the rules of relational data design, leading to increased flexibility and reduced data duplication and redundancy – also known as normalisation.

Relational model of data   A model of data that has the relation as its main logical construct.

Relationship   In a conceptual data model, an association between two entity types, or between one entity type and itself.

Repository   Software in which metadata is stored, manipulated and defined – a repository is normally associated with a corporate data management initiative.

Repository administration   A role in data management concerned with the management and control of the software in which 'information about information' is stored, manipulated and defined.

Schema   A description of the overall logical structure of a database expressed in a data definition language (such as the data definition component of SQL).

Second normal form (2NF)   In relational data analysis, a relation is in second normal form if it is in first normal form and every non-key attribute is fully functionally dependent on the primary key – there are no part-key dependencies.

SQL   Originally SQL stood for structured query language. Now the letters SQL have no meaning attributed to them. SQL is the database language defined in the ISO/IEC 9075 set of international standards, the latest edition of which was published in 2011. The language contains the constructs necessary for data definition, data querying and data manipulation. Most vendors of relational database management systems use a version of SQL that approximates to that specified in the standards.

Structured data   Data that has enforced composition to specified datatypes and relationships and is managed by technology that allows for querying and reporting.

Table   The logical structure used by a relational database management system (RDBMS) that corresponds to the relation in the relational model of data – the table is the main structure in SQL.

Third normal form (3NF)   In relational data analysis, a relation is in third normal form if it is in second normal form and no transitive dependencies exist.

Tuple   In the relational model of data, the construct that is equivalent to a row in a table – it contains all the attribute values for each instance represented by the relation.

Unified Modeling Language (UML)   A set of diagramming notations for systems analysis and design based on object oriented concepts.

Unstructured data   Computerised information which does not have a data structure that is easily readable by a machine, including audio, video and unstructured text such as the body of a word-processed document – effectively this is the same as multimedia data.

XML   Acronym for eXtensible Markup Language – the markup language used to convey the definition, structure and meaning of the information contained in a document.

PREFACE

I think I first decided that I wanted to be a soldier when I was about three years of age. In 1960, aged 16 and with a slack handful of GCE 'O' Levels, I joined the Royal Armoured Corps as a junior soldier. I suppose I thought that driving tanks would be fun, but my time with the Royal Armoured Corps was short-lived and, in 1962, I joined the Royal Corps of Signals and trained as an electronics technician. I learned to repair and maintain a range of electronics equipment that used logic AND, OR, NAND and NOR gates, multivibrators, registers and MOD-2 adders, all of which are the building blocks of the central processing units at the heart of computers. Nine years later, I attended a course that turned me into a technical supervisor. This course extended my knowledge to include the whole range of telecommunications equipment. I now knew about radio and telephony as well as being the proud owner of a Higher National Certificate in Electrical and Electronic Engineering. On this course we also met a computer, an early Elliot mainframe, and learned to program it. After this course I found myself in Germany with a brilliant job, responsible for the 'system engineering' of the communications for an armoured brigade headquarters. Not only was I ensuring that my technicians kept the equipment on the road, but I was also designing and having my staff build the internal communications of the headquarters – which involved the interconnection of about a dozen vehicles.

A career change happened in 1978 when, following a year's teacher training, I was commissioned into the Royal Army Educational Corps. I spent the next nine years in classrooms in Aberdeen, London, the Falkland Islands (not sure that some of the places where I taught when I was there could be called classrooms, but...) and Beaconsfield. In Beaconsfield I taught maths, electronics and science; in the other jobs, I taught a mixture of literacy, numeracy, current affairs and management. It was these teaching jobs that gave me my greatest sense of personal satisfaction. I also extended my knowledge of computing by studying for a BA with the Open University and 1987 saw me getting deeper into computing by studying for an MSc in the Design of Information Systems, where I was introduced to databases and structured methods. I left the course thinking I knew about data and data modelling. I now know that I had hardly scraped the surface.

In 1992, after two more educational jobs, I was offered a job in 'data management'. Well, I knew about 'data' and I had taught 'management' so, despite never having before heard the two words used together, I thought it sounded like my thing. I may have been influenced by the belief that the job would involve an office in London that was close enough to home to commute daily. It came as a shock to find that the office was in Blandford, where I had already served for over seven years during my time in the Signals, and it severely disrupted my home life. But this was nothing unusual; disruption of home life is a substantial part of the lot of a soldier.

The Army had commissioned one of the large consultancy companies to conduct a major study into its information systems. This study had recommended that the Army should have a data management team and this team came together in 1992. There were five of us: four officers and a civil servant. All we knew was that data management was to be good for the Army. Nowhere was there a description of what data management was. So we were in a highly desirable position: we had to work out what we had to do. I think this period provided me with the greatest technical challenge of my Army career. What I was aware of was that the Army had a large number of information systems, all independently designed, and it was virtually impossible to share information between them. And the Army was also undertaking a large programme of information systems procurement, in some important cases into areas that had not previously had information systems support. To make the Army more effective on the battlefield and, at the same time, to reduce our casualties, it was vital that the information systems could share information. The Army had a vision of a single, fully integrated information system. This would not, of course, be a single system but a federation of systems that appeared to the user as a single system. This could not be achieved without data management.

Thus began my interest in data management. Three years later I was promoted and became the head of the team until I retired from the Army in 1998. I now work as an independent consultant and lecturer. As well as teaching commercial courses in data management and business analysis, I was a tutor with the Open University for 10 years from 1999, tutoring database and general computing courses in the undergraduate and postgraduate programmes. Since 2005 I have been involved with Working Group 2 of Sub-Committee 32 of the Joint Technical Committee formed by ISO and IEC to develop international standards in the general Information Technology area. The remit of Sub-Committee 32 is data management and interchange and Working Group 2 is responsible for the development and maintenance of standards for handling metadata. Thus my data management journey continues.

I believe that all medium to large organisations, commercial and government, need a corporate data management service. I see many instances where the inability to share information between information systems leads to mistakes and misunderstanding, which in turn lead to poor customer service (even government departments have customers) and extra expenditure. These organisations cannot really afford to be without data management, yet very few recognise the problems, let alone that data management is the solution. Regrettably this ignorance exists not only amongst business managers; it is rare to find an IT or IS manager who sees the need for data management. In fact most, like me 20 years ago, have never heard the two words 'data' and 'management' used together. I hope that this book goes some way to bring data management to the attention of those who really ought to know about it.

This book, therefore, represents the knowledge I have gained over the last 20 years. Some of this knowledge came from doing the job, some from the people I have taught and some from the many books sitting on my bookshelves, most of which are listed in the bibliography.

I owe a debt of gratitude to a number of people who have helped me on my data management journey. Ian Nielsen, Martin Richley, Duncan Broad and Tim Scarlett were my colleagues in that original Army data management team who shared those many hours around a whiteboard trying to work out what it was all about. There were others involved as well. David Gradwell and Ken Allen were our first consultants, introducing us to the mysteries of metadata models and naming standards. Later on, when we started data modelling in earnest, we had the benefit of the experience of Harry Ellis and Ron Segal (who is now in New Zealand). I learned masses from working with all of these people and I think we were all (including our experienced consultants) on a learning curve. At the start of my data management journey I attended a Principles of Data Administration course run by Chris Newton for Stehle Associates. This course set data management and data administration in context. It is Chris's Principles of Data Administration course that is the skeleton on which I have built my own Principles of Data Management course, which I now deliver for Stehle Associates. Dave Beaumont, the principal of Stehle Associates, has encouraged me to develop data management courses and he and I have spent many hours discussing data management issues. He kindly reviewed early drafts of some of the chapters of the first edition and has reviewed the whole of the second edition. Thanks, too, to Ian Sinclair, one of my former colleagues on the committee of the UK chapter of DAMA International, who reviewed the chapter on data quality for the first edition; to Matthew West, who reviewed the original appendix on generic data models; and to Tony Jenkins who reviewed the whole text for the first edition and provided many useful recommendations for its improvement. I would also like to thank the many people I have not mentioned but whom I have either worked with or discussed data management issues with over the last 20 years. I have learned from you all.

Particular thanks are due to Matthew Flynn of BCS and his team who have been instrumental in getting both editions of this book into print.

Finally, a massive thank you to my wife, Vivienne, for her unstinting support over the last 47 years. Being a soldier's wife for 32 years was never going to be a picnic and she had a right to expect things to be more relaxed and easier when I retired. Instead, with consulting, teaching, committee membership and the writing of two editions of this book, I have neglected her and our grown-up children, Stuart and Lorna, far more than I should have done. Despite all this, Vivienne is still there looking after me and supporting me. Thank you.

Keith Gordon
High Wycombe
June 2013

INTRODUCTION

This book is called *Principles of Data Management* but it is really about having the policies and procedures in place within an organisation so that the various information systems that the organisation uses to support its activities can provide high-quality information to their users, even if that information did not originate in the information system with which the user is currently interacting. For this to happen the organisation's information systems must be able to share information. If there is no automatic sharing of information between the information systems, some departments may be kept in the dark about what is going on in other departments and information may have to be keyed into more than one system. Neither of these situations helps the organisation's effectiveness or efficiency. The key to the provision of high-quality information and the sharing of information between information systems is to have an effective policy for corporate data management in place. Yet very few senior business and IT or IS managers have heard of data management, let alone have an effective policy for data management in place.

This book is aimed at three audiences. First there are the data management practitioners themselves. They are presumably already committed to data management but may be struggling to find all the information that they need to set their role in the wider business context or to perform the myriad tasks that fall within the scope of data management. This book will not have all the answers, but it may provide an indication of what the answer should be and, perhaps, where to go and look for the answer. Second, there are the IT or IS managers who have heard of data management and are probably aware that it might be a good idea, but are not sure what it involves or what the implications of having a corporate data management function will be. Maybe they already have a team responsible for data management working within their department but are not sure what that team does or what it should do. The third group who should read this book – or at least the sections that are not too technical – are the business managers who want to understand why they are being asked to pay for a team of data managers who do not look as if they are going to deliver the much-sought-after return on investment within the current budgetary cycle. For the data management practitioners I commend the Certificate in Data Management Essentials qualification offered by BCS. This book covers the current syllabus for the Certificate in Data Management Essentials as well as providing additional material. So to meet the requirements of practitioners, IT or IS managers and business managers, this book covers the whole range of data management activities.

This second edition is divided into four parts with some supporting appendices. The four parts are:

- **Part 1: Preliminaries** – where we set the scene, describing the importance of data to the enterprise, introduce the concept of database design and consider the roles and responsibilities of data management within an enterprise.

- **Part 2: Data Administration** – where we describe the tasks and areas that are the responsibility of data administrators, such as corporate data modelling, data definition, data naming, metadata, data quality and data accessibility. It also includes a new chapter on master data management.

- **Part 3: Database and Repository Administration** – where we describe the tasks and areas that are the responsibility of database administrators and repository administrators.

- **Part 4: The Data Management Environment** – where we consider a number of fads, advances and developments, including the use of software application packages such as accounting packages, distributed data, business intelligence, object orientation, multimedia or unstructured data and web technology. The discussion on web technology is much expanded from that in the first edition.

PART 1
PRELIMINARIES

In this part we describe the importance of data to the enterprise, introduce the concept of database design and consider the roles and responsibilities of data management within an enterprise. This part has three chapters.

Chapter 1 – Data and the Enterprise – introduces the idea that information is a key business resource. It starts by exploring the relationship between information and data. We then move on to a discussion of the importance of the quality of the data that underlies the information. If the quality of data is important, what are the common problems with data? Why must we take an enterprise-wide view of data? The chapter concludes by highlighting that the management of data is a business issue and not a technical issue.

Chapter 2 – Database Development – is a long, largely technical chapter that provides an explanation of how the databases at the heart of all information systems are designed. It introduces the concepts of database architecture and then provides examples of two analysis techniques – conceptual data modelling and relational data analysis – and how these lead to a physical database design.

Chapter 3 – What is Data Management? – first considers the problems encountered without data management, then introduces the scope of the responsibilities of data management. We then look at the three separate roles within data management – data administration, database administration and repository administration. We end this chapter by summarising the benefits of data management.

1 DATA AND THE ENTERPRISE

This chapter introduces the concepts of information and data and discusses why they are important business resources within the enterprise. We start to discuss some of the problems caused by data which is of poor quality or inconsistent, or both.

INFORMATION IS A KEY BUSINESS RESOURCE

When asked to identify the key resources in any business, most business people will readily name money, people, buildings and equipment. This is because these are the resources that senior business managers spend most time managing. This means that in most businesses there is a clear investment by the business in the management of these resources. The fact that these resources are easy to manage and that the management processes applied to these resources can be readily understood by the layman means that it is seen to be worthwhile investing in their management. It is usually easy to assess how much the business spends on managing these resources and the return that is expected from that investment.

But there is a key resource missing from that list. That missing resource is 'information'. Without information, the business cannot function. Indeed, it could be said that the only resource that is readily available to senior management is information. All important decisions made within an enterprise are based on the information that is available to the managers.

Despite its importance, most business people do not recognise information as a key business resource. Because of its association with technology (with 'information technology' having become in effect one word, generally with more emphasis on the 'technology' than on the 'information'), information is seen as something mystical that is managed on behalf of the business by the specialist information technology or information systems department. The management of information is seen, therefore, as something requiring special skills beyond the grasp of the layman. It is very difficult to determine how much the business spends on managing information or, indeed, the return it can expect from that expenditure.

Information is a business resource that is used in every aspect of a business: it supports the day-to-day operational tasks and activities; it enables the routine administration and management of the business; and it supports strategic decision making and future planning.

For a supermarket chain the operational tasks and activities include the processing of customers' purchases through the electronic point-of-sale system and the ordering of goods from suppliers; for a high street bank they include the handling of customers' cash and cheques by the cashiers, the processing of transactions through ATMs and the assessment of the credit status of a customer who is requesting a loan; for an online book 'store' they include the collection of customers' orders, the selection and dispatch of the books and the production of a customer profile enabling the 'store' to make recommendations to customers as they log on to the website.

For all types of business, information in various forms is routinely used by managers to monitor the efficiency and effectiveness of the business. Some of this information comes in the form of standard reports. Other information may come to the managers as a result of their ad hoc questions, perhaps directed to their subordinates but, increasingly, directed to the information systems that support the business.

All businesses need to plan for their future and take high-level strategic decisions. In some cases the consequence of making an incorrect strategic decision could be the ultimate collapse of the business. To carry out this future planning and strategic decision making, the senior management of the business relies on information about the historic performance of the business, the projected future performance of the business (and this, to a large extent, will be based on an extrapolation of the historic information into the future), its customers' present and future needs and the performance of its competitors. Information relating to the external environment, particularly the economy, is also important. For a supermarket chain these decisions may include whether to diversify into, say, clothing; for a high street bank they may include the closure of a large number of branches; and for an online book 'store' whether to open new operations overseas.

Information is important, therefore, at every level in the business. It is important that the information is managed and presented in a consistent, accurate, timely and easily understood way.

THE RELATIONSHIP BETWEEN INFORMATION AND DATA

Wisdom, knowledge, information and data are all closely related through being on the same continuum – from wisdom, to knowledge, then to information and, finally, to data. This book is about managing data to provide useful information so we will concentrate on the relationship between information and data.

An often-heard definition of information is that it is 'data placed in context'. This implies that some information is the result of the translation of some data using some processing activity, and some communication protocol, into an agreed format that is identifiable to the user. In other words, if data has some meaning attributed to it, it becomes information.

For example, what do the figures '190267' represent? Presented as '19/02/67' it would probably make sense to assume that they represent a date. Presented on a screen with other details of an employee of a company, such as name and address, in a field that is labelled 'Date of Birth' the meaning becomes obvious. Similarly, presented as '190267 metres', it immediately becomes obvious that this is a long distance between two places, but for this to really make sense the start point and the end point have to be specified as well as, perhaps, a number of intermediate points specifying the route.

While these examples demonstrate the relationship between data and information, they do not provide a clear definition of either data or information.

There are many definitions of data available in dictionaries and textbooks, but in essence most of these definitions basically say that data is 'facts, events, transactions and similar that have been recorded'. Furthermore, as I pointed out earlier, the definition of information is usually based on this definition of data. Information is seen as data in context or data that has been processed and communicated so that it can be used by its recipient.

The idea that data is a set of recorded facts is found in many books on computing. However, this concept of data as recorded facts is used beyond the computing and information systems communities. It is, for example, also the concept used by statisticians. Indeed, the definition of data given in Webster's 1828 Dictionary – published well before the introduction of computers – is 'things given, or admitted; quantities, principles or facts given, known, or admitted, by which to find things or results unknown'.

However, developing our definitions by looking at data first appears to be starting at the wrong point. It is information that is important to the business and it is there that our definitions, and our discussion about the relationship between information and data, should really begin.

We start by considering the everyday usage of information – something communicated to a person – and with that we can find a definition of data that is relevant to the theme of this book. That definition is found in ISO/IEC 2382-1, 1993 (*Information Technology – Vocabulary – Part 1: Fundamental terms*) and it states that data is 'a re-interpretable representation of information in a formalised manner suitable for communication, interpretation or processing'. There is a note attached to this definition in the ISO/IEC standard which states that data can be processed by human or automatic means; so this definition covers all forms of data but, importantly, includes data held in information systems used to support the activities of an organisation at all levels: operational, managerial and strategic.

Figure 1.1 provides an overview of the relationship between data and information in the context of a computerised information system. The user of the system extracts the required information from their overall knowledge and inputs the information into the system. As it enters the system it is converted into data so that it can be stored and processed. When another system user requires that information, the data is interpreted – that is, it has meaning applied to it – so that it can be of use to the user.

For most of this book we consider data stored in a database. This is often called 'structured data'. However, it must be understood that a considerable proportion of an organisation's information may be held in information systems as 'unstructured data' – in word-processed documents, drawings and so on.

Figure 1.1 The relationship between data and information

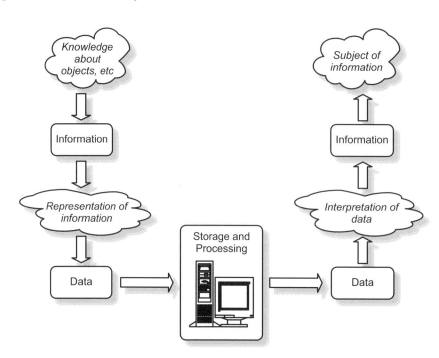

THE IMPORTANCE OF THE QUALITY OF DATA

Since information is an important resource for any organisation, information presented to users must be of high quality. The information must be up to date, complete, sufficiently accurate for the purpose it is required, unambiguously understood, consistent and available when it is required.

It is essential that information is up to date. When customers buy their shopping at the supermarket they need to be charged the current price for the items they have bought, not the price that was current yesterday before the start of today's cut-price promotion. Similarly, managers reordering stock need to be aware of the current, not last week's, stock levels in order to ensure that they are not over- or under-stocked.

Only when the information available is complete can appropriate decisions be made. When a bank is considering a request for a loan from a customer, it is important that full details of the customer's financial position are known to safeguard both the bank's and the customer's interests.

Information on which important decisions are made must be accurate; any errors in the potential loan customer's financial information could lead to losses for the bank, for example. While it is important that information is accurate, it is possible for the information to be 'too accurate' or 'too precise', leading to the information being misinterpreted. Earlier I quoted '190267 metres' as the distance between two points, say London and Birmingham. But the figure '190267' implies that this distance has been measured to the nearest metre. Is this realistic? Would it be more appropriate to quote this figure as '190 kilometres (to the nearest 10 kilometres)'? I cannot answer that question without knowing why I need to know the distance between London and Birmingham. Information should be accurate, but only sufficiently precise for the purpose for which it is required.

To be accurate from a user perspective, information must also be unambiguously understood. There should be no doubt as to whether the distance the user is being given is the straight-line distance or the distance by road. The data should also be consistent. A query asking for the distance between London and Birmingham via a specified route should always come up with the same answer.

Information has to be readily available when and where it is required to be used. When it is time to reorder stock for the supermarket, the information required to decide the amount of replacement stock to be ordered has to be available on the desk of the manager making those decisions.

Information is derived from the processing of data. It is vital, therefore, that the data we process to provide the information is of good quality. Only with good-quality data can we guarantee the quality of the information. Good-quality data is data that is accurate, correct, consistent, complete and up to date. The meaning of the data must also be unambiguous.

THE COMMON PROBLEMS WITH DATA

Unfortunately, in many organisations there are some major, yet unrecognised or misunderstood, data problems. These problems are generally caused by a combination of the proliferation of duplicate, and often inconsistent, occurrences of data and the misinterpretation and misunderstanding of the data caused by the lack of a cohesive, enterprise-wide regime of data definition.

Whenever it is possible for any item of information to be held as data more than once, there is a possibility of inconsistency. For example, if the addresses of customers are held in more than one place – or, more specifically, in more than one information system – and a customer informs the company that they have changed their address, there is always the danger that only one instance of the address is amended, leaving the other instances showing the old incorrect address for that customer. This is quite a common scenario. Another scenario is where the marketing department and the finance department may have separate information systems: the marketing department has a system to help it track customers and potential customers while the finance department has a completely separate system to support its invoicing and payments received accounting functions. With information systems independently designed and developed to support individual business areas or specific business processes, the duplication of data, and the consequent likelihood of inconsistency, is commonplace. Unfortunately, in most organisations, the potential for inconsistency through the duplication of data is getting worse because of the move away from centralised mainframe systems, the proliferation of separate departmental information systems and the availability of personal desktop computing power, including the provision of spreadsheet and database software.

Even where it is understood that it would be to the advantage of the organisation for information to be shared between these separate systems, this is often impossible without there being the possibility of misinterpretation or misunderstanding of the information that is shared.

In its 1994 publication *Corporate Data Modelling*, the Central Computer and Telecommunications Agency – now part of the Office of Government Commerce – recognised that there are a number of possible reasons for sharing information. These are:

- when central reference data is used by independent operational units, such as product codes and product prices;

- when public domain datatypes are used and exchanged, for example when publicly available statistical data sets are to be used;

- when operational results need to be collated across several profit centres, for example to collate or compare the sales figures from stores within a supermarket chain;

- when the output from one system forms the input to another, for example the output of a forecasting system is used by another system to determine resource and budget implications;

- when application systems performing a similar function for distinct autonomous units are required to harmonise their data to permit close collaboration, for example the command and control systems for the police, fire and ambulance services need to 'work together' in the event of an emergency.

The sharing of information between independently designed and developed information systems is technically straightforward. It is a relatively simple matter to electronically connect two or more information systems together using a network and then to transfer data between them. The difficulties come after the data has been transferred and the receiving information system cannot interpret the data or, worse still, interprets the received data according to its understanding of the meaning of the data, but this interpretation differs from that used in the originating system. This possibility of the misinterpretation of transferred data is very common in organisations and the situation is getting worse.

This is also a consequence of the proliferation of independently designed and developed departmental or single-function information systems. At the heart of an information system is a database whose purpose is to provide persistent storage of the data. Each of these databases is designed to ensure that the data is available when required by the applications supported by that information system and, possibly, to maintain the integrity of the data within that particular database. A database is designed to provide effective and efficient support to the business area or function that the information system is being designed to support by meeting the immediate data requirements for that business area or function as they are understood by the database designer. It is very rare for a wider view of current or future data requirements to be taken.

The proliferation of departmental or function-specific information systems, each with its own database designed without recognition of wider data requirements, has led to widespread problems of data inconsistency caused by duplication across different information systems and data misinterpretation when data is shared between information systems.

AN ENTERPRISE-WIDE VIEW OF DATA

In order to improve the quality of information across an organisation, we must first understand the data that provides that information and the problems that are associated with that data. We must also look at business information needs and move the organisation to a position where the required data is made available to support the current information needs in a cost-effective manner while providing the flexibility to cope with future needs in a reasonable timescale. We need to consider the information needs of the whole organisation and then manage the data in such a way that it supports the organisation's total information needs.

In order to manage the organisation's data resources effectively, we must first understand it. This requires more than just recognising data as being the raw material in the production of information. It implies knowledge of what data is important to the business and where and how it is used. What functions and processes use the data? When is it created, processed and destroyed? Who is responsible for that data in all stages of its life?

It is also essential that we produce a clear and unambiguous definition of all data that the organisation uses. Such a definition must be a common view, accepted and agreed by all business areas.

Effective management of data also requires an understanding of the problems that relate to data. These problems often cross departmental boundaries and their solutions consist of both technical and organisational aspects.

Organisations vary tremendously in size and nature. A large multinational organisation tends to have different data-related problems from a small company, although even in a small company the problems can be quite complex. The type of business may also affect the nature of the problems. A large proportion of the information systems in a finance or insurance company relate to customers or potential customers. In a manufacturing environment, however, dealing with customers is only one part of the overall business processes.

At the more technical level, data-related problems are affected by the types of computer system in place. Are the systems networked or distributed? Is extensive use made of personal computers? Are there multiple computer sites? And so on.

Individual departments do not necessarily perceive a given problem as having a potential impact across the whole organisation. One of the difficulties often faced by a central team responsible for managing the data for the whole organisation is bridging the gap between different departmental views. This requires patience and tact. It certainly requires authority, or access to appropriate authority, as the implementation of a solution may well involve co-operation with several managers within the organisation. Most importantly, it demands an understanding both of the information needs of the whole business and of the nature of the associated technical and organisational problems.

In reality the problems relating to data are often very complex and affect many different areas within an organisation. Data is used in different ways by different business functions. Data can take many forms and the technologies for handling and storing data are constantly changing. Data problems do not appear in a form that enables a neatly packaged, stand-alone solution for the handling and management of data.

A number of vendors now supply enterprise resource planning (ERP) software that is supposed to provide a single integrated database that meets an organisation's entire data needs for the management of its resources. In general these products do not appear to be providing the advantages claimed. Unless the organisation is prepared to replace all of its information systems in one go, there will still be a need for the data held by the ERP system to be integrated with the data held by the existing information systems that are still in use. Also, to really take advantage of ERP software, the organisation probably needs to change its business processes to conform to the processes supported by the software and many businesses are not prepared to make these changes.

MANAGING DATA IS A BUSINESS ISSUE

We identified money, people, buildings and equipment as the key resources in any business and we added information to that list.

For all of these resources some special responsibilities exist within the organisation:

- The finance department has special responsibilities for managing the organisation's money including the allocation of budgets, managing investments and accounting.
- The personnel department has special responsibilities for managing the organisation's employee base including the provision of advice on legislation affecting personnel issues and the recruitment of staff.
- The estates department has special responsibilities for managing the buildings used by the organisation including ensuring that the buildings meet legal requirements in respect of health and safety issues, buying, selling and leasing of buildings and ensuring that the estate is adequately insured.
- The stores and maintenance department has special responsibilities for managing the organisation's equipment including the provision of a central purchasing function, the accounting for equipment in use and the storage of equipment until it is required for use.
- The IT or IS department has special responsibility for data and information including the physical storage, distribution, security, backup and archiving of data.

In most organisations it is now common practice for line management to have responsibility for the day-to-day administration and management of these resources, with the specialist departments only providing specialist advice to the line management. People have to be managed on a day-to-day basis; money is allocated to budget holders to use and manage according to specific rules; buildings are run and administered; equipment is used and maintained.

Additionally, information is collected, validated and used. This is very much the responsibility of the business. All the decisions about what is collected and how it is validated are business decisions. So are the decisions about how information is to be handled and stored as data. Any data management function must, therefore, support the business. Data management is not purely a technical issue; the definition of the data to be stored should be the responsibility of the business. Most organisations are counting the cost of ineffective data management. Real business opportunities may be lost as a result of the inability to respond quickly to changing requirements. There are many situations where information exists but is not accessible in the right time frame.

In many cases the only way that information may be shared between information systems is by reading information from one screen and keying it into another system or, worse still, systems. The cost of continually rekeying information in this way is significant in terms of both the resource required to carry out this task and potential errors through misinterpretation of the information that is to be rekeyed. Such costs impact on the business as well as on the IT or IS department, although the greater impact is on the business. Surprisingly, this approach to information sharing is still in use in some organisations today.

There are many claimed benefits for having a data management function within the organisation. These benefits nearly all make sound business sense and can be recognised as such. However, not all of them can be related to direct cost savings. Consequently, it requires a degree of faith on the part of management that the end result, the benefits, will justify the costs.

The benefits split into two areas: those that are business-oriented and those that are systems-oriented. The former include cost savings through, for example, the reduction in duplicated marketing mailings and improved customer service, while the latter include reduced time to develop new applications, which also translates into financial savings. I firmly believe, however, that the systems-oriented benefits are a natural by-product of a business-oriented data management initiative. The reverse is not necessarily true. There may be no additional benefits to business effectiveness and efficiency if the IT or IS function implements data management in order to save on development costs.

It is relatively easy to quantify the costs of today's problems, both in financial terms and as lost business opportunities. Thus it is possible to demonstrate relatively easily the potential benefits of reducing or even eradicating such problems and enabling the business to exploit the huge investment it has already made in data for optimum returns. It is possible to make the business case for the establishment of a data management function.

SUMMARY

In this chapter we have seen that information, an often neglected key business resource that needs to be shared across an enterprise, is developed from data. To provide quality information, data has to be properly managed. There has to be an enterprise-wide view of data, and the business, not the IT or IS function, has to take the lead in the management of data.

2   DATABASE DEVELOPMENT

This is a long chapter that takes a look at the complex subject of the development of databases. Some concepts are only briefly explained while others are discussed in more detail. The intention is not to teach the reader how to develop a database – that would take a complete book many times the size of this one, and even then the reader would probably need help and guidance from an experienced practitioner before they could put the ideas into practice.

This chapter is here to help those who have not been involved in the development of databases to put the other material in this book in context; because of the complex nature of the subjects being discussed it may need to be read more than once. The experienced database developer can safely miss out this chapter, although they may discover some new insights by reading it.

THE DATABASE ARCHITECTURE OF AN INFORMATION SYSTEM

This section introduces the concept of a database and the software used to manage it – a database management system, commonly called a DBMS.

File systems

Before the advent of databases, any data that was required by an application program was stored in specially constructed files designed for and associated with the application programs. These file-based approaches to the storage of data presented many problems and it was to overcome these problems that databases were developed.

Each of these files would contain many records, with each record being a collection of data values held in fields within the record. There are a number of ways of organising records within files, leading to many different methods of data access. These include sequential access, where data is accessed by searching through the file from the beginning until the data is found, and direct access, where there is a mechanism that knows the 'location' in the file of the required data and knows how to go directly to that location. Any application program has to be written for a specific file structure with a specific access method. This means that each application program becomes closely coupled to its data structure. The application program is both logically and physically dependent on the data structure; any change to the data structure of the file requires a corresponding change to the application program and, probably, any change to the application program requires a corresponding change to the data file.

The database approach

A database is an organised way of keeping records in a computer system. Databases provide a means of overcoming the problems caused by storing data in files that are closely coupled with application programs. If properly applied, the database approach manages data as a shared resource, providing both logical and physical data independence. The data still has to be stored (usually on disks these days) and that storage is in a file physically similar to those used in the old file-based approaches. The difference is that between the file and the application programs there is a suite of software called a database management system, as shown in Figure 2.1.

Figure 2.1 A model of a database system

This model shows a number of user processes interacting with the general-purpose database management system. It also shows that the database management system interacts with two 'datastores', physical storage areas for data in files. One datastore is the database itself, providing persistent storage of the data required by the various user processes. The other datastore contains the data definitions. The set of data definitions is generally known as a schema. The schema contains the specification of the properties of all the data in the associated database. It is used by the database management system to determine how the data in the associated database is to be processed. The schema is independent of the database management system and the user processes and is normally expressed in terms of easily understood conceptual constructs. The data definitions are, therefore, not embedded in the application programs. This overcomes one of the main problems of the file-based approach to the storage of data.

There are a number of claimed advantages of the database approach over the file-based approaches. Assuming that databases are properly designed and used, these advantages include:

- **Data independence** – there is a layer of software, the database management system, between the users and their applications and the stored data; this layer of software insulates the users from changes to the way that data is physically stored.

- **Integration and sharing of data** – a database can store all the data needed by many different business areas so that many users from different business areas can access the same database.

- **Consistency of data** – with the data being integrated in a database, the data inconsistency problems associated with separate application-specific data files are prevented.

- **Minimal data redundancy** – with many applications sharing an integrated set of data, the redundancy of data caused by duplication is avoided; there may, however, be some planned and controlled data duplication to meet specific requirements.

- **Uniform security and integrity controls** – since the controls necessary to maintain the security and integrity of the data are handled by the database management system software, these controls are applied uniformly to all users of the database. Security and integrity are explained in more detail in Chapter 8.

- **Data accessibility and responsiveness** – within the database there may be many different ways to access any required set of data; it is even possible to answer ad hoc queries in addition to the pre-planned queries encoded in the application programs.

- **Ease of application development and reduced program maintenance** – the application developers and those responsible for the future maintenance of those applications do not need to know and understand the way that the data is physically stored; instead, they only need to understand the conceptual constructs used in the schema.

Database management systems may be specifically developed for particular purposes, but most databases in use today are built on general-purpose database management systems. Most general-purpose database management systems on the market are based on the standard SQL database language (ISO/IEC 9075, 2011), which is itself based on the relational model of data, although it is possible to purchase database management system software based on other models of data.

Irrespective of whether the database management system software is specifically developed or general purpose, there are a number of common functions that should be provided by all database management systems. These are:

- **Data definition** – the ability to use easily understood conceptual constructs to define the way that the data is to be organised and structured within the database.

- **Constraint definition and enforcement** – the ability to define semantic constraints on the data (for example restrictions that are to be applied to data values) and then to enforce those constraints universally.

- **Access control** – the ability to define the rights of users to access all or some of the data and to prevent access by users without the appropriate rights.

- **Data manipulation** – the ability to retrieve and update data as well as the ability to perform calculations and structuring for presentation purposes.

- **Restructuring and reorganisation** – the ability to change a database in some way, either to logically restructure – that is, to change, add or delete some element of the data structure – or to physically reorganise how the data is stored – for example to add an index.

- **Transaction support** – the ability to ensure that a database is in a consistent state both before and after a transaction has been completed.

- **Concurrency support** – the ability to allow many user processes – and, therefore, many users – to access a database at the same time without conflict or interference.

- **Recovery** – the ability to return the database to a usable state after a hardware or software failure, including the return of the database to a consistent state if a transaction fails to complete.

The first of these functions of a database management system is the ability to define the way that the data is to be conceptually organised and structured within the database. This is the ability to define the database schema.

There are a number of ways to think of the organisation of data. In the pre-database file-based approach, the conceptual view of the data taken by the application program had to match exactly the physical structure of the file. This was often complex and understanding of it was complicated by the requirement to fully understand any coding used in the file structure. These complex structures are difficult for people to visualise and understand. With a database management system the data can be conceptually organised in a more convenient form, with the database management software taking care of the translation to and from the file format in which the data is actually stored.

If the database management system is based on the SQL database language, this conceptual view of the data is based on interrelated tables, which are a representation of the mathematical relations at the heart of the relational model of data. Each table comprises a number of columns with each column holding data of a common type. For example an Employee table may well have columns called Payroll Number and Start Date, amongst others. Each row of such a table holds data about a single employee.

For an object oriented database management system, the conceptual view of the data is a series of object classes whose instances interact through the passing of messages. Objects of the Employee class may be able to respond to messages asking questions such as 'What is your payroll number?' and 'What date did you start employment?'

The three-level schema architecture

In attempting to understand how a database management system works, it is useful to think in terms of a layered approach of three separate levels of schema within the database management system. These are the logical (or conceptual) level, the internal (or storage) level and the external level, as shown in Figure 2.2.

Figure 2.2 The three-level schema architecture

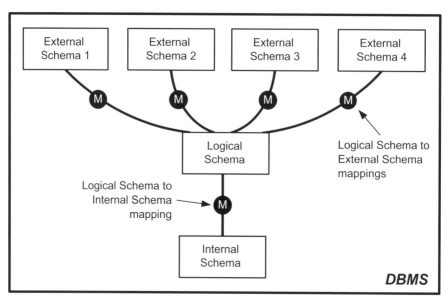

This three-level schema architecture was originally proposed by the American National Standards Institute (ANSI) Standards Planning and Requirements Committee (SPARC) in 1975. It is a theoretical concept only, but it provides a valuable insight into the way that the use of a database avoids data dependence.

The schema at the logical level is the central, and main, component of the architecture. It defines the properties of all the data. It includes the data definitions and the associated constraints, using the appropriate conceptual constructs – tables, object classes and so forth – appropriate to the database management system being used.

The schema at the internal level defines how the database is physically stored in files and how these files are accessed. The addition of indexes to speed retrieval may be viewed as an addition to the internal or storage schema.

Each schema at the external level defines the data required to support one or more user processes. Each schema at the external level may be viewed as a subset or an abstraction of the schema at the logical level, although it is not necessary for the same conceptual constructs to be used at both the logical and external levels. For example the logical schema may have the relational table as its main construct, while one or more of the external schemas may have the object class as its main construct.

The separation between the schema at the logical level, where the data is conceptually visualised – tables and columns, object classes and so forth – and the schema at the internal level – where the way that the data is actually stored is known – provides a level of data independence that we call 'physical data independence'. It is necessary to be able to translate the conceptual constructs at the logical level to the physical file definitions at the internal level, and this translation is handled by the mapping from the schema at the logical level to the schema at the internal level. We generally say that the mapping provides the physical data independence. This separation of the two levels and the mapping between them mean that the schema at the logical level is immune to changes in the schema at the internal level. Changes affecting the way that the data is physically stored (such as the addition of new indexes to speed up querying of the data or a restructuring of the file) should not require any changes to the schemas at the logical and external levels. The only additional changes required are to the mapping. The only effect, if any, seen by the users is a change in performance. Indeed, changes to the internal schema are often made in response to a need to improve the performance of the database.

Similarly, the mappings from the schema at the logical level to the schemas at the external level provide logical data independence. These mappings specify how the conceptual constructs used at the logical level correspond to the conceptual constructs used at the external level. A schema at the external level is immune to changes in the schema at the logical level that are outside the scope of the external schema. Changes in the schema at the logical level, such as the addition of a new table or the addition of a new column in an existing table, are possible without having to change any of the schemas at the external level or to amend any of the application programs, except of course for the external schema and the associated application program for the users for whom the changes have been made. It is only the external schema and application program associated with those users that are affected; the rest are not.

AN OVERVIEW OF THE DATABASE DEVELOPMENT PROCESS

All information systems are developed to meet a set of information needs or requirements that belong to a set of users. An important part of the overall development process is to understand and document those requirements so that the information system that is developed and eventually delivered does in fact help the users by meeting their requirements.

There are a number of different approaches to the development of information systems, with a number of formalised methods available to the development team. All of these methods use diagramming techniques to record the results of the analysis of the information requirements.

All systems, whether supported by information technology or not, help to improve business processes – those specific activities that are designed to achieve defined goals or objectives. All systems also have to record information as data in order to provide their processes with something to work on.

The use of recorded data by specific processes is likely to be sequenced in the business; there are liable to be restrictions or constraints in the business that limit the application of processes to recorded data. Thus it may be that certain processes must precede others or, once a particular process has been applied, certain other processes are prohibited.

So for each system there are three facets that need to be considered: the information (or its associated data), the processes and the timing or sequencing. The diagramming techniques of information systems development methods provide ways to document these three facets of the system. Depending on the method, the diagrams may provide views of the data, processes and timing from the perspective of the business system that the information system needs to support; they may provide views of the data, processes and timing as they will be implemented in the information system; or they may provide both.

Our focus is on data management and, therefore, we concentrate on how information requirements are documented and understood to lead to the development of a database. However, anyone involved in data management will also find it helpful to understand the techniques used to document processes and timing.

Any database at the heart of an information system has to be designed so that it meets the information requirements of the user community. The relationship between the information requirements and the implemented database is shown in Figure 2.3. It can be seen that there is a defined process that delivers the final implemented database based on the set of information requirements.

Figure 2.3 A simplified view of the database development process

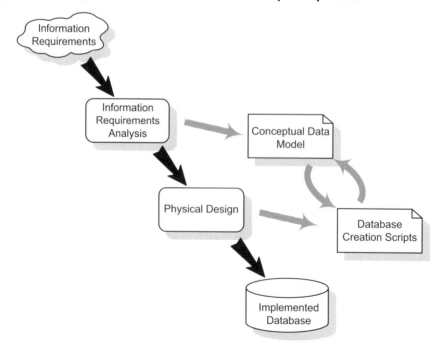

Figure 2.3 shows that to get from the stated requirements to the final implemented database there are at least two main stages in the process: the information requirements analysis phase and the physical database design phase. The results of the information requirements analysis phase are recorded in a conceptual data model. Such a model probably consists of a diagram and a set of supporting documentation. An example of a conceptual data model diagram is shown in Figure 2.4.

This conceptual data model is for a small subset of the information normally used by a human resources function. It shows personal details of the employees: their addresses, their qualifications and their next of kin, and, additionally, some company-related information such as the employees' grades and their assignments to departments and projects. This conceptual data model may have been arrived at as a result of discussions with the staff of the human resources department or through an analysis of the information in the manual records currently held by the department, or by a combination of both.

There are a number of different data modelling notations in use, and some analysts even use object class models from object oriented analysis and design methods such as the Unified Modeling Language (UML) in place of data models. Some of these notations are easier to use and to understand than others. The Ellis–Barker notation used in Figure 2.4 is my preferred notation. I have found it very easy to discuss models drawn using this notation with non-modellers such as business representatives. Appendix A provides a discussion of the capabilities of some other data modelling notations.

There are also a number of different approaches to the development of data models and it is not the intention of this book to teach you how to model data. There are many excellent data modelling books already on the market. The one I would recommend to anyone new to data modelling is *CASE*METHOD: Entity Relationship Modelling* by Richard Barker (1990). One approach to the development of the data model in Figure 2.4 will be used in the 'Conceptual data modelling (from a project-level perspective)' section later in this chapter to demonstrate some of the ideas behind data modelling. Having completed the requirements analysis phase and produced an appropriate conceptual data model, the next step is to design the database. In many methods this stage is (mistakenly) called 'physical design', but what we are doing at this stage is developing a schema using the appropriate conceptual constructs for the proposed database management system. This schema may be considered as the equivalent of the schema at the logical level in the three-level database architecture we discussed earlier.

If the database is to be implemented using a database management system based on the SQL database language, the schema is defined in terms of tables and columns. The most convenient method of achieving this is to document the schema in a 'script' – a listing in plain text of the commands needed by the database management system to build the database (see Figure 2.5 for a small portion of the script needed to create the database developed from the conceptual data model in Figure 2.4). This script can then be executed by the database management system to create the database.

Figure 2.5 shows the command to create a table called **person**. This table has six columns: **person_identifier**, **name** and so on. The data held in the **person_identifier** column is an integer number. This is shown by the declaration of the datatype for that column as **INTEGER**. There must also always be a value in the **person_identifier** column. This is shown

Figure 2.4 A conceptual data model diagram

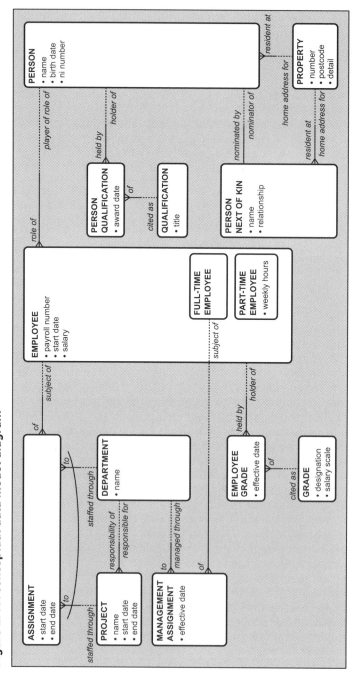

Figure 2.5 A portion of an SQL create script

```
CREATE TABLE person
(
    person_identifier                     INTEGER    NOT NULL,
    name                                  CHAR(30)   NOT NULL,
    resident_at_property_number           CHAR(25)   NOT NULL,
    resident_at_property_post_code        CHAR(8)    NOT NULL,
    birth_date                            DATE,
    ni_number                             CHAR(9),
    PRIMARY KEY person_identifier,
    FOREIGN KEY (resident_at_property_number,
                 resident_at_property_post_code)
                 REFERENCES property
);
```

by the **NOT NULL** constraint declaration for the column. **NULL** is an indicator in SQL that a value is missing. A column is said to be **NULL** at a row and column intersection if no value is specified for that column for that row. The constraint declaration **NOT NULL** says that missing values are not allowed. Each person, therefore, must have an identifier recorded in the database. In the UK it ought to be a reasonable assumption that **ni_number** (National Insurance Number) uniquely identifies a person, but this cannot be relied upon to be true.

The data held in the **birth_date** column will be a date (the datatype is **DATE**) and it is possible that, for some employees, the birth date is not recorded – **NOT NULL** is not specified for the **birth_date** column. Note that database management systems from different vendors handle dates in different ways despite the fact that SQL is supposed to be an international standard.

The declaration of a primary key identifies a column (or a number of columns) that uniquely identify each row in the table. In this case each person's identifier is managed to be unique and can be used to identify a person.

The declaration of a foreign key identifies a column or columns that represent a relationship between this table and another table. In this case the combination of the values in the **resident_at_property_number** and **resident_at_property_post_code** columns should match corresponding values in the **property** table; the **number** and **post_code** columns in the property table are declared as the primary key of that table.

The script includes a comparable **CREATE TABLE** command for each table in the database. There may also be a number of other commands within this script, or in another script, to implement any constraints that may need to be placed on the data. It is not included in Figure 2.5 but there may, for instance, be a constraint that an employee must be between the ages of 16 and 75 when they start employment. If such a constraint were implemented, it would be impossible to insert data about an employee who did not meet these age restrictions.

Figure 2.3 shows that there is a possibility of iteration between the conceptual data model and the database creation scripts. It could well be that the conceptual data model contains a constraint that it is not possible to implement in the chosen database management system. Or it could be that, on testing of the database, it is found that there is an error in the logic of the database (perhaps some important data is missing) and the creation script has to be amended and the database created afresh. In many cases these later amendments to the creation scripts are not reflected back into the conceptual data model and the documentation for the database becomes inconsistent and unreliable.

CONCEPTUAL DATA MODELLING (FROM A PROJECT-LEVEL PERSPECTIVE)

Figure 2.4 showed a conceptual data model diagram for the data required to support part of a human resources function. It is a very small data model and represents only a small part of the business of a commercial enterprise. Any information system built using this data model would probably end up as what is known as a 'small system' – a system to support a small, clearly defined community of users. It is a data model developed purely from the perspective of the small part of the business that the information system will be developed to support. It takes no account of any corporate need to share information across the enterprise. The problems associated with developing data models that do take account of the corporate need are discussed in Chapter 4.

Although it is not my intention to teach data modelling I am going to show, using just one of the many approaches available, the development of the model in Figure 2.4. The main purpose of this is to demonstrate the concepts used in data modelling. An understanding of these concepts will help you to 'read' a new conceptual data model that you come upon in the future.

Introducing the entity type concept

Figure 2.6 shows the first of our data modelling concepts. The single box, labelled **EMPLOYEE**, represents the concept known as an entity type. In fact the box represents all the employees of the company; it represents all the instances of the type or class of 'things' called employees. Entity types are always named with singular nouns despite representing all instances of the concept represented by the entity type.

An entity, an instance of an entity type, is usually defined as 'something of significance to the business about which information is to be recorded'. The 'something' may be physical, such as an employee or an item of equipment, or it may be conceptual, such as an order (although there may be a physical representation of the order on a piece of paper). It may even be details of the specification of something else about which information is to be recorded. An example of this latter situation may be found in the airline industry. An airline may wish to record details about the individual aircraft in its fleet, such as their current location and the date they were last serviced. But all aircraft come off a production line where they are built to a specification, and all aircraft of a particular type have a number of common characteristics that the airline may wish to record, such as maximum range and average speed. The conceptual data model would, therefore, have two entity types: the first would probably be called **AIRCRAFT** and would record the location and date last serviced while the other would probably be called **AIRCRAFT MODEL** and would record maximum range and average speed.

Figure 2.6 The EMPLOYEE entity type

Introducing the attribute concept

In Figure 2.7 I have added details of the information that we wish to record about our employees. You may or may not agree with this particular list of information, but it is a list that was developed interactively by a group of students on a course I ran. In real life the information required would be determined from the actual requirements of the human resources department.

Figure 2.7 The attributes of the EMPLOYEE entity type

Each of these items of information is known as an attribute, a 'detail that serves to qualify, identify, classify, quantify or express the state of an entity'. Each of the attributes of **EMPLOYEE** listed in Figure 2.7 does one or more of these. The value of **payroll number** identifies the employee. It could be argued that the value of **name** also identifies the employee, but it is unlikely that names are guaranteed to be unique within the organisation and, therefore, it would be inappropriate to say that the value of **name** identifies the employee. It does, however, help to qualify the employee in that it helps to distinguish one employee from another. An employee's **grade** helps to classify the employee.

Each of these attributes is then investigated to see if it is truly an attribute of the **EMPLOYEE** entity type or whether it should be represented by another data modelling construct. Consider the **address** attribute. What if more than one employee lives at the same address? It may be important for the company to know that, and then addresses or, more particularly, the properties with an address become significant to the business. Because it is now considered to be significant to the business, the property becomes an entity type in its own right (as shown in Figure 2.8).

Figure 2.8 The PROPERTY entity type

EMPLOYEE
* payroll number
* name
* birth date
* next of kin
* ni number
* start date
* qualifications
* grade
* department
* salary

PROPERTY
* number
* postcode
* detail

PROPERTY now appears as an entity type with three attributes, **number**, **postcode** and **detail**. The attributes **number** and **postcode** are there because, in the UK at least, house number (or name if there is no house number) and post code are sufficient to uniquely identify any property. The attribute **detail** is there to hold the rest of the address. (For the purposes of this exercise I am deliberately hiding details, such as how addresses are structured, to make the explanation of the key concepts easier.) Note that the **address** attribute in the employee entity has now been deleted.

Introducing the relationship concept

We now have two entity types, **EMPLOYEE** and **PROPERTY**, but we still need to represent that employees live at addresses. For this we need our third data modelling concept, the relationship. This is shown in Figure 2.9.

Figure 2.9 The 'resident at' relationship

The fact that there is a relationship between the **EMPLOYEE** and **PROPERTY** entity types is represented by a line on the diagram joining the two entity types together. This line has a specific set of notation that I will describe soon. But first the definition.

A relationship is simply defined as 'an association between two entity types'. In fact a relationship may exist between instances of the same entity type. A relationship such as this is known as a recursive relationship. The possibility of a recursive relationship leads to a fuller definition of relationship as 'an association between two entity types, or between one entity type and itself'. For example we may have a relationship to represent the fact that some employees manage subordinate employees: Joe Smith manages Phil Jones and Jenny Rogers; Jenny Rogers manages Barbara Watson, Roger Harrison and Henry Phillips. Joe Smith, Phil Jones, Jenny Rogers, Barbara Watson, Roger Harrison and Henry Phillips are all instances of the entity type **EMPLOYEE**.

Data models need to be interpreted both by business people, who are required to negotiate or approve the data requirements to be met by the system, and by technical people, who have to implement the system. It is important that the models are interpreted unambiguously and an important contribution to this unambiguous understanding is to have a formal method of 'reading' these relationships.

For example, consider the relationship between **PROPERTY** and **EMPLOYEE** that is introduced in Figure 2.9. Reading this relationship from bottom to top – from **PROPERTY** to **EMPLOYEE** – we have the sentence:

Each **PROPERTY** <u>may be</u> *home address for* <u>one or more</u> **EMPLOYEES**

I have used text formatting, **BOLD SMALL CAPITALS**, <u>underlining</u> and *italics*, to indicate the different elements of the sentence, which is constructed using the following rules:

- The word 'Each' is used because the box with the word 'property' inside it is an entity type (that is, it represents all instances of the type – all the properties) but we want to refer to a single instance of the type (that is, a single property).

- 'Each' is followed by the name of the entity type at the end from which we are starting the sentence – in this case **PROPERTY**.

- The term '<u>may be</u>' is used because not every property has to be the home address for an employee – this is represented on the diagram by a dotted line at the **PROPERTY** end of the relationship; a dotted line is always read as '<u>may be</u>'.

- '*home address for*' comes from the name of the relationship at the **PROPERTY** end of the relationship.

- The term '<u>one or more</u>' is used because there is an inverted three-pronged arrowhead (known as a crow's foot) at the **EMPLOYEE** end of the relationship – a crow's foot is always read as '<u>one or more</u>'.

- The sentence ends with the name of the entity type at the end of the line; we make it plural so that the sentence reads easily, in this case **EMPLOYEES**.

Each relationship should also be read in the opposite direction. Reading the relationship from top to bottom – from **EMPLOYEE** to **PROPERTY** – we have the sentence:

Each **EMPLOYEE** <u>must be</u> *resident at* <u>one and only one</u> **PROPERTY**

This sentence is constructed as follows:

- 'Each' because we want to refer to a single instance of the type.
- **EMPLOYEE** from the name of the upper entity type.
- '<u>must be</u>' because every employee has to be resident at a property (their home address) – this is represented on the diagram by the solid line at the **EMPLOYEE** end of the relationship and a solid line is always read as '<u>must be</u>'.
- '*resident at*' comes from the name of the relationship at the **EMPLOYEE** end of the relationship.
- The term '<u>one and only one</u>' is used because there is no crow's foot at the far end, the **PROPERTY** end, of the relationship – the absence of a crow's foot is always read as '<u>one and only one</u>'.
- **PROPERTY** comes from the name of the lower entity type.

In data modelling parlance this relationship is known as a one-to-many relationship. A property can be associated with many employees (Each **PROPERTY** <u>may be</u> *home address for* <u>one or more</u> **EMPLOYEES**) but an employee can only be associated with one property (Each **EMPLOYEE** <u>must be</u> *resident at* <u>one and only one</u> **PROPERTY**) through this relationship. There could be other legitimate relationships between **EMPLOYEE** and **PROPERTY** that may mean that an employee can be associated with more than one property overall, but an employee can only be resident at one property.

Further development of the model

We now turn our attention back to the attributes of **EMPLOYEE**.

The first thing we notice is that some of the remaining attributes, ***name***, ***address***, ***birth date***, ***ni number***, ***next of kin*** and ***qualifications***, have nothing to do with the employment of the person who is employed but are attributes of the person in their own right. So our '**EMPLOYEE**' entity type needs to be split into two entity types, **PERSON** and **EMPLOYEE**, with a relationship joining the two entity types. This is shown in Figure 2.10.

Figure 2.10 Splitting the EMPLOYEE entity type

The new relationship can be read from left to right as follows:

Each **EMPLOYEE** <u>must be</u> *role of* <u>one and only one</u> **PERSON**

And from right to left as follows:

Each **PERSON** <u>may be</u> *player of role of* <u>one or more</u> **EMPLOYEES**

This allows for any individual person to be employed by the company more than once.

One of the remaining attributes of **PERSON** is *qualifications*. Since this is plural we can deduce that each person may have more than one qualification and, of course, some people may have no qualifications at all. For those people who do have qualifications we may need to know when these qualifications were awarded.

We can now enhance our data model to show this. These enhancements are shown in Figure 2.11.

Figure 2.11 The QUALIFICATION and PERSON QUALIFICATION entity types

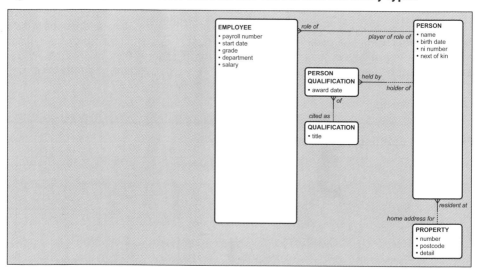

We have introduced two new entity types: **PERSON QUALIFICATION** with an *award date* attribute and **QUALIFICATION** with a *title* attribute.

The new relationship between **PERSON** and **PERSON QUALIFICATION** is read from right to left as follows:

Each **PERSON** may be *holder of* one or more **PERSON QUALIFICATIONS**

And from left to right as follows:

Each **PERSON QUALIFICATION** must be *held by* one and only one **PERSON**

And the new relationship between **PERSON QUALIFICATION** and **QUALIFICATION** is read from top to bottom as follows:

Each **PERSON QUALIFICATION** must be *of* one and only one **QUALIFICATION**

And from bottom to top as follows:

Each **QUALIFICATION** may be *cited as* one or more **PERSON QUALIFICATIONS**

As with the **address** attribute, the **qualifications** attribute of **PERSON** has been deleted.

One of the attributes of **EMPLOYEE** is **grade**. Every employee must have a grade but this grade probably changes over time and the human resources department may need to know the history of how an employee's grade has changed. This leads to further enhancements to the model as shown in Figure 2.12.

Figure 2.12 The GRADE and EMPLOYEE GRADE entity types

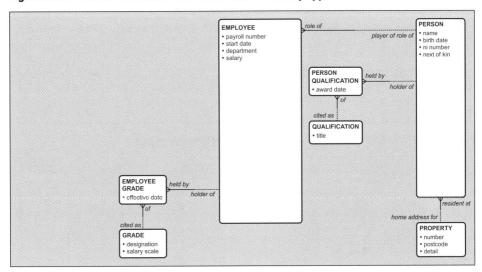

As before, we have deleted the **grade** attribute of **EMPLOYEE** and introduced two new entity types: **EMPLOYEE GRADE** with an **effective date** attribute and **GRADE** with a **designation** attribute and a **salary scale** attribute.

The new relationship between **EMPLOYEE** and **EMPLOYEE GRADE** is read from right to left as follows:

Each **EMPLOYEE** may be holder of one or more **EMPLOYEE GRADES**

And from left to right as follows:

Each **EMPLOYEE GRADE** must be held by one and only one **EMPLOYEE**

And the new relationship between **EMPLOYEE GRADE** and **GRADE** is read from top to bottom as follows:

Each **EMPLOYEE GRADE** must be of one and only one **GRADE**

And from bottom to top as follows:

Each **GRADE** may be cited as one or more **EMPLOYEE GRADES**

29

The **EMPLOYEE GRADE** entity type records both the current and past grades for each employee. The **effective date** attribute of **EMPLOYEE GRADE** records the date that an employee is appointed to a new grade. There is no record of the date that an employee ceases to hold a particular grade because it is assumed that this is the date of the next appointment to a new grade and so could be determined from other data in the database. In companies or organisations where there is a more complex grade structure with, for example, the concept of temporary grades, this simple model would not be sufficient to record all of the data.

The entity type **EMPLOYEE** has a **department** attribute. The human resources department needs to record information about employees from the time that they are first given a contract, but they are not formally assigned to a department until they arrive for their first day's work. This means that not every employee has a department recorded for them, but most do. Employees may move between departments and the human resources department may need to know the history of which departments an employee has worked in. This leads to further enhancements to the model as shown in Figure 2.13.

Figure 2.13 The DEPARTMENT and ASSIGNMENT entity types

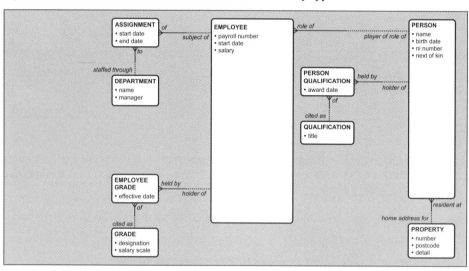

We have deleted the **department** attribute of **EMPLOYEE** and introduced another two new entity types: **DEPARTMENT**, with **name** and **manager** attributes, and **ASSIGNMENT**, with **start date** and **end date** attributes.

The new relationship between **EMPLOYEE** and **ASSIGNMENT** is read from right to left as follows:

Each **EMPLOYEE** may be subject of one or more **ASSIGNMENTS**

And from left to right as follows:

> Each **ASSIGNMENT** <u>must be</u> *of* <u>one and only one</u> **EMPLOYEE**

And the new relationship between **ASSIGNMENT** and **DEPARTMENT** is read from top to bottom as follows:

> Each **ASSIGNMENT** <u>must be</u> *to* <u>one and only one</u> **DEPARTMENT**

And from bottom to top as follows:

> Each **DEPARTMENT** <u>may be</u> *staffed through* <u>one or more</u> **ASSIGNMENTS**

All assignments of employees to departments can, therefore, be recorded and the human resources department can determine all the departments to which an employee has been assigned. They can also determine the start date of each current assignment and the start and end dates of each completed assignment. The human resources department can also produce a listing of all the employees who are or have been assigned to a particular department, with the appropriate dates of the assignments.

The new department entity has a ***manager*** attribute with which we can record who manages the department. But a manager of a department is also an employee and we have already provided, with the **EMPLOYEE** and **PERSON** entity types, the means to record details of employees. The ***manager*** attribute in a department should, therefore, be replaced by a relationship between **DEPARTMENT** and **EMPLOYEE** as shown in Figure 2.14.

Figure 2.14 The one-to-one 'managed by' relationship

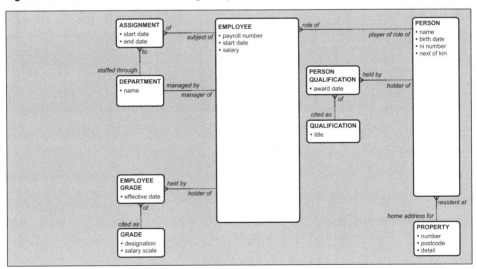

This new relationship is a one-to-one relationship and can be read as follows:

Each **DEPARTMENT** <u>must be</u> *managed by* <u>one and only one</u> **EMPLOYEE**

Each **EMPLOYEE** <u>may be</u> *manager of* <u>one and only one</u> **DEPARTMENT**

Using this relationship the human resources department can determine which employee currently manages each department, but they cannot determine who managed a department in the past or which departments were managed by a particular employee in the past. To achieve this would require a relationship such as:

Each **DEPARTMENT** <u>must be</u> *managed by* <u>one or more</u> **EMPLOYEES**

Each **EMPLOYEE** <u>may be</u> *manager of* <u>one or more</u> **DEPARTMENTS**

This is known as a many-to-many relationship and is shown in Figure 2.15.

Figure 2.15 The many-to-many 'managed by' relationship

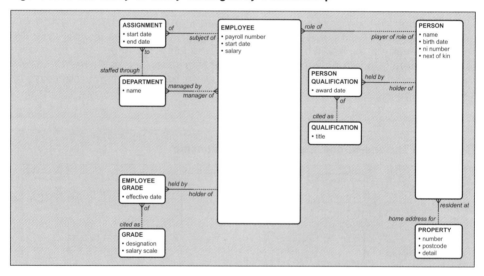

But with this relationship, although the human resources department can determine who managed a department in the past and which departments were managed by a particular employee in the past, they cannot put any dates to these management assignments.

To achieve this requires a new entity type and associated relationships to replace this many-to-many relationship as shown in Figure 2.16. This replacement of a many-to-many relationship by a new entity type and relationships is known by data modellers as 'resolving the many-to-many relationship'.

This new entity type, **MANAGEMENT ASSIGNMENT**, has an ***effective date*** attribute and relationships such that:

Figure 2.16 The resolution of the many-to-many 'managed by' relationship

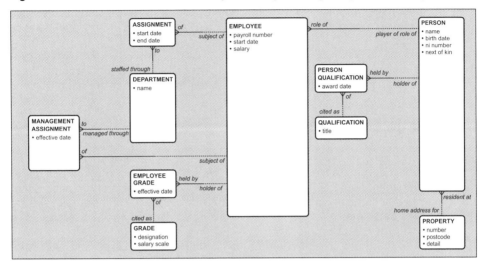

Each **EMPLOYEE** may be *subject of* one or more **MANAGEMENT ASSIGNMENTS**

Each **MANAGEMENT ASSIGNMENT** must be *to* one and only one **DEPARTMENT**

Each **DEPARTMENT** may be *managed through* one or more **MANAGEMENT ASSIGNMENTS**

Each **MANAGEMENT ASSIGNMENT** must be *of* one and only one **EMPLOYEE**

This simple model clearly allows all assignments to departments to be recorded and also allows details of who manages a department at any one time to be recorded, but there are a number of issues that must be considered.

Jenny Rogers manages the Finance Department and, therefore, has an instance of the **MANAGEMENT ASSIGNMENT** entity type associated with her instance of the **EMPLOYEE** (and **PERSON**) entity type(s), but it is not clear whether she should also have an instance of the **ASSIGNMENT** entity type associated with her instance of the **EMPLOYEE** entity type. That is, it is not clear whether a department manager is also recorded as an employee working within that department or not. This is not a big issue provided a decision one way or the other is made and then this rule is applied consistently. If it is not and the database is queried to list all the current employees of each department, the following inconsistencies could occur:

- If only the **ASSIGNMENT** records are queried, those managers who are only recorded through instances of **MANAGEMENT ASSIGNMENT** do not appear.

- If both the **ASSIGNMENT** and the **MANAGEMENT ASSIGNMENT** records are queried, those managers who are recorded through instances of **ASSIGNMENT** as well as through instances of **MANAGEMENT ASSIGNMENT** appear twice in the lists produced as a result of the query.

Furthermore the fact that each **DEPARTMENT** <u>may be</u> *managed through* <u>one or more</u> **MANAGEMENT ASSIGNMENTS** means that the business requirement that there can only be one current manager for each department could be compromised. It could be possible to record two overlapping instances of management assignment for any one instance of department.

There are a number of modelling conventions that can be used to overcome these problems but, as it is not the intention to teach data modelling, they are not discussed further here.

Introducing the subtype concept

Sometimes we need to express the idea that there may be differences as well as similarities between instances of an entity type and that there may be groups of instances that share some of those differences. For example some of the people that are employed by a company may be employed full-time while the other employees are only employed part-time.

In Figure 2.17 there are two new entity types, **FULL-TIME EMPLOYEE** and **PART-TIME EMPLOYEE**. They are called entity subtypes but they are entity types in their own right, so we use the same entity type notation – the 'soft-cornered' box. We identify them as subtypes of **EMPLOYEE** by placing the new entity types within the **EMPLOYEE** box. **EMPLOYEE** is known as the supertype of **FULL-TIME EMPLOYEE** and **PART-TIME EMPLOYEE**. A subtype may itself be subtyped, that is it may itself act as the supertype of further subtypes. A hierarchy of supertype and subtype entities is sometimes known as a specialisation hierarchy.

Figure 2.17 Adding entity subtypes

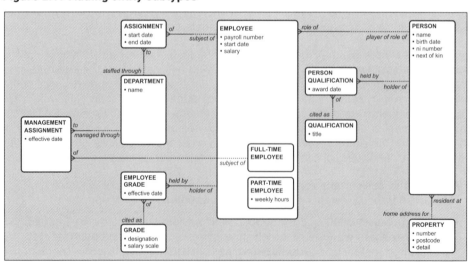

The entity subtypes of an entity supertype are mutually exclusive. In our example, a person is either employed full-time or is employed part-time, but not both. Furthermore every instance of the supertype is also an instance of one of the subtypes. There is no instance of the supertype that is not also an instance one of the subtypes. Every employee is employed either full-time or part-time; there is no other form of employment. Another rule of subtypes is that the mutually exclusive nature extends for all time. This means that for our example, a part-time employee can never become a full-time employee or vice versa.

Aside: In real life this may not be true. The implication of modelling these as subtypes is that the transfer of a full-time employee to part-time employment is treated as a new employment. The full-time employment record is closed and a new employment record is created. You might consider that this is not a sensible approach – and you would be correct – but these subtypes of **EMPLOYEE** enable me to demonstrate the principles of subtyping even if the situation is somewhat artificial.

Entity subtypes may have attributes or relationships in their own right. For part-time employees there is a need to record the number of hours they are contracted to work each week, but there is no requirement to record this information for full-time employees. Thus a part-time employee has a **weekly hours** attribute. There is also a business rule that only full-time employees may manage a department. This is represented by moving the relationship between **EMPLOYEE** and **MANAGEMENT ASSIGNMENT** so that it is between **FULL-TIME EMPLOYEE** and **MANAGEMENT ASSIGNMENT** such that:

Each **FULL-TIME EMPLOYEE** may be *subject of* one or more **MANAGEMENT ASSIGNMENTS**

Each **MANAGEMENT ASSIGNMENT** must be *of* one and only one **FULL-TIME EMPLOYEE**

Although the attributes or relationships that are specific to a single entity subtype are shown explicitly in the model, each subtype also implicitly inherits all the attributes or relationships of its supertype. The attributes **payroll number**, **start date** and **salary** apply to both of the subtypes **FULL-TIME EMPLOYEE** and **PART-TIME EMPLOYEE**. The relationship between **EMPLOYEE** and **ASSIGNMENT** also applies between **FULL-TIME EMPLOYEE** and **ASSIGNMENT** and between **PART-TIME EMPLOYEE** and **ASSIGNMENT** so that:

Each **FULL-TIME EMPLOYEE** must be *subject of* one or more **ASSIGNMENTS**

Each **ASSIGNMENT** may be *of* one and only one **FULL-TIME EMPLOYEE**

and:

Each **PART-TIME EMPLOYEE** must be *subject of* one or more **ASSIGNMENTS**

Each **ASSIGNMENT** may be *of* one and only one **PART-TIME EMPLOYEE**

Entity subtypes are useful in that they enable the data modeller to indicate real-world differences between groups of instances of entity types. They show explicitly in the conceptual data model how real-world 'things' may be classified. They are also useful in that they enable the clear specification of constraints in the model, such as the constraint that the hours to be worked each week are only to be recorded for part-time employees and the constraint that only full-time employees are allowed to manage a department. Without the use of subtypes these constraints would need to be expressed in words, which might later be misunderstood or missed altogether.

Introducing the exclusive arc

Another useful technique is the ability to indicate where only one of two or more relationships applies for any one instance of an entity type. These are known as mutually exclusive relationships and are usually marked on a conceptual data model diagram with an arc, commonly known as an 'exclusive arc'.

Figure 2.18 introduces a new entity type, **PROJECT**, so that employees can be assigned to projects as well as departments, where each project is the responsibility of a single department. There are no restrictions constraining employees to only be assigned to projects managed by their own department; employees can be assigned to projects managed by departments other than their own. Assignments to both departments and projects are to be recorded. The **ASSIGNMENT** entity type has a relationship to the **PROJECT** entity type as well as to the **DEPARTMENT** entity type. These two relationships are crossed by an arc at the **ASSIGNMENT** entity type end, indicating that they are mutually exclusive as far as **ASSIGNMENT** is concerned.

Figure 2.18 Adding an exclusive arc

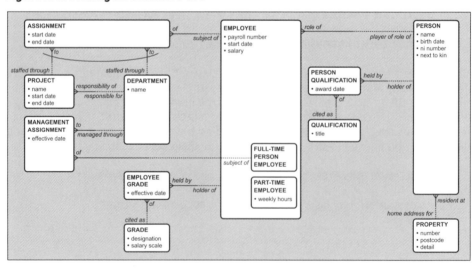

These mutually exclusive relationships are read as follows:

Each **ASSIGNMENT** must be to one and only one **DEPARTMENT**
OR to one and only one **PROJECT**

Each **DEPARTMENT** <u>may be</u> *staffed through* <u>one or more</u> **ASSIGNMENTS**

Each **PROJECT** <u>may be</u> *staffed through* <u>one or more</u> **ASSIGNMENTS**

Exclusive arcs are useful in enabling the data modeller to indicate a real-world situation – the exclusive nature of relationships between entities. The arc also explicitly shows the clear specification of a constraint in the model: for any one instance of the entity type only one of the mutually exclusive relationships may be recorded. In the real world an assignment can be to either a department or a project but not to both. This means that, within any database, an **ASSIGNMENT** instance may be associated with either a **DEPARTMENT** instance or a **PROJECT** instance but not both.

The mutual exclusivity shown by the exclusive arc in Figure 2.18 involves two relationships and the mutually exclusive ends of these relationships are both 'mandatory' (<u>must be</u>) and 'many' (<u>one or more</u>). Mutual exclusivity is not restricted to the 'mandatory many' type of relationship ends. A set of mutually exclusive relationships may include relationship ends that are 'many' (one or more), 'one' (one and only one) or a mixture of both. However, a set of mutually exclusive relationships must include ends that are either all 'mandatory' (<u>must be</u>) or all 'optional' (<u>may be</u>); a mixture of mandatory and optional is not allowed.

When developing a conceptual data model it is sometimes difficult to decide whether to use the subtyping technique or to mark relationships as being mutually exclusive. This is because the two concepts are really saying the same thing in different ways. With subtyping we are saying that the instances of the supertype may be classified into distinct groups; with mutually exclusive relationships we are saying that each relationship only applies to certain instances of the relevant entity type – the instances of that entity type are grouped according to the relevance of the relationships.

For example instead of using the exclusive arc to indicate that assignments may be either to a department or to a project but not to both, we could have subtyped **ASSIGNMENT** into **DEPARTMENT ASSIGNMENT** and **PROJECT ASSIGNMENT**.

Entity subtypes can often be replaced by a set of mutually exclusive relationships. Exclusive arcs, identifying mutually exclusive relationships, can always be replaced by entity subtypes. You may therefore question why we have the exclusive arc notation. Indeed some data modelling notations, such as IDEF1X (see Appendix A), do not have an exclusive arc notation. It is then necessary to use entity subtypes to show the 'mutually exclusive relationship' concept.

Our final enhancement to the data model comes through further consideration of the *next of kin* attribute of the **PERSON** entity type. A next of kin must live somewhere and it would be useful to know the address of the next of kin and their relationship to the employee as well as their name. This requires a **PERSON NEXT OF KIN** entity type with relationships such that:

Each **PERSON** <u>may be</u> *nominator of* <u>one and only one</u> **PERSON NEXT OF KIN**

Each **PERSON NEXT OF KIN** <u>must be</u> *resident at* <u>one and only one</u> **PROPERTY**

Each **PROPERTY** <u>may be</u> *home address for* <u>one or more</u> **PERSON NEXT OF KIN**

Each **PERSON NEXT OF KIN** <u>must be</u> *nominated by* <u>one and only one</u> **PERSON**

These enhancements are shown in Figure 2.19.

Figure 2.19 The PERSON NEXT OF KIN entity type

Since a person can only have one next of kin, this could have been modelled with two attributes in the **PERSON** entity type (*next of kin name* and *next of kin relationship*) and a relationship between **PERSON** and **PROPERTY** such that:

Each **PERSON** <u>must be</u> *related to next of kin resident at* <u>one and only one</u> **PROPERTY**

Each **PROPERTY** <u>may be</u> *home address for next of kin of* <u>one or more</u> **PERSONS**

However, the construct in Figure 2.19 is preferred for two reasons. First, it more clearly represents the semantics that there are two separate 'things' of interest to the business – the person and the next of kin of that person. Second, should there be a later decision to allow a person to record more than one 'next of kin', the changes required are relatively simple – the addition of a crow's foot at the **PERSON NEXT OF KIN** end of the relationship between **PERSON** and **PERSON NEXT OF KIN** and, possibly, a means of identifying (through an additional attribute in **PERSON NEXT OF KIN**) the principal next of kin of an employee where more than one is recorded.

This is now the final model as seen in Figure 2.4. While the intention was not to teach you how to data model, I hope that by working through this example you now understand the concepts embodied in a data model and the way in which it can represent the data requirements of a business, or business area, to be supported by an information system.

Our conceptual data model only covers some of the data requirements of our business area – the human resources function. It is restricted to the perspective of a single project. In Chapter 4 we will look at data modelling from a corporate perspective.

RELATIONAL DATA ANALYSIS

In the previous section we saw one approach to the development of a conceptual data model. This was typical of the approach that might be taken when there is no formal documentation of the requirements that are to be met. The model is developed by the analyst as a result of information about the business data requirements gathered through interviews, workshops or observation of working practices.

There is another much more formal approach to the analysis of data requirements that relies on there being some document or other existing record (such as a program file) that lists the items of data that are to be recorded. This set of data items is then analysed using this process, which is known as relational data analysis. The result is a set of relations in third normal form (more about these terms in a short while) and this set of relations can be shown diagrammatically in a form that looks remarkably similar to our previous conceptual data model, although there are some significant differences.

Although relational data analysis is based upon the relational model of data proposed by Edgar F. Codd (1970), there is no presumption that relational data analysis is followed by an implementation using a relational database. The implemented database could be object oriented or follow some other model of database implementation.

As with our look at the development of a conceptual data model, the easiest way to explain relational data analysis is to work through an example. Before we can do that, however, it is necessary to explain the relational model of data, which is founded on well-established mathematical set theory.

The relational model of data

In the relational model of data, the data is recorded in a set of linked relations. The relation used as the main concept of the model is not the same as the relationship in a conceptual data model and it is inappropriate to use these two terms interchangeably in the data/database community, despite the fact that they are used interchangeably in general usage.

A relation has two parts – a heading and a body. The heading consists of a set of attributes; the attribute in the relational model of data is a similar concept to the attribute we saw in the conceptual data model, although there are some differences. The body is a set of elements that are called tuples (which rhymes with 'couples'). Each tuple is, in turn, a set of data values, one value for each of the attributes defined in the relation heading. More formally a tuple is a set of attribute-name:attribute-value pairs. The set of values from which the individual values of an attribute may be taken is known as a domain. More than one attribute can take its values from any one domain. The domain is a very important concept in relational theory, but it plays no part in the relational data analysis process described later in this chapter.

The easiest way to visualise a relation is as a table (although in some important respects a table is an inappropriate representation of a relation). The representation of a relation as a table is shown in Figure 2.20. The relational concepts are highlighted in the diagram.

Figure 2.20 A relation shown as a table

The heading of the relation comprises five attributes called **Person Identifier**, **Family Name**, **Given Name**, **Birth Date** and **NI Number**. The body of the relation comprises six tuples, one for each of the employees Joe Smith, Phil Jones, Jenny Rogers, Barbara Watson, Roger Harrison and Henry Phillips. The set of values for each of these four attributes for each employee forms a tuple. The tuple for Barbara Watson is highlighted. The domain for the attribute **Family Name** is also highlighted. We can see that this has at least six values, but there may be more values in the domain that are not used by the **Family Name** attribute in this particular relation.

There are a number of rules associated with relations. Without going into too much technical detail these are:

- There is no significance to the order of the attributes within the relation heading; this is because the relation heading is a set of attributes and one of the properties of a mathematical set is that the elements of the set are unordered. The fact that in Figure 2.20 the attributes are arranged in a particular order from left to right is purely for presentational purposes; that order has no significance to the relation that Figure 2.20 is representing.

- Similarly, since the body of the relation is a set of tuples, there is no significance to the order of the tuples within the body of the relation. Again the fact that in Figure 2.20 the tuples are arranged in a particular order from top to bottom is purely for presentational purposes.

- Attributes within the relation heading should be unique; that is, there should be no duplication of attribute names within a relation.

- There should be no attributes whose values can be derived from the values taken by other attributes, whether those attributes are in the same relation or in another relation.

- Relations have unique identifiers known as primary keys; the primary key comprises the attribute, or combination of attributes, whose values are the minimum required to uniquely identify each instance of the relation. The primary key of the relation represented in Figure 2.20 is the **Person Identifier** attribute; each person has a person identifier that is managed to be unique.

- No two tuples in a relation may have the same value of primary key. If the **Person Identifier** attribute is the primary key of the relation representing persons, no two persons can have the same personal identifier.

- In each tuple each part of the primary key must have a value. Every person must have a person identifier.

- The attributes of a relation represent characteristics that are determined by the primary key; that is, they describe the 'thing' defined by the primary key. The name of the employee with personal identifier P6793 is Barbara Watson, her date of birth is 6 December 1952 and her national insurance number is AA756242C.

- In any tuple no attribute may take more than one value; that is, each attribute is single-valued – there are no multiple-valued attributes within a relation.

Normalisation

We use the process of relational data analysis – the development of a set of relations in third normal form – to develop a conceptual database design in which there will be no update anomalies when data is input into the database or later updated. In general terms this means that for any piece of information there is only one place in the database where the data representing the information can be stored and that place is unambiguously recognised. This process of relational data analysis allows us to confirm that we are associating attributes that are all about one thing (person, product and so on) or concept (promotion, order, account, transaction and so on) of interest to the business.

This is exactly what we were trying to achieve when we earlier developed the conceptual data model using the entity-relationship notation.

The example we use to demonstrate relational data analysis is also based on the human resources department that we saw earlier, although now our starting point is the existing paper records in use within that department. An example of one of these paper records is shown in Figure 2.21.

The first stage in the process is to list all the 'data items' (fields on the form) that we can identify. The result of doing this is shown in Figure 2.22. You will notice that the data items are split into different groups. All of the data items in the first group (from **Title** to **Head of Department Tel No**) are fields for which only a single value is allowed on the form. The remaining data items can take many values. These are known as 'repeating groups'.

Figure 2.21 The human resources paper record

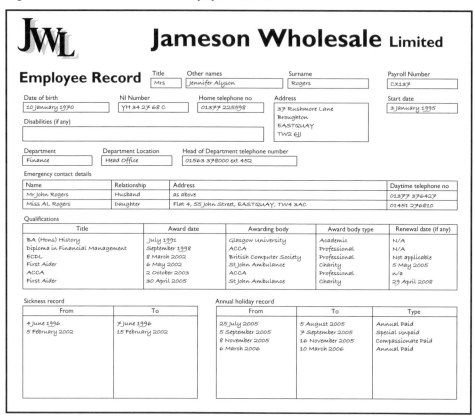

This simple listing of the data items provides us with a 'relation' in what is known as the un-normalised form. This is often abbreviated to UNF. You should note that un-normalised 'relation' does not comply with all of the rules of relations and that is why the word relation is in quotes.

One of the data items, **Payroll Number**, is of particular interest. This is because the payroll number of an employee uniquely identifies that employee within the company. When we start the normalisation process, **Payroll Number** will become the primary key of the main relation, in this case the **EMPLOYEE** relation.

First normal form

The first stage in our normalisation process is to move from this un-normalised form to produce a set of relations that are in first normal form (often abbreviated to 1NF). A relation is in first normal form if all the values taken by the attributes of that relation are atomic or scalar values – we say that the attributes are single-valued. This is to comply with the rule that there must not be any multiple-valued attributes in a relation.

Figure 2.22 The 'data items' identified from the human resources paper record

```
Title
Other Names
Surname
Payroll Number
Date of Birth
NI Number
Home Tel No
Address
Disabilities
Start Date
Department Name
Department Location
Head of Department Tel No

Emergency Contact Name
Emergency Contact Relationship
Emergency Contact Address
Emergency Contact Day Tel No

Qualification Title
Qualification Award Date
Qualification Awarding Body
Qualification Award Body Type
Qualification Renewal Date

Sickness From
Sickness To

Annual Holiday From
Annual Holiday To
Annual Holiday Type
```

To move to first normal form we need to remove the repeating groups from the initial 'relation'.

Each of the repeating groups then becomes a relation in its own right. In our example we have four new relations: one for the emergency contact details; one for the qualifications held by the employee; one for the periods that the employee has been absent through sickness; and one for the periods that the employee has been on holiday. From the information on the form in Figure 2.21 we can see that the form records sickness absences since the employee started with the company, whereas holiday periods are only recorded for the current holiday year. This is not something that we need to take into consideration in our relational data analysis. We are only interested in the data that needs to be recorded; we are not interested, in this process, in when that data is recorded and for how long it is recorded.

For each of these new relations we need to identify a primary key. For the employee's emergency contacts the name is sufficient to uniquely identify one amongst the contacts recorded for a single employee. But we need to uniquely identify an emergency contact amongst all the emergency contacts recorded in the company. In any but the smallest company it is possible for two employees to have an emergency contact called John Rogers, and for them to be two different people. The name of the emergency contact is, therefore, insufficient to uniquely identify an emergency contact within the company. What we really need to uniquely identify an emergency contact is both the name of the contact and an indication, such as the payroll number, of the employee for whom this person is an emergency contact. The primary key of this relation is, therefore, the combination of **Payroll Number** and **Emergency Contact Name**.

Our first normal form relations are shown in Figure 2.23. These are now relations as they comply with all the rules we listed earlier. Each of the data items listed is now an attribute.

Figure 2.23 The first normal form relations

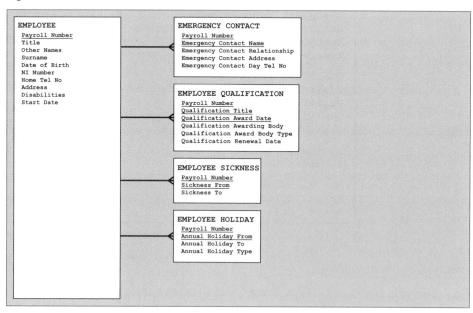

All our new relations have a primary key identified (in this case by underlining the relevant attributes). All of these primary keys comprise at least two attributes: the primary key of the main relation and sufficient extra attributes to uniquely identify each instance of the real-world thing that the relation represents. As explained above for the emergency contact relation, this is the combination of the employee's payroll number, the **Payroll Number** attribute, and the name of the emergency contact, the **Emergency Contact Name** attribute. For the relations representing sickness absence periods and holiday periods, it is the combination of the employee's payroll number and the start date for the relevant period. For the relation representing the employee's qualifications there are three elements to the primary key since three items of data are required to uniquely identify each employee's qualification. One of these is the employee's payroll number as before. There is also the title (or name) of the qualification. But the combination of the employee's payroll number and the title of the qualification is insufficient to uniquely identify a qualification held by an employee. Inspection of the form shows that Jenny Rogers holds two first-aid qualifications, one of which is now out of date. So to uniquely identify a qualification held by an employee we also need another item of information, the date that the qualification was awarded. Hence the primary key of the relation representing the qualifications held by employees is the combination of **Payroll Number**, **Qualification Title** and **Qualification Award Date**.

When the primary key of a relation appears as an attribute in another relation it is known as a foreign key in the other relation. In this case **Payroll Number** is a foreign key in our four new relations.

Figure 2.23 approximates to the notation of our previous conceptual data model. Every relation that has a foreign key amongst its attributes has a relationship line drawn to the relation with the corresponding primary key. This relationship line has a crow's foot at the end of the relationship with the relation with the foreign key. At the other end of the relationship, the end with the relation with the primary key that corresponds to the foreign key, there is a plain end (i.e. there is no crow's foot). This diagram is less expressive than our conceptual data model because we cannot show the 'may be' or 'must be' nature of the relationships and we do not have any names for the relationships. The diagram does, however, help to demonstrate our progress through the relational data analysis process.

Second normal form

The next stage of our relational data analysis process is to move our relations to second normal form (2NF). For a relation to be in second normal form it has to be in first normal form and, in addition, it must meet the condition that every attribute that is not part of the primary key is dependent on the whole of the primary key. More formally a relation is in second normal form if and only if it is in first normal form and every non-key attribute is irreducibly dependent on the primary key.

In this context, 'dependence' means that if we have two attributes, **Payroll Number** and **Employee Surname**, and we know the value of the attribute **Payroll Number**, we can determine the value of the attribute **Employee Surname** (for example given the payroll number CX137, we know that the surname of that employee is Rogers). We say that **Employee Surname** is dependent on **Payroll Number**. The reverse is not true. If we know that an employee's surname is Rogers, we cannot determine that employee's payroll number – there may be more than one Rogers working for the company. So **Payroll Number** is not dependent on **Employee Surname**.

We achieve second normal form by reviewing every attribute that is not part of the primary key in the first normal form relations to see if any of those attributes are dependent on one or more parts of a multiple-part primary key but not the whole primary key. If so, those attributes need to be removed.

Our main first normal form relation (labelled **EMPLOYEE** in Figure 2.23) has **Payroll Number** as its primary key. This is a single-part primary key and, therefore, each of the attributes in that relation must be dependent on the whole of the primary key. This first normal form relation is, therefore, also in second normal form.

Let us now consider the **EMERGENCY CONTACT** relation shown in Figure 2.23. This relation has a multiple-part primary key of two attributes – **Payroll Number** and **Emergency Contact Name** – and three non-key attributes – **Emergency Contact Relationship, Emergency Contact Address** and **Emergency Contact Day Tel No**. If we know the combined values of **Payroll Number** and **Emergency Contact Name**, we can determine the values of the non-key attributes. The test is to take each non-key attribute in turn and see if it is possible to determine its value using only a part of the primary key. For **Emergency Contact Relationship** we need to know the values of both **Payroll Number** and **Emergency Contact Name** to know its value. Knowing just the value of **Payroll Number** is insufficient. The employee with payroll number CX137 has both a husband and a daughter as emergency contacts.

Similarly knowing just the value of **Emergency Contact Name** is insufficient; it is possible that more than one employee has an emergency contact called Mr John Rogers. The same is true for both **Emergency Contact Address** and **Emergency Contact Day Tel No**. This **EMERGENCY CONTACT** relation is, therefore, also in second normal form.

Similar inspection also indicates that the relations **EMPLOYEE SICKNESS** and **EMPLOYEE HOLIDAY** are also already in second normal form.

Let us now consider the employee qualification relation. This has a multiple-part primary key of three attributes – **Payroll Number, Qualification Title** and **Qualification Award Date** – and three non-key attributes – **Qualification Awarding Body, Qualification Award Body Type** and **Qualification Renewal Date**. We need to know the values of all three elements of the primary key to determine the value of **Qualification Renewal Date**. The same is not true for **Qualification Awarding Body** and **Qualification Award Body Type**. The values of these two attributes are not dependent on the value of **Payroll Number** or on the value of **Qualification Award Date**. They are only dependent on the value of **Qualification Title** (assuming that only one body issues any qualification of a given name or title; this may not be true in the real world but we make that assumption for the purposes of this exercise).

To create our second normal form relations we need, therefore, to remove **Qualification Awarding Body** and **Qualification Award Body Type** to another relation, which I shall call **QUALIFICATION**. But this new relation also needs **Qualification Title** as its primary key since we know that the values of **Qualification Awarding Body** and **Qualification Award Body Type** are dependent on **Qualification Title**.

The second normal form relations are now shown diagrammatically in Figure 2.24. As before, every foreign key is at the crow's foot end of a relationship to the relation with the corresponding primary key.

Third normal form

We now need to move our relations from second normal form to third normal form (3NF). For a relation to be in third normal form it has to be in second normal form and also has to meet the condition that every attribute that is not part of the primary key is not dependent on an attribute that is also not part of the primary key. More formally a relation is in third normal form if and only if it is in second normal form and every non-key attribute is nontransitively dependent on the primary key.

Figure 2.24 The second normal form relations

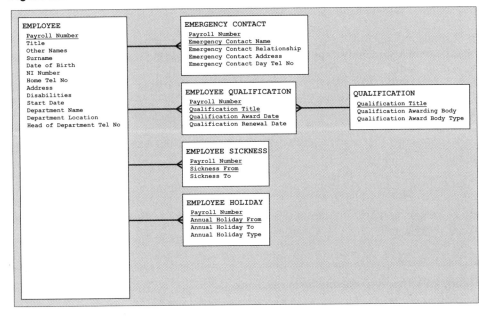

We achieve third normal form by reviewing every attribute that is not part of the primary key in the second normal form relations to see if any of those attributes are dependent on another attribute that is not part of the primary key. If so, those attributes need to be removed.

In the second normal form **EMPLOYEE** relation, the value of **Title** is dependent on the value of **Payroll Number**, the primary key. If I know that the value of the **Payroll Number** attribute is CX137, I can determine that the value of the **Title** attribute is Mrs. The same is true of the **Other Names**, **Surname**, **Date of Birth**, **NI Number**, **Home Tel No**, **Address**, **Disabilities**, **Start Date** and **Department Name** attributes. However, if I know the value of the **Department Name** attribute, I can determine the values of both the **Department Location** and **Head of Department Tel No** attributes. The attributes **Department Location** and **Head of Department Tel No** are not, therefore, directly dependent on the primary key, the **Payroll Number** attribute. We say that **Department Location** and **Head of Department Tel No** are transitively dependent (that is, indirectly dependent) on **Payroll Number** through **Department Name**.

The attributes **Department Location** and **Head of Department Tel No** are, therefore, removed from the **EMPLOYEE** relation to form a new relation, called **DEPARTMENT**. This new relation also needs **Department Name** as its primary key since both **Department Location** and **Head of Department Tel No** are dependent on **Department Name**.

The attribute **Department Name** remains in **EMPLOYEE** as a foreign key, but it is not part of the primary key. So that it can be identified as a foreign key that is not part of the primary key it is marked with an asterisk (*).

In the second normal form **EMERGENCY CONTACT** relation, all the non-key attributes are directly dependent on the primary key. The relation **EMERGENCY CONTACT** is, therefore, also in third normal form.

In the second normal form **QUALIFICATION** relation, the value of the attribute **Qualification Award Body Type** is determined by the value of the attribute **Qualification Awarding Body**. This means that we need a new third normal form relation, say called **QUALIFICATION BODY**, with **Qualification Awarding Body** as its primary key and **Qualification Award Body Type** as its only non-key attribute. The relation **QUALIFICATION** retains the attribute **Qualification Awarding Body** as a foreign key.

Inspection shows that both the **EMPLOYEE SICKNESS** and **EMPLOYEE HOLIDAY** relations are already in third normal form.

The third normal form relations are now shown diagrammatically in Figure 2.25. As before, every foreign key is at the crow's foot end of a relationship to the relation with the corresponding primary key, but note that when moving to third normal form the foreign keys are not part of the primary key.

Figure 2.25 The third normal form relations

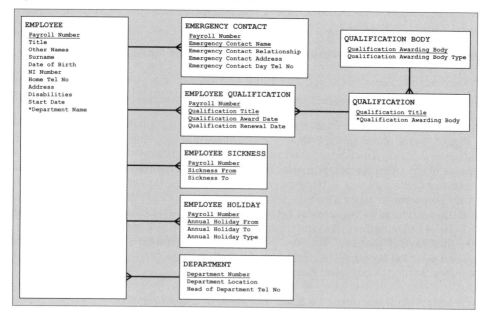

Our relations are now in third normal form and this is as far as we can go with the process of relational data analysis.

Further normal forms

There are, however, a number of higher normal forms, the most significant of which is known as Boyce–Codd normal form (BCNF).

Until now we have been talking about the primary key for a relation as if there is only one possible primary key. Sometimes there is more than one possible primary key. Consider our human resources department. For our **EMPLOYEE** relation, we almost intuitively selected the attribute **Payroll Number** as the primary key. If the company issues unique payroll numbers to its employees, we know that the payroll number can be used to uniquely identify an employee and it makes sense to use the **Payroll Number** attribute as the primary key. There may, however, be other possible combinations of attributes that could have been used as a primary key. It could well be that, for all except very large organisations, the combination of the values of **Other Names**, **Surname** and **Date of Birth** is sufficient to uniquely identify any employee. These three attributes could have been chosen as the primary key. All possible primary keys are known as candidate keys. So our **EMPLOYEE** relation has two candidate keys: **Payroll Number** on its own and the combination of **Other Names**, **Surname** and **Date of Birth**. One of the candidate keys, in this case **Payroll Number**, is chosen as the primary key. The choice of which candidate key to use as a primary key is sometimes quite arbitrary, although there is often a clear preferred option. Candidate keys not selected to be the primary key are sometimes referred to as alternate keys.

With our discussion of first, second and third normal forms we have been focusing on the dependencies of the non-key attributes to the primary keys.

With Boyce–Codd normal form the emphasis has shifted from the primary key to all the candidate keys. For most practical purposes Boyce–Codd normal form and third normal form are equivalent. The only exceptions occur when there are two or more candidate keys, where those candidate keys are composed of more than one attribute and where the multi-attribute keys overlap (that is, they share a common attribute). In this situation it is possible for update anomalies to occur at third normal form, but not if the relations are restructured to be in Boyce–Codd normal form. Boyce–Codd normal form is really just a stricter form of third normal form.

For example consider the third normal form relation to hold data about employee interviews shown in Figure 2.26.

Figure 2.26 The employee interview relation

Interviewee Payroll Number	Interview Date	Interview Time	Interviewer Payroll Number	Room Number
BZ987	2010-05-02	1030	AQ327	G101
CA446	2010-05-02	1200	AQ327	G101
CX137	2010-05-02	1200	BY669	G102
CA446	2010-07-02	1030	AQ327	G102

This relation has three candidate keys as follows:

- **Interviewee Payroll Number** and **Interview Date**;
- **Interviewer Payroll Number**, **Interview Date** and **Interview Time**;
- **Room Number**, **Interview Date** and **Interview Time**.

Each of these candidate keys is multipart and has one or more overlapping attributes.

If the room allocation for the interviewer with the payroll number AQ327 on the 2 May 2010 is changed then this needs to be updated in two places, leading to a potential update anomaly.

To resolve this the equivalent Boyce–Codd normal form relations are shown in Figure 2.27.

Figure 2.27 The equivalent Boyce–Codd normal form relations

Interviewee Payroll Number	Interview Date	Interview Time	Interviewer Payroll Number
BZ987	2010-05-02	1030	AQ327
CA446	2010-05-02	1200	AQ327
CX137	2010-05-02	1200	BY669
CA446	2010-07-02	1030	AQ327

Interviewee Payroll Number	Interview Date	Room Number
AQ327	2010-05-02	G101
BY669	2010-05-02	G102
AQ327	2010-05-02	G102

The first of these two relations has the following candidate keys:

- **Interviewee Payroll Number** and **Interview Date**, allowing us to determine the interview time and the payroll number of the interviewer;
- **Interviewer Payroll Number**, **Interview Date** and **Interview Time**, allowing us to determine the payroll number of the interviewee.

The second of these two relations has the combination of **Interviewer Payroll Number** and **Interview Date** as its only candidate key, allowing us to determine the room number allocated to the interviewer for that day.

Further normal forms – fourth normal form, fifth normal form and, most recently, sixth normal form – have been proposed. They are beyond the scope of this book and are not discussed further.

Surrogate keys

Many database developers prefer to use a meaningless primary key (sometimes called a surrogate key) instead of constructing a primary key from real-world attributes such as **Payroll Number**, **Surname**, **Other Names** and **Date of Birth**. There are many advantages to taking this approach, not the least being that any values for real-world attributes may be subject to change (for example following real-world changes, a change in company policy or the need to correct errors). If surrogate keys are to be used, it is still sensible to use relational data analysis to check normalisation using candidate keys involving appropriate real-world attributes.

Relational data analysis and conceptual data modelling

The application of relational data analysis, essentially a 'bottom-up' approach, to the employee record in Figure 2.21 has produced the diagram in Figure 2.25. This is notationally very similar to the conceptual data model in Figure 2.19 that we developed using a less formal 'top-down' approach. The model in Figure 2.19 is in Boyce–Codd normal form, although we did not apply the relational data process. An experienced data modeller intuitively produces a model that is in Boyce–Codd normal form without applying the rigour of relational data analysis.

Inspection of the two models developed using the two approaches reveals that there are similarities in content between them. This is to be expected as they are models of the same business area – the human resources department. There are also some differences in the content of the models. This is also to be expected. When discussing requirements with management and staff who are very familiar with their job, some significant details are often missed. On the other hand the documentation used for relational data analysis may be out of date. It is by no means clear which of these two models is more correct than the other. The discrepancies need to be resolved by further discussion with the subject-matter experts in the business and a consolidated data model produced.

THE ROLES OF A DATA MODEL

Conceptual data models can be developed to understand the information requirements of a business and to form the basis for a physical database design to support the business.

Understanding information requirements

In the first case the data model is used to document the information that is used by the business and the way in which that information is grouped and related. The aim here is either to highlight inconsistencies in the information used by the business or, if the conceptual data model is being developed as a prelude to the development of an information system, to enable an expert in the business to agree that all the information requirements have been completely and faithfully documented. Business experts could even be involved in the development of the model. Irrespective of whether the analyst developing the model is primarily a business person or an experienced data modeller, it is the duty of the analyst to develop a model that can be meaningfully discussed with the business. All the information that is needed by the business must be explicitly included in the model. All the names of entity types, attributes and relationships in the model must be meaningful to the business. The analyst who is an experienced data modeller must resist the temptation to include constructs in the model that hide or distort the business relevance of the information. The model must be easy to read and interpret.

A conceptual data model that is to be used to understand the information requirements of a business, or a business area, should be the result of the analysis of those information requirements alone. No design considerations should be included in the model. The model should be the result of pure analysis, untainted by design.

The basis for physical database design

A conceptual data model, that is a data model that has been developed to understand the information requirements of the business, could also be used as the basis for the design of a database that is to be at the heart of an information system that supports that business. However, such a design may be inappropriate. It may not meet some future information requirement without some significant restructuring of the logical schema for the database. It could be that the data modeller has identified that some of the information requirements are similar to those of a previous project for which a good data modelling solution is already known or for which there is a published 'data model pattern'.

When the modeller has used their experience to create a data model that creates an effective logical schema design, the conceptual data model may well use data modelling constructs and names that are alien to the business. Although such a model provides a well-considered and robust input to the 'physical design' of the database, it is no longer correct to claim that the model completely and faithfully documents the information requirements of the business. These information requirements may be hidden by a data modelling construct that has been introduced into the model for sound reasons. For example a business that buys and sells products would expect to see **CUSTOMER** and **SUPPLIER** entity types in their conceptual data model but these two concepts may be wrapped up in a single entity type, often called **PARTY**, to recognise the fact that a company that is the supplier of some products may also be the customer for other products. It is not unknown for the **PARTY** entity type to also include the employee concept because sometimes employees can also be customers. In this case it is incorrect to call the data modelling activity 'analysis'. It has gone beyond analysis; it is the start of design.

PHYSICAL DATABASE DESIGN

Once the conceptual data model is complete it provides the start point for the design of the physical database.

Aside: When new to data modelling some 20 years ago (before the widespread use of drawing packages and tools to support data modelling), I naively asked a consultant when I would know that a data model was complete. The answer I got was 'when the correction fluid on the model is so thick that it is able to stand on its edge'. The implication is that even an experienced data modeller has to rework the model many times.

The conceptual data model, with its entity types, attributes and relationships, does not presuppose the form of the implemented database. Because the model is in Boyce–Codd normal form, it is very easily translated into a design for a relational database (a database managed by a database management system based on SQL). The model could, however, be translated into a design for a database managed by some other form of database management system such as an object oriented database management system. We assume, however, that the database is to be implemented using an SQL-based relational database management system where the main construct at the logical level is the database table.

This 'physical database design' process has two stages:

- first-cut database design;
- optimised database design.

First-cut database design stage

In the first-cut database design stage, the aim is to use the conceptual constructs of the logical-level schema of the target database management system to develop a design that matches the conceptual data model as closely as possible.

Each entity type in the conceptual data model becomes a table, with each of the attributes of the entity type becoming a column of that table. If the foreign keys needed to implement the relationships are not already identified as attributes, they need to be identified and become additional columns of the table.

There should be a consistent approach to the naming of tables and columns. It should be possible to relate the schema design back to the conceptual data model from which it is derived, so the names of the tables and columns should be as close to the names in the conceptual data model as possible within the limitations that all database management systems place on the lengths of names. Ideally each table name should be identical to the entity type name and this is normally possible within the naming length restrictions. The table corresponding to the **EMPLOYEE** entity type in Figure 2.19 would be called **employee** and the table corresponding to the **EMPLOYEE QUALIFICATION** entity would be called either **employee_qualification** or **employeeQualification** to cope with the restriction that spaces are not allowed in SQL names.

Column names must be unique within a table, so it is possible to have an **effective_date** column in both the **employee_grade** table and in the **assignment** table, distinguishing between the two if necessary by using 'dot notation', for example **employee_grade. effective_date** for the **employee_grade** table and **assignment.effective_date** for the **assignment** table. It is common practice to name foreign key columns with the same name as the column that they correspond to in the table that is referenced by the foreign key. Following this approach the **assignment** table would have two foreign key columns – **payroll_number** referencing the **employee** table and **name** referencing the **department** table. Because of the large number of 'name' columns that normally appear in a database, many designers would use **department_name** for the second case but this means that there is not an overall consistent approach to naming.

One recommended approach to the naming of foreign keys is to concatenate the relationship name, the 'distant' entity name and the 'distant' column name to give names to the foreign key columns that fully explain their role. In this case the two foreign key columns in the assignment table would be called **of_employee_payroll_number** and **to_department_name**.

Each column is defined with a datatype such as **CHAR(10)**, a fixed-length string of 10 characters; **VARCHAR(10)**, a variable-length string with a maximum length of 10 characters; **DATE**, a calendar date; and **DECIMAL(5,2)**, a number such as '234.56'. If the domain for each attribute was specified as part of the conceptual data model, it is usually fairly straightforward to determine the appropriate datatype. If domains have not been specified, it is normally necessary to review some specimen data in order to determine the appropriate datatype.

There has to be an explicit primary key declaration for each table (naming the column or columns in the table whose values uniquely identify a row in the table). If required, there must also be explicit foreign key declarations (naming the column or columns that comprise each foreign key) to implement each relationship from the table to another table.

Another important element of the first-cut database design is the specification of the physical file storage for the database. Database management systems manage the actual storage of data but most provide mechanisms for the designer to control the allocation of tables to particular physical structures. These physical structures may be called tablespaces, filegroups or some other name. It is possible to allocate more than one table to a single tablespace and in some database management systems it is possible to split a large table over a number of tablespaces. The allocation of tables to tablespaces is determined principally by the likely volumes of data for each table and how data is to be collected from different tables to answer the anticipated queries. These are not trivial questions to answer.

Optimised database design stage

The first-cut design gives a database design that closely resembles the conceptual data model. Such a design should be robust, easy to understand and meet all the data requirements of the business areas being supported. However, within the stated requirements for any information system are a number of non-functional requirements that specify performance targets for the overall system such as the maximum time a user must wait after submitting a request for information (a query on the database) before that information is available. It may be necessary for the database designer to enhance or move away from the first-cut design to improve the performance of the database.

The two main strategies for improving performance of a database are to:

- make use of the built-in facilities of the database management system;
- compromise on the design of the logical schema.

Two facilities provided by most database management systems are the ability to cluster data and the ability to create indexes. Data clustering means arranging data on the disk in such a way that logically related data is placed as closely together as possible. This improves performance because fewer disk access requests are required to answer queries on the database or to update data. An index provides the database management system with an alternative way to access data other than searching through all the physical records associated with a particular logical table. A database index is analogous to the index at the back of this book. It enables the database management system to know where to go to access any particular piece of data. An index may be built on a single column or on multiple columns from the same table. Using an index improves retrieval performance by reducing the number of disk accesses required to query the data. Database update is, however, slowed down if data is indexed; each database update requires updating the index (which normally requires some restructuring of the complete index) as well as updating the main data file. Changes to the clustering of data and the addition or removal of indexes are the equivalent of altering the schema at the internal level of the three-level architecture. These changes can be made without affecting the schema at the logical level and without affecting the application processes.

Physical data independence is maintained and data clustering and indexing can, therefore, be altered once the database is in use.

On the other hand a compromise to the design of the logical schema affects data independence. Such a compromise is often called denormalisation. You will recall that our aim is to design a logical schema that is in Boyce–Codd normal form; indeed we may even seek to design a logical schema that is in a higher normal form. The rationale for this is that it provides only one place to store any item of data, reducing data redundancy and eliminating the possibility of data inconsistency (at least within that single database). This means, however, that data that may be logically related is dispersed throughout the database. Collecting this dispersed data together to answer any particular query can require a large number of disk access requests, which can in turn impact performance. Denormalisation can involve returning 'repeating groups' to their master table (or relation). It can also mean joining two tables that are often queried together. Introducing new columns to hold data that can be derived from other data already held elsewhere in the database can also be considered as denormalisation. An example of this would be the recording of the total cost of an order where the costs of the individual items ordered are already recorded. While denormalisation can improve retrieval performance, it can slow down update performance (data needs to be recorded in more than one place) and introduce the possibility of inconsistency (because the users or the application programs need to manage the duplicated updates). Denormalisation should, therefore, be avoided if possible; if used, all decisions to denormalise should be carefully documented.

SUMMARY

This chapter has taken a detailed look at the development of databases. First the database concept and the three-level schema architecture were introduced. Having taken a brief look at the overall process for database development, we then looked in more detail at the information requirements analysis phase. We saw examples of top-down development of a conceptual data model and the bottom-up relational data analysis process. Finally we looked at the way that a conceptual data model is translated into a physical database design.

3   WHAT IS DATA MANAGEMENT?

This chapter starts by looking at what can happen if data is not adequately managed. It then looks at the responsibilities of a data management function and the separate roles within that function. It finishes by looking at the benefits that data management can bring to an enterprise and the relationship between data management and enterprise architecture.

THE PROBLEMS ENCOUNTERED WITHOUT DATA MANAGEMENT

At its simplest, data management is the management of data, information represented in a formalised manner suitable for communication, interpretation or processing. This far-reaching but simple statement implies that all aspects of the management of data, including the storage of data in a file or a database to support a limited set of business processes, are 'data management'. However, data management as a formal term is normally associated with the provision of an enterprise-wide service. The definition that has been in use within the BCS Data Management Specialist Group for some time is:

Data management is a corporate service which helps with the provision of information services by controlling or co-ordinating the definitions and usage of reliable and relevant data.

From this definition it can be seen that data management is a far-reaching function. It is involved with the definition of data to enable that data to be shared between information systems and become a corporate resource. It is also involved with the management of the data in active information systems to ensure that it is reliable (that is, of good quality) and that the relevant data is available to the users that need it.

Data management, and its 'big cousins' information management and information resource management, can be compared to other corporate business functions, for example personnel and finance. The data management function looks after the data resource in the same way as the personnel department looks after the personnel in the organisation and the finance department looks after the organisation's money. I have used the term 'data management function' here because the data management responsibility may not reside in a single organisational department.

It is important to recognise that the majority of data does not 'belong' to the data management function, as indeed the majority of personnel within a company do not 'belong' to the personnel department. The management of a large proportion of the data is normally the responsibility of the different functional departments in the organisation. The data management function should, however, provide the essential quality control of the enterprise's data and be recognised as an authoritative source of information about the organisation's data.

Only a very few organisations have managed to implement an effective corporate data management function. The remainder are counting the costs of ineffective or non-existent data management. These costs come from the development of information systems to meet narrow departmental or business function and process needs without recognising that each information system in an organisation should be a subsystem of a larger integrated enterprise-wide federation of information systems, designed so that the appropriate information is provided to the appropriate user in the appropriate place at the appropriate time. At the heart of such a federation of information systems is the requirement to share data; for this to happen there has to be common enterprise-wide definitions of data and a co-ordinated enterprise-wide control of the actual live data. In other words there has to be data management as defined by the BCS Data Management Specialist Group and this data management has to be properly resourced, supported and managed in order to be effective.

> **Aside:** Unless an organisation is prepared to replace all its information systems with a single enterprise resource planning (ERP) system, any ERP system that is introduced is yet another system that needs to share data with other information systems. The introduction of ERP systems does not remove the need for effective data management. Indeed it probably exacerbates the data management problem.

Without effective enterprise-wide data management in place within the organisation:

- **The information systems within the enterprise cannot be interfaced.** Because they have not been defined and developed to work together, the information systems cannot be 'joined' other than at the most rudimentary technical level.

- **Data is not shared between the information systems.** Even if it is possible to technically connect the information systems, it is still usually impossible to share data between those systems because of the incompatible data definitions in use in the disparate information systems.

- **Communication breaks down and information gets lost.** Without true data sharing it becomes impossible for departments to obtain the information they need to carry out their jobs effectively within the necessary time frame.

- **Data is unnecessarily transcribed and rekeyed.** If there is a need for information to be shared between incompatible information systems, the only option that is often available is to have the information from one system rekeyed into the other system or systems. This is not only very resource-intensive but there is a danger of the data being incorrectly transcribed if the definitions are ambiguous or the concepts underlying those data definitions are incompatible.

- **The wheel keeps being reinvented.** A substantial portion of the time and cost of the development of any information system is taken up with the analysis of the information and data requirements and the subsequent development of the database to meet those requirements. Without effective data management this effort is required for each new information system, irrespective of whether the same or similar information or data requirements have been analysed before. With enterprise-wide data management in place the new information system can reuse existing data definitions, producing savings in both the time and cost of the development of the new system. Implementing data management specifically to save system-development costs is unlikely to lead to an increase in information sharing across the enterprise, whereas if data management is implemented to improve information sharing, there is almost certainly going to be a reduction in system-development costs in the long term.

- **The competitive edge of the organisation is reduced.** If information is delayed or lost, for example because the mechanisms for the sharing of data between information systems are inefficient or are not even provided, the ability of the organisation to provide an efficient service to its customers, and thus to compete with its rivals, will be impeded.

- **Frustration sets in.** Users of information systems who consistently find that they do not have the right information at the right time to carry out their job effectively soon become frustrated. The staff of the IT or IS department who are providing support for those users find that they are constantly being criticised and they become frustrated at their inability to provide an effective service. The IT or IS department staff involved in the development of new and replacement systems find themselves having to develop from scratch those systems whose requirements overlap systems developed before, either by themselves or their colleagues. They also become frustrated.

The requirement for information is changing all the time. Where data is poorly or ambiguously defined, it may be difficult to respond to requests for new information or information presented in a different manner. Real business opportunities may be lost as a result of the inability to respond quickly to changing requirements. There are many situations where information exists in systems as data but is not accessible to the users within the right time frame.

Such costs impact on the business, which is the user of the information, as well as on the IT or IS department that provides the technical infrastructure to provide the information to the users.

DATA MANAGEMENT RESPONSIBILITIES

From the BCS Data Management Specialist Group definition it can be deduced that data management is a corporate service that:

- **strategically** supports the corporate definition, management and use of business data;
- **operationally** supports the development and maintenance of computerised information systems.

To meet its remit to provide strategic and operational support to the organisation, the data management function has a number of responsibilities. The key areas amongst these responsibilities are:

- achieving recognition of data, both structured and unstructured, as an enterprise-wide valuable business resource;

- improving the quality of the data held within the enterprise's information systems and ensuring that there are procedures in place to maintain the quality of the data;

- facilitating information sharing across the business by the provision of corporate data definitions and support to the teams involved in systems development to ensure that these definitions are used;

- making the various levels of management within the business accountable for the development and ownership of data definitions – it is within the business, not in IT or IS, that the real meaning of data and information is known;

- achieving a single source for reference data to support all the information systems within the enterprise – this includes internal reference data such as product codes and prices as well as external reference data such as UN country codes.

The degree of accountability that the data management function has depends on its reporting level in the organisation. The lower the position in the organisational hierarchy, the more limited the responsibilities are likely to be. It naturally follows that the more limited the responsibilities are, the less impact the data management function can have on the organisation's use of data and thus the benefits reduce accordingly.

DATA MANAGEMENT ACTIVITIES

To fulfil the above responsibilities, the data management function needs to identify the specific activities that it needs to carry out and then obtain sufficient resources to perform the activities. These activities are shown in Figure 3.1.

An important early activity for the success of any data management initiative is to educate all concerned about the importance of data management to the organisation and the role that they play in data management. This education, of course, involves the staff directly concerned in the data management function. It must also be directed towards the business and user community at all levels, from senior management through to the end-users of the information systems who may be responsible for collecting and inputting data, and also at the technical staff in the IT or IS department who need to follow and use the products delivered through data management. If application development is 'outsourced', those involved in the procurement procedures must also be made aware of the importance of data management so that they can ensure that adherence to the data management standards is included in the contracts with the development company.

Another important early task is to develop the organisation's data management policy and strategy. The policy document sets out what the business expects from the data management initiative and how business managers, end-users of the information systems and the IT or IS staff relate to the data management staff. This needs to be endorsed at the highest level within the organisation. Once the policy is endorsed, it is possible to develop the strategy of how to meet the data management goals and targets.

Figure 3.1 Data management activities

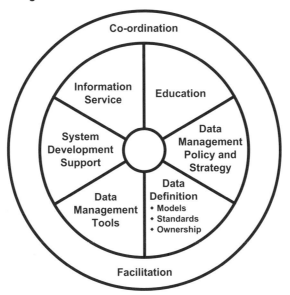

One of the principal tasks of data management is to develop the corporate data definitions for the organisation. Key to this is the development of a data model or a set of data models that encapsulate all of the business organisation's information needs. The data definitions can then be derived from these models. Each data definition must be 'owned' by an appropriate business authority, and data management must seek out a suitable owner. The data models and the ownership are the 'front of house' facets of data definition. Behind the scenes there needs to be a number of standards covering the way that data models are to be developed, the format that data definitions are to take and the way that data 'objects', such as entity types, attributes, tables and columns, are to be named.

Data management is a complex activity and it is doubtful if much will be achieved without some automated tool support. There is a need, therefore, to identify and procure these tools and a need to have procedures in place to ensure that the tools are used consistently and that the information stored in the tools is available when required.

If data management is to be successful, it must influence the way that data is defined and handled in any new or replacement systems. It is very important, therefore, that the staff who are charged with the responsibility for data management interact with and support the staff involved in developing future information systems. It is too easy for systems developers to see any standards, including standard corporate data definitions, as constraints on their freedom of action and, perhaps, a potential source of delay to the completion of their project. The interaction between data managers and system developers must be managed so that the system developers see the data managers as a positive resource that are of benefit to their project.

Once data management is up and running, the data managers probably have a greater knowledge than the business staff of what data and information is available within the organisation, where it is available and how it is used. The data management staff can, therefore, provide a valuable information service to the business and to the IT or IS staff. They can, in effect, provide a 'one-stop shop' for information about information and data.

As with any other function, functional management has to be in place to ensure that all of these activities are co-ordinated and facilitated. There must be adequate resources to carry out the activities. The activities must be prioritised and planned so that the service provided by the data management function provides the support to the organisation that is expected and required.

Figure 3.2 shows the key deliverables to be expected from each of these activities.

Figure 3.2 Data management deliverables

The IT or IS department is often cast in the role of 'advocate' for the creation and implementation of a data management function. It is often the view of the business that the management of data is solely the responsibility of the IT or IS staff. Certain aspects of physical data management, such as database administration, do naturally fall within the overall IT or IS responsibility, but the management of data and its associated information, as an asset to enable the business to exploit its huge investment in data, is very much the responsibility of the business and, as such, the business must sponsor it and be involved in it. The business must drive data management.

ROLES WITHIN DATA MANAGEMENT

The BCS Data Management Specialist Group has identified three distinct roles within the data management function. These roles are data administration, database administration and repository administration.

In its publication *Data Management*, the Central Computer and Telecommunications Agency (1994b) showed the relationship between data management, these three roles and the broader concept of information management using the diagram in Figure 3.3.

The roles in this particular view of information management that are outside the scope of data management include process management, which looks at the business processes that use data; system management, which is the management of the computer systems that support the business processes; and business information support, which provides a service to the business users to enable them to exploit the information available. System management is now more commonly known as IT service management.

Figure 3.3 The relationship between data management and information management

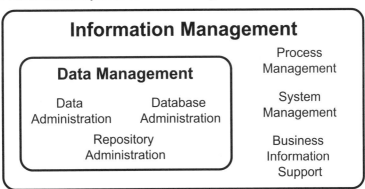

You should be aware that this is not the only view of what constitutes information management. However, this view is good enough for our purposes because it happens to coincide with the three roles within data management as seen by the BCS Data Management Specialist Group.

Data administration is concerned with mechanisms for the definition, quality control and accessibility of an organisation's data. This is the role that takes a corporate view of data as it is used by the business. It is a policy-making role in that it must set down the rules and procedures for data definition, data quality and data usage, but it may also be involved in developing, on the business's behalf, draft data definitions, carrying out data quality audits and the consequent cleansing of the data. It is often called upon to provide advice and expertise on data modelling to system-development projects. Alternatively it may be called upon to assure the quality of data models developed by system-development project staff. Data administration is the least technical of the three data management roles. Further discussion of the areas included within the responsibilities of the data administration role is provided in Chapter 4 to Chapter 9.

Database administration is concerned with the management and control of the software used to access physical data. Database administrators carry out the day-to-day administration of the various databases and their associated database management systems. Routinely this involves monitoring the performance of the database, removing or archiving data that is obsolescent and maintaining backups in case of emergencies. It may also involve reordering or restructuring the database to improve performance. Database administration may also be called upon to provide expertise on physical database design to projects that are developing IT systems. Alternatively it may be called upon to assure the quality of physical database designs to ensure that they conform to corporate standards. See Chapter 10 for further discussion of the database administration role.

Repository administration is concerned with the management and control of the software in which 'information about information' is stored, manipulated and defined. As such it is a role whose scope is the internal support of the data management function and I normally refer to repository administration as being the 'provision of database administration specifically to support data administration'. It is the most technical of the three data management roles. See Chapter 11 for further discussion of the repository administration role.

THE BENEFITS OF DATA MANAGEMENT

Many benefits are claimed for data management. Nearly all these benefits make sound business sense and can be recognised as such. Unfortunately not all of them can be related to direct cost savings. It therefore requires a degree of faith on the part of senior management that, when embarking on data management, the end result will justify the cost and the effort.

Every organisation is different. It is useful to consider the potential benefits in two areas:

- those that are business related;
- those that are related to information technology and systems.

The main benefit that is business related is the increased availability of information through the sharing of data between the disparate IT systems. There should also be an improvement in data quality. These will lead to an improvement in the overall efficiency and effectiveness of the organisation. This will, in turn, lead to an enhanced level of customer service, improving the organisation's competitive edge.

It should also be possible to identify tangible benefits that are business related, such as a financial 'return on investment', that follow on from the implementation of data management, for example staff savings through a reduction in rekeying of data or a reduction in the cost of marketing mailings through the eradication of duplicate customer data.

The benefits from data management related to information technology and systems will be more tangible than the benefits related to the business. The reuse of information and data analysis products (data models and so forth) and data definitions will result in an increase in productivity in systems development, leading to cost savings. Because of the use of common data definitions and a common approach to the management of data in general, there will also be savings in the cost of the maintenance of applications.

THE RELATIONSHIP BETWEEN DATA MANAGEMENT AND ENTERPRISE ARCHITECTURE

If an organisation is far-sighted enough to implement data management, there is also a good chance that the organisation has embraced the concept of enterprise architecture. In general, enterprise architecture is about understanding the different elements that make up the enterprise, including the people, the information, the processes, the communications and, very importantly, how those elements interrelate. By implementing an enterprise architecture, an organisation attempts to determine how these elements work together to meet its current and future goals.

There are a number of enterprise architecture frameworks publicly available including:

- US Department of Defense Architecture Framework (DoDAF);
- UK Ministry of Defence Architecture Framework (MODAF);
- Open Group Architecture Framework (TOGAF);
- Framework for Enterprise Architecture developed by John Zachman (also commonly known as the Zachman Framework).

DoDAF (dodcio.defense.gov/dodaf20.aspx) and MODAF (www.modaf.com) are specifically targeted at the defence communities of the respective nations. Both of these architecture frameworks see the overall enterprise described using a number of separate views, particularly an operational view (organisations, locations, processes, information flows and so on), a systems view (interfaces, data specifications, protocols and so on), and a technical standards view (the supporting standards and documents).

TOGAF (www.opengroup.org/togaf) is an enterprise architecture framework, developed by members of The Open Group Architecture Forum (www.opengroup.org/architecture), that uses models at four levels: Business, Application, Data and Technology. TOGAF can be used by any organisation that wishes to develop an enterprise architecture.

DoDAF, MODAF and TOGAF look at various aspects of an enterprise from different viewpoints. The Framework for Enterprise Architecture developed by John Zachman (www.zachman.com) exemplifies this idea. His framework consists of six columns and six rows.

The columns of the Framework for Enterprise Architecture are:

- the 'what' – the 'inventory sets' of the enterprise – this is the perspective that looks at the information and its representation as data used by the enterprise;

- the 'how' – the 'process flows' of the enterprise;

- the 'where' – the 'distribution networks' of the enterprise;

- the 'who' – the 'responsibility assignments' of the enterprise;

- the 'when' – the 'timing cycles' of the enterprise;

- the 'why' – the 'motivation intentions' of the enterprise.

The first five rows of the Framework for Enterprise Architecture are:

- the 'executive perspective' – the view of the business context planners with models for each column that document the scope of the enterprise;

- the 'business management perspective' – the view of the business concept owners with models for each column that document the business concepts within the enterprise, the business definition models;

- the 'architect perspective' – the view of the business logic designers with models for each column that document the system logic within the enterprise, the system representation models;

- the 'engineer perspective' – the view of the business physics builders with models for each column that document the technology of the enterprise, the technology specification models;

- the 'technician perspective' – the view of the business component implementers with models for each column that document the tools of the enterprise, the tool configuration models.

The sixth row of the Framework for Enterprise Architecture represents the functioning enterprise.

All of these enterprise architecture frameworks involve the specification of information or data, or both, at a number of different levels. It is highly likely, therefore, that there will need to be close co-operation between the data management function and whoever is responsible for the development of the enterprise architecture.

SUMMARY

This chapter started by looking at the problems encountered when there is no data management. The formal definition of data management was presented, followed by the responsibilities of a data management function and the activities and deliverables associated with those responsibilities. The three roles within data management (data administration, database administration and repository administration) were then introduced. The business-related and systems-related benefits of data management were discussed and the chapter concluded by looking at the relationship between data management and enterprise architecture.

PART 2
DATA ADMINISTRATION

As shown in Chapter 3, data administration is concerned with mechanisms for the definition, quality control and accessibility of an organisation's data.

In this part we describe the tasks and areas that are the responsibility of data administrators, such as corporate data modelling, data definition, data naming, metadata, data quality, data accessibility and master data management. This part has six chapters.

Chapter 4 – Corporate Data Modelling – looks at data modelling when applied to an enterprise's total data requirements as opposed to being applied to the smaller set of requirements that are to be met by a single information system. We explain why corporate data models are required. We discuss where corporate data models should lie on the continuum from 'abstract' to 'detailed'. We then suggest how the development of a corporate data model may be approached and introduce six principles to be applied to the development of corporate data models.

Chapter 5 – Data Definition and Naming – introduces the key data definition and naming 'standards' used by data managers. We discuss the principles underlying these standards and provide some examples.

Chapter 6 – Metadata – introduces the concept of 'data about data' and the way that it is used.

Chapter 7 – Data Quality – provides an overview of this important area. We define the term 'data quality', we look at how poor-quality data can affect a business, we consider what causes poor-quality data and we look at techniques for improving data quality. The fact that the achievement of data quality requires an ongoing procedural and cultural change, and not just a one-off project, is stressed.

Chapter 8 – Data Accessibility – brings together in one chapter the related issues of data security, protecting the database against unauthorised users, data integrity, protecting the database against authorised users and data recovery, bringing the database to a usable consistent state after a failure.

Chapter 9 – Master Data Management – introduces master data and its management. Master data is defined and explained, including the reasons why some of the problems with master data arise. MDM Hubs and some of the approaches to their implementation are discussed.

Data governance, which has been defined as the formal orchestration of people, process and technology to enable an organisation to leverage data as an enterprise asset, can be likened to data administration.

4   CORPORATE DATA MODELLING

This chapter looks at the subject of corporate data modelling and sees how it differs from project- or business-area-level data modelling. Three approaches to the development of a corporate data model and six principles of corporate data modelling are introduced and discussed.

WHY DEVELOP A CORPORATE DATA MODEL?

In many respects a corporate data model is very similar to the project-level conceptual data model we described in Chapter 2. It comprises definitions of the things of significant interest to the business (the entity types), definitions of what we need to know about those things (the attributes) and the associations between them (the relationships). A corporate data model is different because its scope extends beyond a single project; ideally it extends to cover the data requirements of the whole business.

There is no definitive role for a corporate data model. While each 'corporation' has specific motives for the development of its corporate data model, the most common reason is to facilitate the sharing of data between applications or information systems. Irrespective of the reason for the development of the corporate data model, the 'corporate data model initiative' will only be successful if the intended role of the corporate data model is clearly understood across the whole enterprise.

There are a number of questions to be addressed when embarking on the development of a corporate data model:

- **What is the definition of 'corporate'?** It is my view that 'corporate', in the context of a corporate data model, should mean the entire enterprise. It is not unknown, however, for those who seek to avoid being involved in (or, as they see it, constrained by) data management to see 'corporate' as equating to 'the corporate headquarters', so not applicable to them in their particular business area.

- **What is 'corporate data'?** Again it is my view that, in the context of a corporate data model, 'corporate data' covers all the data used by the enterprise. The corporate data model should, therefore, cover all of the enterprise's data requirements. There are many, both within the business and within the IT or IS staff who are supporting them, who believe that the data generated in their business area is only of use to them and it should, therefore, be outside the scope of the corporate data model. A counter-argument is that nobody can be sure that any data has only local relevance until the data requirements of the whole enterprise have been analysed and documented.

- **Is the corporate data model to be used as ...**

  ... a business model? In this role the corporate data model will not necessarily be used as the basis for information systems development. It expresses a view of data from the perspective of the business. Such a model could be used, for example, to inform business process reengineering.

  ... a database design model? In this role the corporate data model will be used to inform a common database design. This common database design, or appropriate subsets of it, can then be used in all future information systems design. This will ensure that data is commonly and unambiguously defined in all information systems, facilitating the sharing of data across those systems. Note, however, that if a common database design is to be used, it will not be possible to optimise the database design as discussed in Chapter 2. Any optimisation to enhance the performance of one application program will almost certainly adversely affect the performance of other application programs.

  ... an interface design model? In this role the corporate data model provides a standard with which all information systems must comply at their interfaces with other information systems. The intention is not to direct the design of the databases in the individual information systems, thus preventing optimisation to enhance performance, but to direct how data must be presented to other information systems when there is a requirement to share data with them. This approach means that there has to be some extra processing to translate the data from the definitions used in the design of the database to the definitions specified by the corporate data model, and vice versa. In this way each information system appears to the other information systems as if they were using a common database design based on the corporate data model.

THE NATURE OF A CORPORATE DATA MODEL

In Chapter 2 we saw the development of a conceptual data model that recorded the information requirements of a specific business area to inform the development of the database that would be at the heart of an information system to support that business area and only that business area. This information system, like most information systems, supports a limited set of users carrying out a limited set of business processes. We also saw how the technique of relational data analysis could be used to complement that model. However that conceptual data model is developed, it is restricted to that subset of the total information requirements of the enterprise that is required to support the current business processes, or the business processes under consideration, for that restricted business area.

This approach to data modelling, therefore, provides a data model that, within the bounds of a single project, is relatively easy to understand but leads to a database design that is usually based on the current use of information and data. Any requirement to store new 'data items' or to change the 'business rules' that apply to information or data means a change to the conceptual data model, with subsequent changes to the database structure and the application programs that access the structure. The problem is often compounded because a database supporting a single system is normally optimised to improve the performance of the applications developed for that system. In the worst case, the scale of the changes to the system required when the business processes change may be so prohibitively costly, in both time and money, that the systems start to constrain rather than enhance the business.

The scope of a corporate data model must extend beyond a single information system or business area. In my view any attempt to produce a corporate data model using an approach similar to the development of the conceptual data model of a single project is bound to fail, especially if the purpose of the initiative is to develop a corporate data model that forms the basis of the database design for all future systems. There are two interrelated reasons for this:

- Since the complexity of the corporate data model is proportional to the complexity of the enterprise, for a very complex organisation the corporate data model could be exceedingly large and exceedingly complex, requiring many years (or decades) of development. It is also very probable that because of its complexity and its size the finished product will be unintelligible to all except those who have been intimately involved in its development.

- Physical database design and application development must be postponed until the development of the corporate data model is completed. If it is not, the organisation will be continuously developing legacy systems as the development of the corporate data model overtakes the development of the systems.

A corporate data model, by definition, has to cover many different business areas. If the corporate data model is to be used as the basis for all future database design, it also has to be stable. A corporate data model, therefore, has to cope with:

- the different, sometimes conflicting, uses of information and data required by the different business areas;

- the uncertain nature of the future information and data requirements across the enterprise.

Information and data is used in many different ways by the many disparate business areas within an enterprise. While a single project, supporting one business area or a single set of business processes, could produce a conceptual data model encapsulating that functional area's use of information, this becomes increasingly more difficult the broader the scope of the data model. In the development of a conceptual data model to support all of an enterprise's activity – to inform the development of a large number of inter-operating systems – I believe that it will become necessary to develop a data model that is ever more generic or abstract in nature. The implications of this are discussed later. Examples of the different uses of information that lead to this increasing 'genericity' of a corporate data model include:

- **Differences between departments over the meaning of the term 'customer'.**
  For the finance department, a customer is someone who has placed an order and needs to pay for the goods or services ordered, while for the sales department a customer could be someone that they are working with to develop a relationship so that they will place an order at some time in the future. Furthermore, for the finance department the customer is the department of the 'customer organisation' who is responsible for paying the invoice, while for the sales department the customer could be the person within the 'customer organisation' with the power to make purchasing decisions.

- **Overlapping roles**. For a company selling computer equipment and consumables, another company can be both a supplier, for example supplying the paper to be sold, and a customer, for example by buying computers to manage its own operations. For a finance company or a bank, an employee may also be a customer.

Also, in any enterprise there is some uncertainty over the future data requirements of the enterprise. If there is not to be continual reengineering of the information systems, their databases must have sufficient in-built flexibility to be able to store and distribute new information. The corporate data model must, therefore, reflect the requirement that databases derived from the corporate data model must be able to store data about 'objects', activities and concepts that have never before been identified or are based on rapidly changing 'business processes' that are updated as procedures are adapted to meet new circumstances. The database structures should be static over time, but capable of accommodating business change.

A corporate data model can either be very large, with very many entities in the model and very detailed and specific, or else can be relatively small, with very few entities and very abstract or generic. A corporate data model that is large and specific encapsulates all the business rules and is expressed using names and terms that are familiar to the business. It is a good model with which to discuss data requirements with the business, but any databases designed with such a model as their basis would be unlikely to cope with business change. A corporate data model that is small and generic leads to stable database designs that cope with business change, but its generic nature means that it is not a suitable vehicle for discussions with the business.

Generic data models and their implications are discussed further in Appendix C.

HOW TO DEVELOP A CORPORATE DATA MODEL

I have identified three possible approaches to the development of a corporate data model: a bottom-up approach that I call 'attribute trawling'; the joining of multiple project or area models; and a top-down approach to the development of a single model.

Attribute-trawling approach

This approach involves studying all the existing information systems, collecting the data definitions from those systems (which are probably not documented, so will need to be extracted from the schema definitions held by the database management system) and, once all the definitions are collected, sorting them out so that good, reusable definitions are obtained. These can then be documented in a corporate data model.

There are three major problems with this approach:

- There may be some areas of the enterprise or some business processes that are not currently supported by information systems; there will, in consequence, be a gap in the analysis.

- It is well known that many information systems do not actually meet the users' expectations or needs; the data definitions gathered during this exercise will, therefore, be of dubious quality.

- It is unclear how the data definitions will be analysed and compared; there may just be too many to be handled without automated support and such support is not readily available.

For these three reasons I do not recommend 'attribute trawling' as an appropriate method for the development of a corporate data model.

Joining project or area models

This approach involves the independent modelling of the information or data requirements of the separate business areas within the enterprise. These models are then amalgamated to form an enterprise-wide corporate data model. This is the approach recommended by many authors. However, this approach often fails, even when a common set of modelling standards is used.

The reason for these failures is exactly because the models are developed independently of each other. Although the models may have been developed to common standards, the reason for the failure is the absence of a common 'theme' in the models. There are often no easily identifiable common points where the models could join. What is needed is a common theme.

Aside: I have personal experience of two corporate data modelling initiatives where the 'join project or area models' approach was taken but which failed as soon as an attempt was made to amalgamate the first two independently developed models, and there were a significant number of other models waiting to be amalgamated later.

Hence I also do not recommend the joining of project or area models as an appropriate method for the development of a corporate data model.

Building top-down

Building top-down implies the development of a single conceptual data model that, from its inception, is intended to cover the complete information and data requirements of the whole enterprise.

If the intention is to model separate project or business areas independently and then to join the models, and it is discovered that a common theme is needed, this implies that there has to be some modelling before the project or business area requirements are themselves modelled. In effect this is the development of a 'framework' model, probably based on the core business of the enterprise. If, for prioritising or staffing reasons, it is necessary to model project or business area requirements separately, the 'framework' model can be used as the skeleton for the separate project or business area models, with the local requirements becoming the flesh on the skeleton. It is then easier to amalgamate the separate models.

It is my view, therefore, that the best approach is to build the corporate data model 'top-down', starting from a core or framework model that represents the major objects and concepts of the business. It can then be used as a skeleton and 'fleshed out' with the requirements of the individual project or business areas.

CORPORATE DATA MODEL PRINCIPLES

As a result of leading the development of a corporate data model, I have developed six principles for the development of corporate data models. These principles are:

- develop the model 'top-down';
- give primacy to the core business;
- cover the whole enterprise;
- future-proof the model;
- develop co-operatively;
- gain consensus, not perfection.

Develop the model 'top-down'

In the previous section of this chapter we looked at various options for developing a corporate data model. We saw that the best approach is to develop the corporate data model using a 'top-down' modelling approach. This, therefore, becomes our first principle.

Give primacy to the core business

Clearly a corporate data model must be developed with the core business of the enterprise uppermost in the minds of the developers. If the corporate data model is to be for an enterprise whose main business is selling goods to retail customers, the core of the corporate data model should be based on sales and products and not on the data requirements of the human resources department. This ensures that the model is correctly focused. Awareness that the core business has been given primacy should also appeal to senior management, adding weight and authority to the development of the corporate data model.

It is only possible to give primacy to the core business if that core business is clearly defined. For some enterprises this is not so and it is difficult to identify an initial focus for the modelling effort.

The developers of the corporate data model need to be aware that by giving primacy to the 'core business' there is a danger of the model becoming too focused, thus making it extremely difficult to include other business areas within the model later on.

Cover the whole enterprise

Despite giving primacy to the core business, a corporate data model must be able to support the information needs across the full breadth of the enterprise. This ensures that the model covers all business viewpoints and that no data requirements are missed.

The resultant model could potentially cover a vast scope, particularly if the enterprise is very complex. This presents a major challenge to the modeller. While developing a section of the model to support one business area, the modeller must be constantly considering all other business areas to ensure that decisions are not being made for one area that will disadvantage other areas. The modeller needs, therefore, to have an extensive knowledge of all the business areas within the corporation. This may determine which members of staff can be used to help develop the corporate data model.

Future-proof the model

For a corporate data model to be of real value, it must be stable over time; it must be 'future-proofed'. The model must, therefore, represent the true underlying nature of the information and data used in the business and not how that information or data is used at the time of the analysis. Provided there are no major changes of business purpose, the underlying nature of the information or data used in the business is unlikely to change, but the way that information and data is used and processed is often subject to change. To demonstrate this principle, I work through an example taken from my time in the Army.

Figure 4.1 shows a snippet of a model from the documentation for a proposed system that was intended to support the issue of stores to deployed units.

Figure 4.1 The 'supply chain' model

This snippet has two major flaws:

- It ignores the fact that a unit within the supply chain that supplies stores (be it a depot, a sub-depot or a supply unit) is also a unit that 'consumes' stores.

- It replicates the supply-chain hierarchy in use at the time of the analysis. It was unfortunate that by the time the system was implemented, all of the sub-depots had been closed as a cost-saving measure!

Figure 4.2 The improved 'supply chain' model

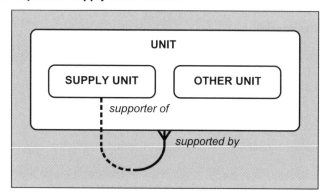

The model in Figure 4.2 provides us with a more stable solution. It uses entity subtyping to recognise that supply-chain units may also be consumer units. It also allows levels of supply-chain units to be added or removed; although the data may change, the data model, and the resulting data structure, is stable.

But this is not very helpful if we need to include a number of different business areas, as illustrated in Figure 4.3.

Figure 4.3 More than one type of support?

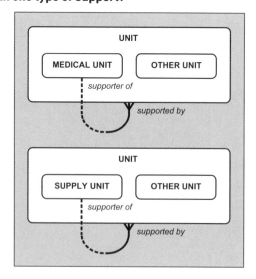

Here we see that as well as support from the supply-chain units we may also have dedicated medical units to provide support. We need a way of bringing these two models together. One approach is shown in Figure 4.4.

Figure 4.4 The combined support model

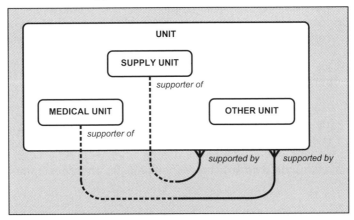

This is technically correct, but now we have the various classifications of support units explicit in the model and, therefore, explicit in the database structure. Any change – addition or removal – of a classification requires a change to the model, which then needs to be reflected in database structures and application programs.

To ensure that changes in business practices that cannot be predicted – such as a change to the classifications of support units – can be handled without expensive changes to the corporate data model that, in turn, require expensive changes to database structures and application programs, our future-proofed design needs to be more generic as shown in Figure 4.5.

Figure 4.5 The generic 'unit' model

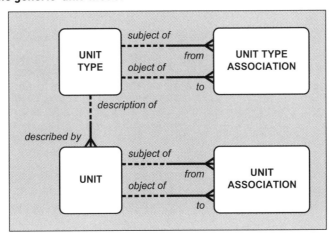

This model is interesting because with a simple name change of the entity types, replacing 'unit' with 'department', 'organisation' or 'party', it could now apply to any business area, military or civilian.

Because of the 'genericity' that comes with future-proofing, the advantages of model stability, database-design stability, interface-design stability and cost saving need to be balanced with the loss of explicit business information within the model, the increased run-time processing load and the need to manage data as well as data definitions. These issues are discussed in more detail when we discuss generic data models in Appendix C.

Develop co-operatively

It is impossible for a data management or corporate data modelling team to develop a corporate data model in isolation. Co-operation is essential. The data modellers must consult widely with subject-matter experts in the various business areas in the enterprise and with the technical people who are familiar with the existing information systems or who will be responsible for the development of future systems.

This co-operation ensures commitment both to the development of the corporate data model and to its subsequent use to inform systems development, enhancing the ability to share data. It is an unfortunate by-product of any collaborative activity that progress is slowed down by the collaboration.

Gain consensus, not perfection

There is a danger that a corporate data modelling team will seek to develop the perfect model. This is laudable but may lead to a delay in the implementation of effective data management. The team should be prepared to publish and support a model that is deemed to be 'fit for role' by all business areas, even if it is not perfect. Although such a model may not be perfect, agreement to a model that can be used across the enterprise is gained earlier than it would have been otherwise. Iterative 'tweaking' of the model by the corporate data modelling team – attempting to develop the elusive perfect model – achieves no good purpose for the business. But strong management of the corporate data modelling team is needed to avoid it; some data modellers are never satisfied and always try to improve their models.

Of course, despite all the advantages of not necessarily seeking out the perfect model, a model that is not deemed to be 'fit for role' should not be accepted. Development and refinement must continue until a model that is deemed to be 'fit for role' is developed.

SUMMARY

This chapter introduced the concept of a corporate data model by looking at the purpose of such a model. The way that the broad scope of a corporate data model affects its form and composition was then discussed. Three approaches to the development of a corporate data model – bottom-up attribute trawling, joining project or business area models and taking a top-down approach – were discussed. We then established six principles of corporate data modelling: develop the model 'top-down'; give primacy to the core business; cover the whole enterprise; future-proof the model; develop co-operatively; and gain consensus, not perfection.

5 DATA DEFINITION AND NAMING

Developing data definitions that can be used as corporate standards is seen by many as the primary role of the data administrator. Data definitions should be developed using conventions or guidelines that specify what constitutes a data definition and how the names of data 'objects' are to be formed. This chapter introduces definition and naming concepts applicable to structured data that is to be implemented using a relational database management system.

THE ELEMENTS OF A DATA DEFINITION

Guidelines are essential to ensure that each data object – entity type, attribute, relationship, table, column and so on – is documented to a particular standard. This standard must provide the minimum acceptable level of descriptive information about data that is to be made available to all the potential users of that data. These potential users are probably first and foremost the developers of future systems, but they may also be people from the business who are interested in knowing what data is available and where.

Although it is possible to suggest what descriptive information about data should be available, these guidelines probably need to be specific to the organisation. This enables the guidelines to cover those aspects of data definition that are important to the management of data within that particular organisation. It is difficult to be prescriptive as to what should be included in a data definition.

Most data definition frameworks or guidelines are based on what is loosely called a 'data item' – roughly equating to a field in a file record, to an attribute in a conceptual data model and to a column in an SQL schema. The elements of such a data definition framework could include:

- a name or label;
- any synonyms or aliases;
- a description or significance statement;
- formats;
- valid value lists or validation criteria;
- valid operations;
- ownership details;

- usage details;

- source;

- comments;

- configuration information.

Fundamental to this standard is that each data item should have a name that uniquely identifies the data item. Naming conventions are discussed later in this chapter. Where there is the possibility of more than one name being applicable, one name must be considered as the primary name and all the other names should be recorded as aliases or synonyms.

Each data item should also have a comprehensive and accurate description of the item. It is preferable if the description is held in the form of a significance statement – a statement of why the data item is deemed to be significant to the business. If the data item has no significance to the business, there is no reason for it to be defined; couching descriptions in terms of the significance of the data to the business helps develop a description that is meaningful to the business, which in turn helps system developers ensure that the data is unambiguously understood when used by application programs.

Details of the format of the data may be included in the definition. This may simply be a statement that the data is currency, a number, a date or a string of characters; but it may also include details of any restrictions that need to be applied, for example the maximum length of a string of characters.

It is also helpful to include lists of valid values or a statement of any validation criteria that may be applied to the data. For some data items there may be a predetermined list of valid values. For 'Gender' the valid values may be restricted to 'Male' and 'Female', or may be 'Male', 'Female' and 'Unknown'; for 'Staff Category' the values might be 'Full-time Employee', 'Part-time Employee' and 'Contractor'. For other data items validation criteria may be needed. For 'Salary' the validation criterion might be 'greater than £0 and less than or equal to £100,000'; for 'Surname' the validation criterion might be 'only include the characters A–Z, a–z, space, hyphen and apostrophe'.

The operations that it is valid to carry out on the data may also be recorded. It is, for example, valid to multiply a length by a number to give a greater (or smaller) length. It is also valid to multiply a length by another length to give an area. It is valid to multiply a currency amount by a number to give another currency amount, perhaps as part of a currency-exchange transaction. It makes no sense, however, to multiply a currency amount by another currency amount and so such an operation would not be valid. For data that comprises strings of characters it is important to record where it is valid to concatenate that data with other string data.

Ownership details may be recorded. Ownership exists at two levels – ownership of the data definition and ownership of the data values. The owner of the data definition is the person in the organisation who has the authority to say that this data should be held and that this definition is the appropriate definition for the data. It should be the responsibility of the owner of the data definition, not the data administrator, to obtain agreement for the data definition across the organisation. The owner of the data definition may also be the owner of the data values once they are recorded, but it may be more appropriate to assign this ownership role to another person (or group of people). Data ownership should not be confused with data stewardship, which is a task normally carried out by the data administrators. Data stewardship involves the maintenance of the data definition on behalf of the owner of the data definition.

Where the data that is defined by this definition is used may also be recorded. This will generally be in the form of a list of the information systems that use data that is the subject of the data definition.

The source of the data definition may be included in the definition. The source may be the owner of the data definition or it may be that the data administrator has developed the data definition using knowledge gained during the analysis of the data requirements. Alternatively it could be that the definition originated in a procedural manual or some other documentation.

It may be necessary to record some extra comments to expand or clarify some other element of the definition. Only in exceptional cases should it be necessary to add extra comments; it should really be possible to include all the detail necessary under the other headings.

Finally the data definition should include information to enable versions of the definition to be controlled. This may include details of the original author and the date of the authorship plus details of any subsequent modifications.

It is important to understand the form of the 'data item' to which a definition built to these standards applies. Is it the definition of a field, an attribute or a column? Is it a definition of the format, structure and values that may be applied to more than one attribute? If it is the latter, it is not a field, attribute or column definition but is a definition of the equivalent of a domain in the relational model of data – a definition of 'a pool of values that an attribute may take'.

Examples of two 'data item' definitions are shown in Figures 5.1 and 5.2. The definition in Figure 5.1 has validation criteria and a set of valid operations while that in Figure 5.2 has a set of valid values.

The data definition elements listed above are those suggested for the definition of a 'data item' or domain. The concepts behind these data definition elements can be adopted to provide the conventions for the definition of other data objects such as entity types, relationships and tables. For example the definition of an entity type could include its primary name, any aliases for the primary name, the relationships the entity type has with other entity types (preferably expressed as sentences reading from the entity type being defined), the attributes of the entity type and the descriptions of any unique identifiers. An example of an entity type definition constructed using these elements is in Figure 5.3.

Figure 5.1 A data definition with validation criteria and valid operations

Name or Label	Salary
Synonyms	Rumuneration
Significance Statement	has significance as the annual reward, expressed in whole pounds Sterling, paid to an employee of the company before the addition of any extra payments for overtime and/or performance bonuses and before the application of any statutory deductions
Format	Currency
Value List	Not applicable
Validation Criteria	> 0
Valid Operations	multiply by number; answer is currency divide by number; answer is currency add currency; answer is currency subtract currency; answer is currency divide by currency; answer is ratio
Ownership	HR Director
Users	HR Management System, Payroll System
Source	Interview Deputy HR Manager, 15 Sep 06
Comments	[None]
Date created	15 Sep 06
Author	K F Gordon
Date last updated	26 Feb 13

Figure 5.2 A data definition with valid values

Name or Label	Relationship
Synonyms	[None]
Significance Statement	has significance as the description of the personal relationship that exists between one person and another person
Format	Character
Value List	Spouse Partner Child Parent Distant relative Friend
Validation Criteria	[None]
Valid Operations	[None]
Ownership	HR Director
Users	HR Management System
Source	HR Manual Edition 3 Section 3-44
Comments	Spouse now includes Civil Partner
Date created	27 Jun 02
Author	J Smith
Date last updated	30 Nov 11

Figure 5.3 An entity type definition

Each **PERSON NEXT OF KIN**

> has significance as the person nominated by one person as the
> other person to be notified in the event of any emergency involving
> that person

Each **PERSON NEXT OF KIN**

> may also be known as a **PERSON EMERGENCY CONTACT**

Each **PERSON NEXT OF KIN**

> must be nominated by one and only one **PERSON**
> must be resident at one and only one **ADDRESS**

Each **PERSON NEXT OF KIN** has attributes:

> name
> relationship

No two **PERSON NEXT OF KIN** can have the same combination of:

> nominated by one and only one **PERSON**
> name

DATA NAMING CONVENTIONS

The purpose of a data naming convention

A data naming convention should be developed to provide consistent, unique and meaningful names for all existing and new items within the enterprise's common data resource. A consistent approach to data naming should be applied across the enterprise to help achieve unambiguous understanding of data. Data names need to be both unique and meaningful to the business; unique so that the data objects to which they refer can be unambiguously identified, and meaningful so that the terms used in the names are terms familiar to the business. Technical terms and abbreviations should be avoided wherever possible.

The data names should, however, also aid communication between all those involved in the use and development of information systems; they must be meaningful to those involved in systems analysis and design as well as to the business.

Consistent, unique and meaningful names can only be achieved if the conventions are well known and easily understood and followed. The conventions must be enforceable.

A typical data naming convention

All data naming conventions rely on using terms, which may be either single words or a number of words, in a precise and predefined manner. Key to this in all naming conventions is what is known as the class word or term. This is also sometimes known as a representation term. Typical class words might be, for example, 'identifier', 'number' and 'text', providing an indication of the form or the representation of the data.

The typical data naming convention that I describe provides names for 'data items' constructed of three terms:

- a mandatory prime term that provides the context of the data, which normally means the entity type or table holding the 'data item';

- one or more optional modifier terms that are used to make the meaning of the data explicit;

- a mandatory class term that indicates the 'class' of the data.

Examples of some names constructed using this convention are:

Person Height
Person Family Name
Person Given Name
Person Hair Colour
Person Eye Colour
Person Birth Date
Person Qualification Award Date
Employee Employment Start Date

In these names 'Person', 'Person Qualification' and 'Employee' are prime terms; 'Family', 'Given', 'Hair', 'Eye', 'Birth', 'Award' and 'Employment Start' are modifier terms; and 'Height', 'Name', 'Colour' and 'Date' are class terms.

With very few exceptions, abbreviations should not be used in the names of objects that are part of a conceptual data model. The only exceptions should be where an abbreviation has achieved common usage and the full term is seldom, if ever, used, for example 'UN' instead of 'United Nations'. Because of constraints in the database management system software, it may be necessary to abbreviate 'physical' names of tables and columns in an SQL schema. The naming convention should include, therefore, a standard approach to abbreviating names when the SQL schema is being derived from the conceptual data model. Appendix D provides an example of a full data naming convention.

Problems associated with data naming conventions

There are basically two problems with data naming conventions: they can be over-prescriptive and they may not deliver what is expected.

Some organisations have decided to adopt the prime-modifier-class term approach to data naming but have then produced a very restricted list of acceptable class terms. The worst case I have seen had only 11 class terms – 'amount', 'quantity', 'code', 'identifier', 'name', 'text', 'rate', 'dimension', 'volume', 'weight', 'date' and 'time'. Within this convention the name 'Person Height' would need to be replaced with 'Person Height Dimension' (i.e. 'Height' has now become a modifier term) and 'Person Hair Colour' would become 'Person Hair Colour Name' ('Hair Colour' now being the modifier term). While data names developed using such a restricted set of class terms are very precise, they do produce names that appear to be very idiosyncratic to those who are not data managers. Exposure of data names such as 'Person Hair Colour Name' to the business community can bring the whole effort to have effective data management into disrepute. While I believe that there should be a standard list of acceptable class terms, I do believe that this list should not be too restrictive.

There is a view that the correct use of a data naming convention enables the identification, through common names, of common 'data items' in different data models. I call this the 'utopian view of data modelling'. Data modelling is largely a subjective activity. While the use of a naming convention to ensure a consistency of approach to the naming of data objects is good practice, it is unlikely that the use of a naming convention alone will lead to the development of identical names by modellers operating independently of each other who are modelling similar business concepts. One modeller might use the name 'Prospect' for an entity that another modeller might quite legitimately call 'Potential Customer'.

The chance of the development of identical or similar names is improved if the naming convention is supported by a thesaurus or controlled vocabulary. A data naming thesaurus contains a list of approved terms, their meanings and their allowed uses as prime, modifier or class terms. It may also include details of terms that are 'broader than' or 'narrower than' an individual term, making it easier to select the appropriate term to use in any particular circumstance. It also contains a list of disallowed terms and the appropriate approved terms to use in their place. For example:

- 'Customer' may be used as a prime term, and is a narrower term than 'External Party' and a broader term than 'Potential Customer' and 'Actual Customer'.
- 'Prospect' is disallowed as a prime term; use 'Potential Customer'.

SUMMARY

This chapter has introduced the concepts of data definition and data naming, and why guidelines or conventions for these need to be in place. Suggestions were given for the detail needed for a data definition and examples were provided. The 'prime-modifier-class' term data naming convention was described and some problems associated with naming conventions were discussed.

6 METADATA

This chapter introduces the concept of metadata and describes its role in data management and elsewhere.

WHAT IS METADATA?

Put very simply, metadata is 'data about data' or 'data that describes other data'. This is a very broad definition of metadata and, in consequence, the term 'metadata' is used in a number of different contexts, principally as:

- metadata for data management;
- metadata for content management;
- metadata for describing data values.

METADATA FOR DATA MANAGEMENT

The classical data management view is that metadata in some way describes the types of data stored in a database. Table and column definitions for a database schema managed by an SQL database management system are metadata. Constraint definitions are also metadata. Rules for accessing data in the database and for maintaining the quality of the data are metadata. Conceptual data models and the data definitions derived from them are also metadata. The relationships in a conceptual data model are metadata. Details of the ownership and source of data definitions are metadata. Any other information that helps business users and system developers with understanding what data is recorded in the enterprise's databases and where it is recorded is metadata.

Metadata may be held on paper (so is not really 'data' according to our definition from Chapter 1) or held electronically. Paper-based metadata may be made available to staff in manuals containing, for example, glossaries of business terms that support the use of the data, descriptions of the information systems owned by the enterprise and the data held by each system, and conceptual data models of the databases for the systems. Electronically held metadata may be stored in the enterprise's information systems. This metadata is used to support the management of the data held in the individual systems, for example the system tables used by a database management system to hold details of the logical schema of the database and the metadata held by a data warehouse describing the schemas of the operational systems that feed the data warehouse. Metadata may also be held electronically in separate stand-alone systems to support data administration. These separate systems are often called data dictionaries or repositories. They are discussed in more detail in Chapter 11.

METADATA FOR CONTENT MANAGEMENT

Increasingly the term metadata is also being used to describe data that describes the content of documents held in libraries and other archives and the content of web pages. A typical example of this use of the term metadata is the Dublin Core Metadata Element Set, often informally known as the Dublin Core ('Dublin' is Dublin, Ohio, USA, the home of the Online Computer Library Center, and not Dublin, Ireland).

The Dublin Core is a standard for describing information resources – video, sound, image, text and web pages – that may be used in many different contexts. The first version of the Dublin Core was designed for simple resource discovery. It has 15 metadata elements, each of which is optional and may be repeated:

- **title** – a name by which the resource is known;
- **creator** – a person, an organisation or a service;
- **subject**;
- **description** – which may include an abstract, a table of contents, a reference to a graphical representation of the content or a free-text account of the content;
- **publisher**;
- **contributor**;
- **date**;
- **type** – whether the resource is a moving image, a still image, sound, text, etc.;
- **format;**
- **identifier** – for example, a Uniform Resource Identifier (URI) or an International Standard Book Number (ISBN);
- **source**;
- **language**;
- **relation** – any related resources;
- **coverage** – spatial, temporal or jurisdiction;
- **rights** – for example Intellectual Property Rights (IPR), copyright and various property rights.

Another version of the Dublin Core, the Qualified Dublin Core, has been developed. There are three additional elements **(audience, provenance and rightsHolder)**. Some of the simple Dublin Core elements may also be qualified; for example the date element may be qualified to be **available, created, dateAccepted, dateCopyrighted, dateSubmitted, issued, modified** or **valid**.

The Dublin Core is not the only standard for content management. Amongst the many others available are the Standard for Learning Object Metadata, published by the Institute of Electrical and Electronics Engineers (IEEE), and the Agricultural Metadata Element Set (AgMES) from the Food and Agriculture Organisation (FAO) of the United Nations.

METADATA FOR DESCRIBING DATA VALUES

As the ability to store multimedia data – moving images, sounds, still images, text and so forth – in a database becomes increasingly available, there is a need to store extra data that describes the content of the multimedia data or how the multimedia data is to be processed by an application when it is retrieved from the database. This extra data is also known as metadata.

Some of this metadata may be held as part of the multimedia itself. Still images (line drawings, photographs and so on) may be stored and exchanged in a number of different formats including JPEG (Joint Photographic Experts Group File Interchange Format), GIF (Graphics Interchange Format), BMP (Windows bitmap format) and TIFF (Tagged Image File Format). All of these standard formats embed metadata within the file itself; the BMP and TIFF formats provide contrasting approaches to the embedding of metadata within a file.

A bitmap file in BMP format contains four blocks of data. The first block is the **Bitmap Header**, which identifies the file as a bitmap file; the second block is the **Bitmap Information**, which stores more detailed information about the bitmap image such as its height and width; the third block is the **Color Palette**, which stores the definition of the colours being used; and the fourth block is the **Bitmap Data**, which describes the image, pixel by pixel, starting from the bottom left corner. The first three of these four blocks of data are embedded metadata.

In a TIFF file, the embedded metadata is held in the file header in the form of tags. These tags indicate, for example, the size of the image, how the image data is arranged and whether image compression has been used.

The purpose of the embedded metadata in these still-image file formats is to describe how the images contained in the files should be processed and displayed. The same is true with embedded metadata in other multimedia file types, for example video clips, audio files or documents in proprietary word-processing formats.

It is generally impossible to query a multimedia data file to find out about its content. You cannot, for example, browse a number of JPEG files to find those that include photographs of dark-haired men without displaying the images held in the files. If there is a requirement to sort through a number of images to find those of people with, for instance, a particular hair colour or another identifying feature, this information must be held as data in the database alongside the multimedia file. There may, therefore, be additional columns in the database to hold hair colour, eye colour, body shape and so forth. The data held in these additional columns is also known as metadata.

SUMMARY

This chapter has introduced the concept of metadata. It has also described its importance in data management (where the metadata describes the types of data stored in a database and includes data definitions and information about them), in content management (where the metadata describes the content of documents held either on paper or electronically) and as additional information about multimedia data values (where the metadata may describe the content of the multimedia value, how the multimedia value is to be processed, or both).

7 DATA QUALITY

The importance of information that is of high quality to a business was discussed in Chapter 1. From this it was determined that the data which underlies the information must also be of good quality. In this chapter we investigate further the issues surrounding data quality. We look at the completeness and correctness dimensions of data quality and how to bring about an improvement in data quality.

WHAT IS DATA QUALITY?

The word quality means different things in different contexts. When talking about the quality of a dish served as part of a meal in a restaurant, I could be talking about the very essence of that dish – the ingredients that the chef uses to create it. On the other hand I could be talking about its character once it has been prepared – its texture, its aroma, how spicy it is and so on. But in discussing the quality of a particular dish on a plate about to be served, the chef is expressing an opinion as to how well that dish comes up to expectations – the extent to which it is fit for eating, the purpose for which it was created or if it meets the restaurant's standards.

It is in this last sense – its 'fitness for use' or its 'goodness' or otherwise – that we use the term quality when talking about data quality. In his book *Data Quality: The Accuracy Dimension* Jack Olson defined data quality by saying that 'data has quality if it satisfies the requirements of its intended use'. He then went on to say:

> It lacks quality to the extent that it does not satisfy the requirement. In other words, data quality depends as much on the intended use as it does on the data itself. To satisfy the intended use, the data must be accurate, timely, relevant, complete, understood, and trusted.

ISSUES ASSOCIATED WITH POOR DATA QUALITY

In their 2004 report entitled *Data Quality and Integrity*, the Butler Group, an independent provider of IT research, analysis and advice, said that 'businesses have failed and will continue to do so, because they neglect to take seriously the management of data quality and integrity issues'.

For their 2004 *Global Data Management Survey*, PricewaterhouseCoopers surveyed 452 large and medium-sized companies in the UK, US and Australia. They found that only 34 per cent of the companies surveyed claimed to be 'very confident' in the quality of their data.

In *Data Quality: The Accuracy Dimension* Jack Olson identified some areas in which costs are created and opportunities lost through poor data quality. These are:

- transaction rework costs, for example needing a department to deal with mishandled orders and shipments;
- costs incurred in implementing new systems, for example errors in data increase the cost of implementing an enterprise data warehouse;
- delays in delivering data to decision makers, for example having to manually massage information before it can be released to managers;
- lost customers through poor service, for example customers not returning because of receiving incorrect shipments;
- lost production through supply-chain problems, for example the wrong quantity of parts is ordered from a supplier.

Poor data quality is common across all business areas and has a major impact on customer service, revenue and profits. As shown in Chapter 1, data of poor quality leads to information of poor quality. Poor data quality has a direct impact on an organisation's decision-making ability.

THE CAUSES OF POOR DATA QUALITY

Poor-quality data can arise for a number of reasons, some technical and some human (although even the technical reasons can probably be traced back to some human error):

- databases having inappropriate schemas;
- errors being made on data entry;
- data decaying over time;
- data being corrupted when moved between systems;
- lack of understanding of the data when it is used.

As discussed in Chapter 2, databases should be designed so that there is no unnecessary duplication of data. They should also be designed so that they can cope with changes in requirements without major cost implications. Update anomalies, which can lead to data inconsistency, are avoided when there is no unnecessary duplication of data. Data inconsistency can lead to inaccurate information being presented to users. When databases are not designed to cope flexibly with future data requirements and the redesign of the database is too costly for the enterprise, there is a potential for reducing the overall data quality because 'work-arounds' are developed that overload or misuse columns in the database, or both. Columns are then used to hold data that they were not designed to hold. Often these 'work-arounds' are not properly documented; knowledge about the meaning of data is held within the heads of a small number of users. Databases must be designed with flexibility and data quality in mind, even if this is at the expense of performance.

There can be a number of reasons why errors are made on data entry. Some of these reasons are accidental and some are deliberate. Accidental errors made on data entry, for example mistyping a date or a name, are the most common source of poor data quality. The number of these accidental entry errors is sometimes increased because insufficient thought has been given to the way that data is entered. Spelling errors, for example, can be reduced by providing the user with a set of valid values from which to select an option. Another source of errors on data entry is where the system is designed so that values are needed for some data but those values are not actually available. Users then either enter fictional data so that they can complete the process or abandon the data entry until the data values are available.

The value of some data decays over time. This is particularly true of databases supporting human resources operations. The qualifications held by employees are normally recorded when they are first employed but it is very seldom that a human resources department has procedures in place to ensure that this data is regularly checked and updated. An employee can, therefore, work hard to gain new qualifications and yet these are not recorded in the company's information systems. A search to find employees with appropriate qualifications for a task may well miss the most appropriately qualified employee. In another environment, the stock figures in a retail store's database are normally amended to take account of the arrival of new stock and of sales but the stock figures can be inaccurate if they are not regularly adjusted to take account of pilfering and shoplifting.

Perfectly good data can be corrupted when it is moved between systems, for example when extracted from operational systems to feed a data warehouse. This corruption is generally because the documentation of the feeder systems has not been kept up to date as they have been modified and, consequently, inappropriate transformations and cleaning procedures have been applied to the data.

Finally there is a danger that data may not be understood when it is presented to users. This is normally caused by the documentation being out of date or metadata being missing or ambiguous.

THE DIMENSIONS OF DATA QUALITY

There are two main dimensions of data quality – completeness and correctness. Completeness assesses the extent to which the data reflects the real-world situation. Correctness, on the other hand, assesses whether the data complies with the appropriate constraints and validation rules and whether it accurately reflects the real-world situation. These two dimensions of data quality apply to both metadata and occurrence data as shown in Figure 7.1. When considering the quality of metadata, all the data models, all the names for the data 'objects' and all of the physical implementations (specified using data definition languages (DDLs) such as the data definition capabilities included in SQL) must be assessed in terms of completeness and correctness.

When considering the quality of the occurrence data, the data used by the business, there are a number of key factors to be considered:

Figure 7.1 The dimensions of data quality

- **Input validation** – ensuring wherever possible that data is validated on input; it should be impossible to input an invalid date such as 35 October 2006 or to input a birth date for an employee that would imply that they were only two years of age when they started their employment with the company.

- **Integrity** – ensuring that data meets all the data integrity rules; no payroll numbers are duplicated for example.

- **Currency** – ensuring that data is up to date; that changes in employee circumstances have been recorded.

- **Duplication** – ensuring that there is no logical duplication of data and that any physical duplication is properly managed.

- **Inconsistency** – ensuring that data remains consistent; this is generally achieved by managing duplication correctly.

DATA MODEL QUALITY

An initial starting point for ensuring that data is of good quality is to have a conceptual data model that is both complete and correct. There are a number of approaches that may be taken to the assessment of the quality of a conceptual data model; some of these approaches are purely qualitative while others are quantitative, applying statistical techniques to the numbers of entity types, attributes and relationships in the model. Many of these approaches have been reviewed in *Information and Database Quality*, a collection of essays published in 2002

An easily applied qualitative model for the assessment of the quality of a data model amongst those reviewed in *Information and Database Quality* is that proposed by Michael Reingruber and William Gregory in *The Data Modeling Handbook*, which is shown in Figure 7.2.

Figure 7.2 The five dimensions of data model quality

In this model Reingruber and Gregory have augmented the correctness and completeness dimensions with two further orthogonal dimensions – the syntactic dimension and the semantic dimension. The syntactic dimension addresses how the modelling language and its syntax have been used while the semantic dimension addresses the relationship between the model and the data requirements of the business area that the model represents. Applying these orthogonal dimensions together we get the four dimensions of syntactic correctness, syntactic completeness, conceptual correctness and conceptual completeness. Reingruber and Gregory have added a fifth overarching dimension that they call enterprise awareness. This recognises that any data model for a specific business area or set of business processes should be seen as a subset of the enterprise or corporate data model. It is the enterprise awareness dimension that is most often overlooked by data modellers working as part of project teams involved in the development of information systems.

IMPROVING DATA QUALITY

In their 2004 *Data Quality and Integrity* report, the Butler Group reported that:

> Too many businesses are caught up in a cycle of managing the downstream impact of data quality with disproportionate resources when compared to implementing a proactive, ongoing data quality strategy. In short, data quality has to start before the physical data actually exists: prevention is better than cure.

This implies that to achieve effective, enduring data quality, an enterprise needs to implement a set of procedures and a culture within the organisation that promotes and sustains good-quality data. Data quality must be the responsibility of a senior business manager. There is no point in having a project to cleanse the data without putting in place the environment to maintain the data in a clean state.

Larry English, one of the leading proponents of data and information quality, has proposed a methodology (or, in his words, a 'value system') called Total Quality data Management (TQdM) that has been developed to achieve just this. The name of this methodology has now been changed to Total Information Quality Management (TIQM), although the principles remain the same. An overview of the methodology is shown in Figure 7.3.

Figure 7.3 Total Quality data Management methodology

The first process, P1, looks at the quality of the design of the databases (that is, the quality of the data definitions) and of the overall information architecture, both from a technical perspective and from a customer-satisfaction perspective. The second process, P2, looks at the data itself. Again there is a technical perspective – does the data comply with the rules – and a customer-satisfaction perspective. The third process, P3, measures the costs of the poor-quality information in terms of reduced profit and revenue. The fourth process, P4, cleans the existing data, giving corrected and good-quality data. The fifth process, P5, improves the enduring information processes to ensure that the data is maintained at good quality. The sixth process, P6, is about effecting a cultural transformation so that there can be a long-term improvement in information and data quality.

The technical perspective of process P2 involves a set of techniques known as data profiling. This involves searching through the data looking for potential errors and anomalies such as similar data with different spellings, data outside boundaries and missing values. For small volumes of data, profiling can be carried out by copying the data into a spreadsheet program and manipulating it using the spreadsheet facilities. Reordering a date column exposes invalid dates. Duplicate names can be identified if a name column is sorted alphabetically. Using filters can make it easy to see incorrect values outside a given range. For larger volumes of data, profiling can be carried out by writing appropriate SQL queries or by using visualisation tools that display graphs or charts based on the data. For very large data volumes these techniques are time-consuming and are unlikely to find any but the most obvious errors or anomalies. There are, however, a number of data-profiling tools on the market that can speed up the process. These tools will not clean the data and they may not even identify the individual dirty data values. But they will provide details of the categories of dirty data that are present so that cleansing may then be applied.

In her book *Executing Data Quality Projects: TEN STEPS to Quality Data and Trusted Information*, Danette McGilvray describes an alternative, but very similar, approach to improving the quality of information and data. This approach is illustrated in Figure 7.4. The individual steps in this approach are clearly named so that it is easy to work out what is involved in each step. My only concern with the TEN STEPS process is that I do not recognise the concept of a 'data quality project'. Projects, by their very nature, have a defined start date and end date. If we wish to have data that is of good quality, the drive to achieve this must be continuous. This is exemplified by processes P5 (Improve Information Process Quality) and P6 (Establish the Information Quality Environment) in TQdM and by steps 7 (Prevent Future Data Errors) and 9 (Implement Controls) in the TEN STEPS process.

Figure 7.4 The TEN STEPS process

Although much of the work to improve data quality is undertaken by technical data management staff, data quality is primarily a business issue. Unfortunately it is often difficult to get the business to recognise that there is a problem. Although there may be information-architecture reasons that cause or allow poor-quality data, much of the poor-quality data arises through poor processes associated with the handling of information in the business. As the Butler Group identified in their 2004 *Data Quality and Integrity* report:

> A typical response to data quality problems is to blame the IT department. Not only is this not helpful, it is not actually correct. Data quality needs to be seen as a business problem, not an IT problem.

Once data that is of poor quality has been cleaned, good data quality can only be maintained through a concerted effort by all in the business who create and use data, as described above. This will not only require the development of appropriate procedures but it will also require an enterprise-wide education programme and a change in the overall culture of the organisation so that the importance of good-quality information and data is recognised.

SUMMARY

This chapter has defined data quality. It has looked at possible causes of poor data quality and looks at how data quality can be improved. It has identified the dimensions of data quality and has looked at data quality from the perspectives of both metadata, including conceptual data models, and occurrence data.

8 DATA ACCESSIBILITY

This chapter brings together three related topics: data security, data integrity and data recovery. Although the mechanisms to control security, integrity and recovery of data are normally controlled and managed by database administrators, the overall policies for the security, integrity and recovery of data fall within the remit of the data administration function.

DATA SECURITY

Data security is about protecting the database against unauthorised users. This is to maintain privacy, to ensure that data is not seen by those who are not entitled to see it, and also to ensure that data is not wilfully corrupted.

There should be an enterprise-wide data security policy in place. This policy should specify the degree of security protection to be applied to the different categories of data in the enterprise and who should have access to what data. The policy should be clear and concise so that all involved in the management of data can easily understand their role in the maintenance of the security of that data.

The policy is then enforced through the use of the security mechanisms provided both by the operating systems and the database management systems in use in the enterprise's information systems. The data security mechanisms available include access controls and encryption. Additionally audit trails may be put in place to track who did what in the event of a breach of security.

Access controls

Most users only need access to a subset of the available data to carry out their duties. They should, therefore, have authorised access to that data and be prevented from accessing the rest of the data. This is where access controls come in.

Access controls rely on authentication procedures such as logins and associated passwords. Groups of data access rights are then granted to individuals, or to groups of individuals with the same or similar roles, based on their logins.

The aim of access control is to ensure that database users can only create, read, update or delete data relevant to their role. One of the functions of the database management system is to provide the facilities to enable this to be achieved. For example, SQL has a subset of the language that is the data control language (DCL) in addition to the data definition language (DDL), the part of SQL that allows for the creation of tables and the various constraints, and the data manipulation language (DML), which allows data to be read, inserted, updated or deleted. Access to data or any database object (table, procedure and so on) is restricted to the creator of the object, usually the database administrator. The creator of an object becomes its owner. No other users can access an object, say to read or update the data, unless privileges associated with that object have been given to that user. The data control statements in SQL allow for the granting and revoking of these privileges, which fall into three groups:

- table privileges;
- function and procedure privileges;
- database object privileges.

Table privileges allow the user to access specific base tables and views (the SQL name for virtual tables) and, perhaps, specific columns within those tables. The privileges may be to **SELECT** (i.e. read) data, to **INSERT** (i.e. create) data, to **UPDATE** data or to **DELETE** data. There is an additional 'privilege', **ALL PRIVILEGES**, that allows the user to create, read, update and delete data. The **SELECT**, **INSERT** and **UPDATE** privileges can apply either to whole tables or to specific columns; the **DELETE** privilege can only apply to whole tables, that is only whole rows can be deleted. Typical table privilege statements are shown in Figure 8.1.

Figure 8.1 Table privilege statements

```
GRANT ALL PRIVILEGES ON employee
   TO human_resources;

GRANT SELECT ON employee
         (payroll_number, salary)
   TO department_head;

GRANT UPDATE, INSERT ON qualification
   TO user27;
```

Function and procedure privileges allow users to execute stored SQL-invoked routines. These are routines that may be written in SQL (using the syntax for functions and procedures) and with the program code stored as part of the logical schema. Alternatively they may be written in some other programming language, such as C, with their definition stored as part of the logical schema. The privilege statement in Figure 8.2 allows the human resources department to execute a function that calculates the current age of an employee.

Figure 8.2 A function privilege statement

```
GRANT EXECUTE ON function_calculate_age
   TO human_resources;
```

Database object privileges control which users can create or alter database structures. These privileges are not part of the SQL standard but are provided by some vendors of database management systems. These privileges are normally reserved for database administrators. In fact, if these privileges are not restricted to database administrators, it will be almost impossible to have enterprise-wide management of data. The privilege statement in Figure 8.3 allows the human resources department to create tables within their database.

Figure 8.3 A database object privilege statement

```
GRANT CREATE table
   TO human_resources;
```

All of these privileges may also be granted to all users by using the pseudo authorisation identifier **PUBLIC**.

Another way that access to data can be controlled is through the use of virtual tables or views. This becomes extremely powerful when combined with access controls. For example, instead of providing department heads with **SELECT** access to the **payroll_number**, **surname** and **salary** columns of the employee table, it is possible to create an appropriate view for that data and grant access to that view as shown in Figure 8.4.

Figure 8.4 A view statement and an associated table privilege statement

```
CREATE VIEW employee_salary
  AS
  SELECT payroll_number, surname, salary
  FROM person, employee
  WHERE person.id = employee.role_of_person_id;

GRANT SELECT ON employee_salary
  TO department_head;
```

Another example of the use of views is to restrict access to data for a particular user, for example so that an employee can see their own employee record but no others. This can be achieved as shown in Figure 8.5 (assuming that a user's authorisation identifier is their payroll number).

Figure 8.5 A user-specific view statement and an associated table privilege statement

```
CREATE VIEW single_employee
  AS
  SELECT *
  FROM employee
  WHERE payroll_number = USER;

GRANT SELECT ON single_employee
  TO PUBLIC;
```

Discretionary and mandatory access controls

There are two levels of access control:

- Discretionary Access Control (DAC) is where the users who are granted access rights are allowed to propagate those rights to other users.

- Mandatory Access Control (MAC) is where access rights cannot be changed by the users.

The access control mechanisms described above, including their use with views, provide Discretionary Access Control. The privileges may be granted and revoked, and once given privileges and the authority to grant them onwards, there is no limit to their propagation amongst users. Under Discretionary Access Control a user could accidentally or maliciously provide access to create, read, update or delete data to unauthorised users. Consequently Discretionary Access Control provides a very low level of data security, yet the use of views and the granting and revoking of privileges are the most common data security mechanisms in use.

Mandatory Access Control needs to be applied where an environment with trusted security is needed. In Discretionary Access Control the user (which may be the database administrator) who created an object can grant access rights to other users. In Mandatory Access Control the access rights are set by the security administrator and are not under the control of the users.

A popular model used in Mandatory Access Control is the Bell–LaPadula Model developed by David Bell and Len LaPadula for the US Department of Defense. Consider a situation where the organisation holds data at three security levels – secret, confidential and public – so that secret is the most sensitive and public is the least sensitive; that is, secret is more sensitive than confidential and confidential is more sensitive than public. Objects in the database are given a security label – one of the specified security levels: secret, confidential, public. That is the level at which the object is classified. Each user or role (known as a subject in the Bell–LaPadula Model) is given a security clearance – again one of the specified security levels: secret, confidential, public. This is the highest level of classification that the subject can access. The model then imposes two restrictions on access to data as follows:

- A subject with a clearance at a given level of classification may not read a database object or data labelled at a higher classification level; that is, there is 'no read up'.

- A subject with a clearance at a given level of classification must not write to any database object labelled at a lower classification level; that is, there is 'no write-down'.

With this model, therefore, users can only view data at or below their own security level; confidential users can view confidential or public data but may not view secret data. On the other hand, users can only create data at or above their own security level; confidential users can create confidential or secret data but may not create public data. This second restriction prevents users from accidentally or maliciously writing highly classified data, say secret data, to a table that is of a lower, say public, classification, which would then be available to subjects with a lower clearance.

Multilevel security

Using a model such as the Bell–LaPadula Model, Mandatory Access Control could be applied to a complete database. For example, all data within the database can be considered as being secret (even though some, probably most, of it should realistically be of a lower classification) and the control is then applied via the operating system. Only subjects with appropriate clearance are allowed access to the database. Applying multilevel security to the whole database in this way is often known as 'system high'. A far greater degree of security can be achieved through the use of multilevel security within the database. This is achieved by applying security labels to database objects, tables, columns and so on, and to the data itself. In the case of the data, a security label is applied to each row so all data in that row is at the same classification level.

One of the implications of the application of multilevel security to database objects and data is that two users (or one user with two different roles, each having a different clearance) may get different answers to the same query applied to the same set of data. Consider a table with 1000 rows of data where 50 rows are labelled as having a secret classification, 100 rows are labelled as having a confidential classification and the remaining rows are labelled as having a public classification. A general query on that table returns 850 rows of data for a subject with a public clearance, 950 rows of data for a subject with a confidential clearance and all 1000 rows for a subject with a secret clearance. The subject with only public clearance is not told that they are denied access to 150 rows; the database management system responds as if there are only 850 rows in the table. Problems can arise when only some of the data in a secret or confidential row should be labelled at that higher level, and most of the data in the row should really be labelled as public. The user with public clearance is then denied access to data that only warrants a public label and should, therefore, be available to them. In the worst case, if they believe that some data about 'x' should be available to them but they do not see that data, they may infer that there is some other data about 'x' that is of a higher classification and this may, of itself, be a breach of security. For this reason the design of a database where multilevel security is to be implemented requires considerably more care than that for a 'system high' or unclassified database. At one time a major database management system vendor was publicly saying that the design of a multilevel secure database would cost 14 times the cost of a standard database. I am not aware that these figures were ever verified through surveys or controlled studies but they do provide an indication of the extra care that needs to be taken when designing a database with internal multilevel security.

Encryption

The access controls discussed above are applied by the database management system, but it is possible to use the operating and file-management systems to directly access the data files, thus bypassing the database management system and its security controls. Generally the average user cannot make sense of these files – the information held within them is of a proprietary format designed by the database management system vendor. However, there are two ways that the data in these files could be compromised. A copy could be taken of the files and then used with another instance of the database management system software to access the files. Under these circumstances the only danger is that the data is read by someone unauthorised to do so. Alternatively a determined 'hacker' with the right knowledge could access these files in situ without going through the database management system. In this case the 'hacker' could corrupt the data as well as reading it.

To prevent either of these situations the database could be encrypted. Either the whole database could be encrypted or the encryption could be applied to just some of the data. The encryption of the whole database is the simplest option but it affects the overall database performance; the database needs to be unencrypted every time some data needs to be read and re-encrypted every time some data is updated. The alternative is to only encrypt data in columns that need encrypting such as columns holding credit card details. Some database management systems come with a built-in ability to encrypt some or all of the data; others provide encryption as an extra module. There are also stand-alone database encryption software products available from third-party vendors.

Audit trails

Most database management systems include facilities to maintain audit trails of database operations, recording what database objects were accessed by whom and when. Some even allow the audit trail to record what data was changed. Audit trails do not prevent unauthorised access but they do provide information that allows security breaches to be detected. As such they help to promote data security.

DATA INTEGRITY

Whereas data security is about protecting the database against unauthorised users, data integrity is about protecting the database against authorised users. As stated in

Chapter 2, one of the roles of a database management system is to allow constraints on data to be defined and to enforce those constraints. It is these constraints that ensure that the data remains consistent and complies with the business rules.

Integrity constraints fall into two categories: those that are inherent in the underlying model of the database management system and those that are encoded into the logical schema.

The inherent constraint rules for all relational databases are, for example:

- All candidate keys are unique; that is, no duplication is allowed.
- No component of the primary key is allowed to be null; this is known as 'entity integrity'.
- Foreign key values must not be unmatched; this is known as 'referential integrity'.

If you purchase a product that claims to be a relational database system, you can expect that if one or more columns is declared as a candidate key and an attempt is made to insert a duplicate set of values into those columns, the insert will be rejected and an appropriate message given to the user. Similarly if there is an attempt to insert a set of values into the primary key columns of a table where one or more value is missing, the insert should be rejected, as should an attempt to insert an unmatched foreign key.

Declaring **person_id** as the primary key of the **PERSON** table in the logical schema therefore ensures that the identifiers allocated to individual persons are unique and are always present. Declaring the combination of **resident_at_property_number** and **resident_at_property_post_code** in the **PERSON** table as a foreign key referencing the **PROPERTY** table ensures that only combinations of **resident_at_property_number** and **resident_at_property_post_code** values that already exist in the **PROPERTY** table can be inserted into the **PERSON** table.

Primary key and foreign key constraints are not the only constraints that can be encoded in the logical schema. It is possible to write more general constraints, some of which can be extremely complex such as:

- The only allowed values for the **relationship** column in the **PERSON_NEXT_OF_KIN** table are 'Spouse', 'Partner', 'Parent', 'Child', 'Distant Relative' and 'Friend' – this is an example of a constraint that applies to a single column of a table.
- The difference between the **start_date** value in the **EMPLOYEE** table and the **birth_date** value in the **PERSON** table must be between 16 and 60 years – all employees must be between 16 and 60 years of age when they are first employed – this is an example of a constraint that applies to different columns in more than one table.

Once constraints have been defined, any attempts to insert data or to update existing data in a way that does not comply with a constraint are rejected. Thus the data within the database retains its integrity, allowing the users a level of confidence in the quality of the data. Data integrity controls are necessary to ensure that data is of high quality, but data integrity controls are not, of themselves, sufficient to maintain the quality of the data.

DATA RECOVERY

Data recovery is about restoring the database to a state that is known to be correct after a failure. Policies must be in place whereby the risks to the data are assessed and then adequate provision is made to ensure that it will be possible to restore the data if necessary. The implementation of these policies must be monitored; when there are no failures from which to recover, it is very easy to overlook the need to prepare for the worst scenario.

Causes of failure

The types of failure that need to be considered can be classified as:

- transaction failures;
- system crashes;
- media failures.

A transaction is a logical unit of work; all or none of the operations within the transaction must be completed to ensure that the database remains in a consistent state. Partial completion leaves the database in an inconsistent state. Thus there are four properties of transactions, known as the ACID properties, that all database management systems are required to maintain. These are:

- **Atomicity** – either all operations of the transaction are reflected properly in the database or none are.
- **Consistency** – execution of a transaction in isolation preserves the consistency of the database.
- **Isolation** – each transaction is unaware of other transactions executing concurrently in the system.
- **Durability** – after a transaction completes successfully, the changes it has made to the database persist even if there is a system failure.

For example, in a transaction to transfer funds from an account, X, to another account, Y, within a bank there are two operations: a debit from account X and a credit to account Y for the same amount. Executing either one of those operations on its own is unacceptable; the database will show an incorrect total for the sum of the funds held by the bank. So both these operations must be committed to the database and hence be held in persistent storage (i.e. on the disk). Alternatively, in the event of failure to complete the whole transaction, those operations that have been completed must be rolled back so that the database is returned to the state that it was in before the transaction started.

Transaction failures can be further classified into those that are the result of logical errors and those that are the result of system errors. Logical errors occur where there is an error in the data input or the transaction will violate some constraint, for example if there are insufficient funds in account X to be transferred to account Y. System errors are where the system has entered a state where it cannot complete the transaction, for example if account X has been debited but for some reason writing to account Y is prevented. In the case of logical errors it is necessary for the user to resubmit the transaction with data that is acceptable. In the case of system errors, however, the system itself should attempt to re-execute the complete transaction on behalf of the user.

System crashes occur when there is some fault with the hardware or there is a bug, either in the database management system software or in the operating system software. The result is that any data held in volatile memory, perhaps as part of a transaction, is corrupted. Data that is already in persistent storage should not be corrupted. System crashes could also be caused by external factors such as a power cut.

Media failures typically occur when a block on a disk loses its data as a result of some malfunction during a read-from-disk operation or a write-to-disk operation.

Recovery mechanisms

Being prepared to recover data after a failure requires that there is some degree of redundancy of data. This redundancy is purely physical; it is not logical redundancy, which could lead to update anomalies. There are a number of forms that this physical redundancy may take.

The commonest form of physical redundancy that allows for recovery after transaction failures is the database log. The log records all the changes to the data held in the database, usually recording both the old and new values of the data. The log record of a change to the data is created before the database itself is modified. When it is necessary to return the database to the last known consistent state that existed before the failure, the log is consulted to discover those operations that must be undone and those operations that must be redone.

The main technique used to recover after system or media failures is to restore a backup of the database. A backup is where the contents of the database and its log are copied onto another storage medium such as a magnetic tape, usually using a utility provided as part of the database management system software. Such backups may be full backups or incremental backups. Incremental backups only record the changes since the last backup. A backup plan could be, therefore, that a full backup is taken at a set time once a week and on the following days only incremental backups are taken. For example, if a full backup is taken at 3 a.m. each Monday morning, the incremental backup at the same time on Tuesday morning records just the changes since 3 a.m. Monday, the Wednesday incremental backup records just the changes since 3 a.m. Tuesday and so on.

There are a number of alternative approaches to using backups. These alternatives could be used instead of backups altogether or could be used to augment a backup strategy. One alternative is to have a standby database, a 'near-identical' copy of an operational database, on a remote server. It is described as 'near identical' because there will always be a slight delay in the posting of changes to the standby database. A standby database will, of course, contain all the errors that exist in the data in the main operational database. Another alternative technique is to employ disk mirroring. This is where another copy of the data is held on another storage device. Both the primary and secondary storage devices are managed by the same instance of the database management system software and modifications are made to both devices simultaneously. Disk mirroring is only really useful to recover from a media failure. A system failure that affects the primary device will almost certainly also affect the secondary device. Disk mirroring should only be used to augment a backup strategy and should not be used instead of backups. Yet another alternative is to employ data replication where data is held in more than one operational database. This is discussed in more detail in Chapter 13 in the context of distributed databases.

SUMMARY

Mechanisms for the application of data security, data integrity and data recovery have been discussed. While database administrators maintain these mechanisms, data administration is responsible for the development of the relevant security, integrity and recovery policies.

9 MASTER DATA MANAGEMENT

This chapter introduces master data and its management. First, master data is defined and explained with some examples. The reasons why some of the problems with master data arise will be discussed. MDM Hubs and some of the approaches to their implementation will then be introduced.

WHAT IS MASTER DATA?

The MDM Institute has defined master data management as 'the authoritative, reliable foundation for data used across many applications and constituencies with the goal to provide a single version of the truth'. Gartner has come up with a competing definition, defining master data management as 'a discipline used by business and IT to ensure uniformity, accuracy, stewardship and accountability of the organisation's shared master data assets' and defining master data as 'a consistent, official set of identifiers, attributes and hierarchies for core entities'.

What is clear about master data management is that the term is relatively new, having appeared within the last decade, but what it is trying to achieve has been one of the goals of data management since data management began.

At its most basic, master data management seeks to ensure that an organisation uses only one version of its 'master data' for all of its operations.

The data within any database (or, indeed, in any enterprise) can be viewed at six different levels, or layers, as shown in Figure 9.1.

Metadata was discussed in Chapter 6. Here we are using the term in the 'metadata for data management' sense, where the metadata describes the types of data stored in a database, such as the table and column definitions for a database schema and the associated constraint definitions.

Reference data consists of the codes and their associated descriptions that are used to categorise other data found in a database or, perhaps, for relating data in a database to information found outside the organisation. The tables that hold this data may be called 'lookup tables'. The values in these tables can be equated to the valid values for an enumerated domain. The tables concerned normally have only a few rows and columns.

Transaction structure data represents the direct participants in a transaction such as suppliers, customers and products. Information about a transaction cannot be recorded unless the details of these participants already exist in the database.

Figure 9.1 The six data layers

Enterprise structure data is data that describes the structure of the enterprise, for example the organisational structure or the financial structure.

Transaction activity data is that data that is seen by many people as the prime purpose of information technology: the recording of the transactions or operations that are carried out by the organisation.

Transaction audit data is the data that keeps track of each transaction. This often involves the use of logs.

Figure 9.2 Different data categories

For example, in the conceptual data model shown in Figure 9.2, **PRODUCT CATEGORY**, **GENDER**, **COUNTRY** and **BRANCH SIZE** are examples of reference data, **PRODUCT** and **CUSTOMER** are examples of transaction structure data, **BRANCH** is an example of enterprise structure data and **ORDER** and **ORDER ITEM** are examples of transaction activity data.

As we move up this 'stack' it is very important that the data is of good quality. There will, however, be less data higher in the 'stack' than lower in the 'stack'. Furthermore the lower we are in the 'stack', the later in the operational life cycle the data is created and the shorter the useful lifespan of the data.

Figure 9.3 The three master data layers

As shown in Figure 9.3 it is the combination of reference data, transaction structure data and enterprise structure data that is normally seen as master data.

Figure 9.4 shows the categories of master data that are used by processes within typical business functions. It highlights the importance of master data to the enterprise. Of the eight business functions, **PRODUCT** is used by all eight, **CUSTOMER** by seven, **DEPARTMENT** by three and **SUPPLIER** by three. It is for a business to determine exactly what data used within the business should be considered as master data.

Figure 9.4 The relationship between business processes and master data

Development	Marketing	Sales	Order Management	Finance	Logistics	Manufacturing	Customer Support
Gather Requirements	Identify Customer Segment	Develop Sales Channel	Fulfil Order	Invoice Customer	Ship Goods	Manufacture Goods	Manage Call Centre
Develop Product	Track Product Performance	Complete Sale	Order Supplies	Receive Payment	Receive Supplies	Check Quality	Provide Service
				Pay Supplier	Manage Inventory	Check Productivity	Receive Returned Goods

Business Functions and Processes

PRODUCT	PRODUCT	PRODUCT	PRODUCT	PRODUCT	PRODUCT	PRODUCT	PRODUCT
	CUSTOMER	CUSTOMER	CUSTOMER	CUSTOMER	CUSTOMER	CUSTOMER	CUSTOMER
		DEPARTMENT	DEPARTMENT	DEPARTMENT			
			SUPPLIER	SUPPLIER	SUPPLIER		

Associated Master Data Categories

HOW DO PROBLEMS WITH MASTER DATA OCCUR?

Problems with what should be considered as master data occur because of two interrelated problems: the 'silo' mentality that exists in many organisations and the independent development of systems to support different 'silos'.

The 'silo' mentality is common in many organisations where groups of employees concentrate on their own function within the organisation. Employees in one part of the organisation often do not know, and do not even care, what employees elsewhere are doing. In large organisations this effect is magnified.

Information technology systems to support the different functions within an organisation are often independently designed or procured 'off the shelf'. In each of these systems data will be defined and stored in different ways.

All of this can lead to inconsistent results. A bank can send marketing material for a mortgage product to a customer who already has a mortgage with the bank because marketing uses a different system to operations, and customer is defined differently in each system. Two branches of a retail company can sell a product at different prices because there is no consistent management of prices.

Generally it is not until there is some problem that either causes the organisation to lose substantial sums of money or to face considerable embarrassment that there is any attempt to manage its master data.

The situation is exacerbated by mergers and acquisitions that bring together data from two or more organisations that then needs to be seen as a single set of data.

You will recognise these problems as very similar to the issues raised in Chapters 1 and 2 which, in turn, led to the setting up of a team to manage data as described in Chapter 3.

With master data management we are concentrating the efforts of data management on the data with the highest value to the organisation.

HOW DO WE MANAGE MASTER DATA?

There are many products on the market that claim to manage master data but technology alone is not enough. The people involved and the processes such as the identification of sources, the collection and transformation of data, error detection and correction and the consolidation of data are also important.

The main technological tool that can be used for the management of master data is the Master Data Management (MDM) Hub, a database and software with two roles: to manage the master data that is stored in the database and to keep it synchronised with the transactional systems that use the master data. An overview of an MDM Hub is shown in Figure 9.5. In this figure, data is imported into the MDM Hub from systems A, B and D, rationalised and then exported to all of the systems where the master data is required.

Figure 9.5 The MDM Hub

One approach to implementing an MDM Hub is storing the complete collection of master data for an organisation in a single database. The data model for this database must include all the attributes required by all the systems that use the master data. The systems that use the master data all need to be modified to use the master data in the hub.

Taking this approach has some advantages such as:

- All systems use the same master data; there is no duplication.
- Duplicate information is easily detected since there is only one place where the master information is held.

However, there are disadvantages such as:

- It may not be possible to change the existing systems to use the new master data.
- The data model for the MDM Hub may be very large and complex.
- Not all of the systems that use the master data will need all of the attributes that have been included in the MDM Hub.

An alternative approach is where the master data is maintained in the current systems and the MDM Hub contains information that can be used to find all of the related records for a particular item of master data.

This approach has the advantage that no change to the existing system is required. Against this, the main disadvantage of this approach is that every query against master data results in a distributed query across all of the existing systems that contain the master data.

Another disadvantage of this approach is the need to know about all of the existing systems before implementing the MDM Hub. This can be overcome by developing the hub with a more generic structure but queries will then be more complex.

When designing an MDM Hub it is important to consider versioning and hierarchies. An example of the need for versioning is where, in addition to knowing the credit limit of a customer today, we may also need to know that customer's credit limit three months ago when a high interest rate was charged because the customer went over their credit limit. Hierarchies recognise relationships between entities in the MDM Hub such as which products are sold by which salesmen, which employees work for a particular manager and in which sales territory a particular customer is resident. And, of course, hierarchies may themselves need versioning.

Populating an MDM Hub involves extracting the data from the source system, transforming the data to the data structure for the hub, checking for duplicates, loading the data into the MDM Hub database and then updating the source systems. This may all take considerable time.

SUMMARY

Master data has been defined and explained and the reasons why some of the problems with master data arise were discussed. MDM Hubs and some of the approaches to their implementation were introduced.

PART 3
DATABASE AND REPOSITORY ADMINISTRATION

As shown in Chapter 3, database administration is concerned with the management and control of the software used to access physical data and repository administration is concerned with the management and control of the software in which 'information about information' is stored, manipulated and defined.

In this part we describe the tasks and areas that are the responsibility of database administrators and repository administrators. This part has two chapters.

Chapter 10 – Database Administration – provides an overview of the roles and responsibilities of database administrators, particularly the monitoring and tuning of the performance of a database.

Chapter 11 – Repository Administration – looks at the management and control of the software in which 'information about information' (or metadata) is stored, manipulated and defined. To do this the chapter expands on the roles of repositories or other software associated with the handling of metadata, such as directories and catalogs, encyclopaedias and data dictionaries in addition to repositories. The features expected of a repository and the ways that a repository can be used as an enterprise-wide knowledge base are also introduced.

10 DATABASE ADMINISTRATION

This chapter provides an overview of the roles and responsibilities of database administrators. It also provides a more in-depth view of one of the jobs carried out by database administrators, the monitoring and tuning of the performance of a database.

DATABASE ADMINISTRATION RESPONSIBILITIES

Database administration is concerned with the management and control of the software used to access physical data. The database administrators, often called DBAs, look after the database management systems in use to record the organisation's data. Database administrators are responsible for:

- development and maintenance of technical standards covering the database administration function;
- physical database design;
- the management of the database management system software;
- database administration education and training.

Technical standards

Just like any other business function the database administration function requires its own technical standards to govern its processes and procedures. These standards need to be developed with data sharing and interoperability across the whole enterprise in mind. They also need to consider the handling and storage of unstructured or multimedia data as well as the more normal structured data. As well as covering all the activities undertaken by the database administrators themselves, these standards need to include how application development teams can test the databases they are developing or test their application programs with existing databases. The standards must specify how end-users are to access data.

Database physical design

The general principles of physical database design were covered in Chapter 2. It is the responsibility of the database administration function to provide the expertise to the enterprise on all matters that impact on database design. In an ideal situation, database administrators who are part of the enterprise-wide data management function design all the enterprise's databases, basing these designs on the corporate data standards.

If, however, database design is decentralised to application development teams, the central database administration team should have the responsibility for reviewing and approving the database designs. This ensures that the designs do not contravene the enterprise's data standards, irrespective of whether they have been developed by in-house application development teams or by external service or software providers. As part of this review process, the database administrators need to be in a position to resolve conflicts between application teams where databases are to be shared. They also need to ensure that the database designs can cope with future data requirements. This implies that there has to be a high level of agreement and collaboration between the data administration and database administration functions.

It is unfortunate that in many cases good database design is sacrificed in the pursuit of enhanced performance. To achieve fast response to queries, the database design may become too tightly coupled to the application design. This not only reduces the scope for data sharing in the short term, it can also lead to data inconsistency and other forms of poor-quality data and could also lead to an inability to cope with future business change.

The database administrators need to be thoroughly familiar with the principles, both theoretical and practical, underlying the various database management systems in use within the enterprise. For example, if relational database management systems are in use (and they almost certainly are), the database administrators need a deep understanding of relational theory and specific detailed knowledge of the particular database management system products in use.

The management of the DBMS software

The duties of a database administrator include:

- management of the security of the database through the correct establishment of new users, the granting of appropriate access rights to users (see Chapter 8) and the investigation of security breaches;
- monitoring of the performance of the database and tuning to improve performance where necessary;
- guarding against catastrophic database failures by taking regular database backups (see Chapter 8) and rehearsing the associated recovery procedures;
- management of upgrades or changes to the database management system software, for example to take account of new features provided by the software.

Education and training

Database administrators must maintain their own expertise and constantly need to update their training and education. They need theoretical education on database issues. In some cases this is to understand the underlying theory of the particular database management systems in use; in other cases it is to understand the advances being made in the field of databases such as the introduction of structured types and collection types into SQL (see Chapter 15) and the impact that has on database design. They also need detailed training on the database management system products they are managing.

Training may cover topics such as:

- the day-to-day activities of administering users and their access rights;
- backup and recovery techniques;
- database configuration and tuning;
- on a more advanced course, how database instances may be incorporated into a federated distributed data system.

The database administrators may also be called upon to provide advice on the training required by different categories of database user.

PERFORMANCE MONITORING AND TUNING

Database administrators should not wait for users to complain about poor performance; they should be constantly monitoring performance and taking appropriate remedial action to ensure that the users receive a good level of service. Nevertheless, however proactive the database administrators are in identifying potential performance problems and taking action to prevent them, they still need to be ready to respond to unexpected poor performance; no matter how hard you try to prevent it, unplanned poor performance problems are always likely to occur.

Not all performance issues that appear at first sight to be due to poor database performance are, in fact, caused by the database; there may be more general system performance issues or there may be something in the application program code that is having an effect on the overall performance. If the poor performance is down to some general system issue, the database administrator needs to collaborate with the system manager to overcome the problem. If the poor performance is down to something in the application code, the database administrator may need to offer advice as to how the code may be rewritten to overcome the problem. This is particularly so if the problem is with embedded database queries hosted within the application code; the query may well be expressed in a way that is inherently inefficient. Database administrators need to be able to guide application developers as to how to write efficient database queries. The database administrator has to be aware, however, that there may be factors other than embedded database queries that cause poor performance. For example the use of poorly designed loops within the application code itself can impact on the performance of the system, giving the impression that there is a database performance problem.

If, after investigation, it is found that the database is the cause of the poor performance, there are a number of steps that the database administrator can take to rectify the situation. Most, if not all, database management system vendors provide tools for the database administrator to analyse the performance of the database and to then tune the database. These vendor-provided tools tend to be for the database management systems sold by that vendor only, but a number of third-party vendors also provide tools, some of which can be used across a heterogeneous environment of mixed database management systems.

The following actions within the control of the database administrator may be used to alter performance:

- the allocation of memory as buffer, or data cache, to store data that is often queried, to reduce the number of disk reads required;

- the allocation of tables, or parts of tables, to files and the allocation of those files to disk space;

- the extent to which database transactions are logged; writing to a log consumes resources, but logs are essential in the event that the database needs to be recovered;

- the application of locks in multiuser situations so that when a user is accessing some data, that data is locked to prevent another user reading incomplete data or attempting to apply a conflicting update; minimising the possibility of deadlocks (two or more applications holding locks on data that others need to be able to proceed); or reducing the timeout interval (the time an application process can be suspended);

- the use of indexes and the clustering of data as discussed in Chapter 2.

All of these parameters may be set during the initial setting up of the database, but they can also be altered when the database is in use.

Another option is to denormalise the database, moving away from the logical design to improve query performance. This was also discussed in Chapter 2. This affects data independence, slows down update performance while improving retrieval performance, and increases the possibility of inconsistent data. Denormalisation should be avoided if at all possible.

SUMMARY

In this chapter we have looked at the roles and responsibilities of database administrators including the development of database administration standards, the physical design of databases, the management of the database management software once it is in use and education and training. We also took a deeper look at the monitoring of the performance of the database and the actions that can be taken to improve performance.

11 REPOSITORY ADMINISTRATION

As we saw in Chapter 3, repository administration is concerned with the management and control of the software in which 'information about information' is stored, manipulated and defined. A repository administrator is, therefore, providing a database administration service to the data management function. The repository administrator needs to follow all of the database administration procedures and techniques discussed in Appendix I. This chapter expands on the roles of repositories or other software associated with the handling of metadata.

REPOSITORIES, DATA DICTIONARIES, ENCYCLOPAEDIAS, CATALOGS AND DIRECTORIES

There are many systems, or subsystems, available that have the common primary purpose of storing, manipulating or defining metadata – 'information about information' – but they appear under a number of different names such as repositories, data dictionaries, encyclopaedias, catalogs and directories.

The last two of these, catalogs and directories, are usually provided as part of a database management system; each directory or catalog is, therefore, associated with a single database instance. Data dictionaries and encyclopaedias are normally associated with tools that are used to support software engineering; an instance of a data dictionary or an encyclopaedia is often associated with a single software development project. Repositories have a broader role and are normally associated with corporate data management initiatives.

Directories and catalogs

As an integral part of a database management system, directories and catalogs are usually associated with physical data as shown in Figure 11.1, a variation on Figure 2.1. Directories and catalogs document the data definitions and the schemas that are used to store the data.

They also provide the mappings between the logical and internal schemas, and between the logical and external schemas if the external schema concept is supported. Although their primary role is to implement and manage the physical environment used for the storage of data, they may also be used to manage the database access controls. Despite their close association with a database management system and the physical data environment, directories and catalogs can also be used to record more conceptual information, such as the conceptual data models, about the database.

Figure 11.1 The role of directories or catalogs

CASE tools

Increasingly system development is supported by Computer-Aided Software Engineering (CASE) tools. These tools usually have a sophisticated user interface that allows the analyst or developer to produce a range of diagrams to support software engineering such as data models, data flow diagrams and process models. These tools are normally associated with one particular software engineering methodology and produce their diagrams using one notation. Some allow the SQL data definition language statements for the logical schema to be automatically generated from the metadata for the data model. Most CASE tools maintain the integrity between the different models so that, for example, something cannot be depicted on a data model that is not supported by the data flow diagram.

An encyclopaedia or data dictionary that supports the CASE tool environment is designed specifically for that purpose. Like any other database it has a schema that is based on a conceptual data model. In this case the conceptual data model is a metadata model that reflects the object types, properties and associations required by the methodology that the CASE environment supports. It is not usually possible to modify this model and it may not even be known to you. The data structure of the encyclopaedia or data dictionary is fixed; any attempt to alter the structure of the encyclopaedia or data dictionary is likely to interfere with the coupling between the user interface, the CASE application code and the underlying database.

As can be seen from Figure 11.2, the encyclopaedia or data dictionary is only accessed via the user interface of the CASE tool environment, but there may be a built-in import/export facility to interface with other tools or dictionaries.

Figure 11.2 The relationship between a CASE tool and its encyclopaedia or data dictionary

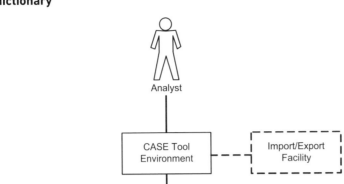

Repositories

Unlike the encyclopaedia or data dictionary supplied as part of a CASE tool, a fully functional repository is based on a flexible information or metadata model. The metadata model and the schema definition of the repository should be available so that the underlying data structure can be modified. This allows an enterprise to add new concepts to the repository to adapt the concepts already supported by it so that the repository structure can match the methodology in use within the enterprise, even if that methodology has been developed in-house. Many of the products available today that are now called repositories were once known as data dictionaries.

A repository should be capable of storing many different types of model (see Figure 11.3) and have a significant level of functionality such that it can fully support the data management activities and co-ordinate the complete 'set' of data management tools. First and foremost, a repository is a software tool to assist data managers to carry out their activities. In theory it is possible to implement a paper-based repository using some type of manual storage, but in practice the complexity of information we need to control and store using the repository soon makes the non-automated approach impossible to manage.

The data management repository provides a centralised source of information about the data of the enterprise. The information held in this repository is of use throughout the

Figure 11.3 The architecture of a repository

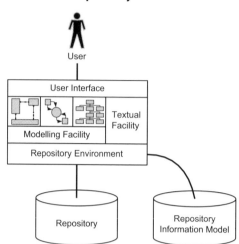

enterprise. To optimise its use it must have interfaces with the other tools that use or manage data, but this can be very difficult to achieve in practice because of the differing environments in which the tools reside and the various personnel who are responsible for them. Nevertheless a well-structured and well-maintained repository becomes a reference point for information that should be readily accessible to all, whether by direct interrogation or by the use of reports generated from the repository.

REPOSITORY FEATURES

The repository acts as an encyclopaedia of knowledge about the organisation and its goals, structure, functions and processes. Conceptual data models and process models should be stored in the repository, as well as information about design details and the different types of data and data structures in use across the enterprise.

The scope of a repository is shown in Figure 11.4. The repository should be capable of dealing with the definition of multiple object types with differing properties and complex relationships. It should provide facilities to handle multiple names for objects in a controlled manner. It should support such things as database design and code generation. It should be possible to partition the repository to represent different views of information corresponding to different stages in the software development life cycle. It should be possible to maintain effective version control.

The repository should have an easy-to-use query language, should have compare and merge facilities, should be able to represent information in graphical format and should be able to generate formal documents. It should be able to import and export information to and from other products such as CASE tools.

Figure 11.4 The scope of a repository

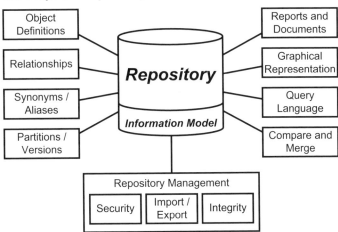

A repository should be perceived as a database of information. The procurement of a repository should follow the procedure for the procurement of any software. Good design is essential if the user requirements are to be satisfied. Ideally, therefore, we should discipline ourselves to produce a suitable conceptual model based on an analysis of the requirements. This will provide a blueprint for the repository that we can use to evaluate the available products.

When evaluating repositories it is important to look at the functionality and flexibility of the products available. The following questions are a small sample of those that should be asked:

- What properties can be defined for each object type?
- How does the repository deal with multiple names?
- Is it possible to support multiple views or versions?
- Is it possible to tailor the information model?
- Are there any performance implications in doing so?
- Does the repository support different types of database management system?
- What types of relationship are supported?
- What types of query can the repository answer?
- Is the query language easy to use?
- How does the repository import or export information?
- What standard reports are offered?

- Can report layouts and terminology be tailored?
- How easy is the product to install and maintain?
- How easy is the product to use?
- Is it menu-driven?
- Does it have online help facilities?
- What features for maintaining integrity and security are there?

The data management staff should not only have authority to select and manage a repository but should also be part of the evaluation process for other systems development software tools in order to ensure correct links can be provided with the repository and that the principles of data management can be upheld.

THE REPOSITORY AS A CENTRALISED SOURCE OF INFORMATION

By setting up a repository, data management is setting up a centralised source of information – a knowledge base – that is of potential use to everyone in the organisation. This is shown in Figure 11.5. As well as information about the data of the enterprise, many repositories also contain other information that is useful to information systems developers, such as process definitions, business rules and interface definitions.

Figure 11.5 A repository as a centralised source of information

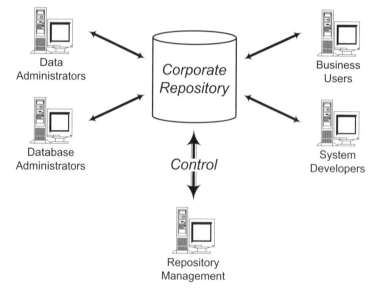

Careful consideration must be given to the methods by which use of this knowledge base can be optimised. The repository has great potential as a vehicle for dissemination of information, both in the form of reports and as an online knowledge base of information.

The type of access we give to users can play a critical part in the success of the repository. Decisions on who is allowed to update the repository, and under what circumstances, are highly dependent on the planned use of the repository. For example, update of the repository with data analysis information could be limited to the data administration function but if the repository is to be highly integrated in the system development process, that approach may prove unacceptable to the system development teams.

As with any other database, the data held in the repository must be of high quality if it is to be useful. The data management team has a fundamental duty to ensure that the information in the repository is accurate and correct and that it is subject to quality assurance.

Of equal importance to the design of the actual repository is the design of the repository infrastructure – the technical environment in which the repository is used. If the infrastructure is set up correctly, the repository should be integrated into the working practices of the IT or IS department and those other departments that are going to make use of it. Each repository user should be provided with an appropriate level of support. This may take the form of menu-driven processing, online help, skeleton screens, tailored reports, customised queries and so on. Training must be geared to meet the needs of the different types of user. It may be useful to develop modular in-house training courses to satisfy these requirements. If the repository is easy to use, it is more likely to be readily accepted by its potential users.

METADATA MODELS

Any system that holds metadata, irrespective of whether it is called a repository, a data dictionary or some other name, needs a database designed to hold that metadata. The conceptual data model for such a database is known as a metadata model. Metadata models are described in more detail in Appendix E.

SUMMARY

This chapter concentrated on the systems that a repository administrator is responsible for. The differences between directories and catalogs, encyclopaedias and data dictionaries, and repositories were discussed. The features of a repository and the way that a repository can be used as an enterprise-wide knowledge base were explored in more detail.

PART 4
THE DATA MANAGEMENT ENVIRONMENT

In this part we consider a number of fads, advances and developments, including the recent developments in SQL. Data management practitioners should not only be aware of these trends, but should ensure that their organisations have policies in place to take account of these developments. This part has six chapters.

Chapter 12 – The Use of Packaged Application Software – discusses some of the issues that the use of application software packages bought 'off the shelf' raises for data management.

Chapter 13 – Distributed Data and Databases – provides an overview of some of the issues that need to be addressed when distributing data.

Chapter 14 – Business Intelligence – discusses business intelligence, the name that has been given to the set of 'techniques' that is used to transform raw data into information that can be used to inform high-level decision making, including data warehousing, data mining and online analytical processing (OLAP).

Chapter 15 – Object Orientation – introduces object orientation, a programming paradigm, and then discusses the Object Definition Language from the Object Data Management Group and the extensions to SQL to make it 'object-relational'.

Chapter 16 – Multimedia – introduces the characteristics of multimedia and then goes on to address approaches for handling multimedia with databases.

Chapter 17 – Web Technology – looks at data and web technology, introducing HTML, XML, web architecture, Big Data, NoSQL databases and the sematic web.

12 THE USE OF PACKAGED APPLICATION SOFTWARE

For most business processes, there are now application software packages that can be bought 'off the shelf'. This chapter discusses some of the issues that the use of such packages raises for data management.

WHAT ARE APPLICATION SOFTWARE PACKAGES?

As stated above, for most business processes there are now application software packages that can be bought 'off the shelf'. A bought-in financial package can handle sales order processing, purchase order processing, general ledger and much more. A human resources package includes recruitment management, payroll, training management and so on. Many organisations have a strategy of using these 'off-the-shelf' application packages wherever possible as this is normally seen as a relatively cheap option for delivering speedy business benefit.

Most application packages provide the functionality that the package designer thinks is appropriate for a broad range of businesses. The database underlying these packages is designed to support the functionality provided by the package. It is highly unlikely that the requirement to share data was taken into account when the package was being designed. In an environment where off-the-shelf application packages are used, it is, therefore, difficult to share data between systems. This is especially true if the organisation is to be supported by a mixture of bespoke systems and packaged systems or by packaged systems from different vendors. It is not unknown, however, for data not to be shareable between packages or systems from the same vendor. If off-the-shelf application packages are to be used and there is to be data sharing, a 'bespoke interface' or a set of bespoke interfaces must be developed.

THE IMPACT ON DATA MANAGEMENT

Where application packages are to be procured to support business requirements, there are a number of issues that need to be addressed from a data management perspective:

- Is a reliable conceptual data model or logical schema available for the package? If not, it will be impossible for the data management team to assess the difficulty of sharing data between this package and the rest of the enterprise's systems before it is procured and implemented.

- Does the package match the functional and data requirements of the business? Business users easily identify if the package does or does not meet their functional and local data requirements but they are unlikely to consider any wider requirement to share data.

- How will the corporation handle the effects of the introduction by the vendor of new versions or releases of the package? New versions may introduce a requirement to reengineer interfaces.

The questions above are based on the assumption that the selected off-the-shelf package meets the business users' requirements. Increasingly, however, packages are being bought that do not quite match the functional requirements – the designer of the package envisaged a slightly different set of processes and procedures for the business area to those in use within the organisation. This is a result of the application of the Pareto Law, also known as the 80:20 principle, to package requirements. This principle says that 20 per cent of the work that we do produces 80 per cent of our income. In the context of the procurement of software, this is taken to mean that 80 per cent of the functionality we need only requires 20 per cent of the total cost. Getting the extra 20 per cent of functionality, to give us everything we need, costs that extra 80 per cent. The assumption is, therefore, that to save money we accept a package that provides 80 per cent of the functionality we require and adapt our procedures and processes to match the product we have bought. This seldom works out in practice but, even if it did, nobody seems to take into account the cost of changing the well-established business procedures and practices. The normal situation is that once the package has been bought, we discover that the business is not prepared to change the way it works and the off-the-shelf package has to be 'tailored' to meet the full business functionality. There are substantial financial costs in implementing this tailoring. However, a package that has been tailored is no longer an off-the-shelf package; it is now a 'bespoke' product.

To use an off-the-shelf package within a federated system always requires the development of an interface so that the package's data can be shared with other packages and systems and, probably, requires that the package's functionality also has to be tailored to meet the existing business processes and procedures.

Aside: I was once told that a study had been undertaken looking at the average whole-life cost overruns for systems development based on bespoke software, on the one hand, and for systems development based on the use of off-the-shelf application packages, on the other hand. The study found that the average whole-life costs for bespoke development ran three times over budget but that the average whole-life costs for a development with an off-the-shelf application package ran 14 times over budget. Unfortunately I have not been able to track down any details of this study.

When the true costs of developing, maintaining and managing interfaces as well as the tailoring required by the business area are included in the cost–benefit analysis, off-the-shelf application packages often turn out to be a more expensive option than bespoke development. All of this is also true for enterprise resource planning packages, which were briefly discussed in Chapter 1.

SUMMARY

This chapter has looked at some of the issues that the use of application software packages raises for data management.

13   DISTRIBUTED DATA AND DATABASES

This chapter looks at some of the issues that need to be addressed when distributing data. Unfortunately all of the theory is based on the distributing of a single set of data – the top-down approach – to improve reliability and availability, but the more likely scenario these days is where an organisation wishes to integrate its disparate systems so that it looks to the users as if there is a single set of data – the bottom-up approach.

THE RATIONALE FOR DISTRIBUTING DATA

Our discussion of database architecture in Chapter 2, and particularly the three-level schema architecture, was based on the assumption that all the data would be held in a single database at a single site. Such an arrangement is the logical solution for a small organisation that is based at a single site. A large enterprise that is geographically dispersed could still use a single centralised database and the users could access that database from the terminals or personal computers on their desks over a communications network. On the other hand, the enterprise could opt to have its data and databases distributed throughout its sites.

There are two principal reasons why the enterprise may choose to distribute its data. The first of these is a conscious decision to distribute data as a result of a business requirement to have data held closer to where it is used, probably to ensure that work is not disrupted by communications failures. The second reason, the most likely reason, is that there are many existing systems dispersed throughout the enterprise, each of which has its own database. In this case there is probably a desire to see this data managed as a cohesive whole; we need the ability to share data between legacy systems.

In both these situations the distributed system should provide greater reliability and availability of data with a reduced response time for any particular query. Reliability is improved because the probability that any one site is working at any particular time is improved since any single equipment failure should not bring the system down. In the event of a failure of any one component of the system, the remainder can continue to operate. Availability is improved for similar reasons. If data is replicated, which we discuss below, availability is improved even more.

If we wish to distribute data (top-down distribution), we need to consider an approach to deciding what data is to be stored where, and how that data is managed so that it appears as a cohesive whole. Similarly if we wish to integrate data from existing distributed independent systems (bottom-up integration) so that it appears as a cohesive whole, we need to know how that integration is approached and how it is managed after integration. Using the terminology from the three-level schema architecture, in the top-down distribution scenario we start with a single logical schema (the global logical schema) and break it down so that we have a number of local logical schemas. In the bottom-up integration scenario, we start with a number of local logical schemas and derive a global logical schema. In both cases it is the responsibility of the 'distributed database management system' to know how the various local logical schemas map to the global logical schema and to manage the distribution of the actual data.

THE PERFECT DISTRIBUTED DATABASE SYSTEM?

In *An Introduction to Database Systems,* Chris Date states a fundamental principle and 12 rules (or objectives) for distributed databases. His fundamental principle is:

> To the user, a distributed system should look exactly like a non-distributed system.

The user in this fundamental principle, and in the 12 objectives below, is not necessarily the 'end-user', the human sitting at the terminal. Anyone or anything that accesses the database is considered to be a user, including application programs. By extension, therefore, the application programmer should see the distributed database as a single non-distributed database. The programmer should not need to say 'get data X from site Y'. The instruction to 'get data X' should be sufficient; the 'distributed database management system' should then know that it needs to go to site Y to get the data.

Chris Date's 12 objectives are:

- **Local autonomy** – local data is owned and managed locally, with local accountability and security; no site depends on another for successful functioning.

- **No reliance on a central site** – all sites are equal, and none relies on a master site for processing or communications.

- **Continuous operation** – installations at one site do not affect operations at another; there should never be a need for a planned shutdown; adding or deleting installations should not affect programs or activities; likewise, portions of databases should be able to be created and destroyed without stopping any component.

- **Location independence** (also known as **location transparency**) – users do not have to know where data is physically stored; they act as if all data is stored locally.

- **Fragmentation independence** (**transparency**) – relations or tables can be fragmented for physical storage, but users are able to act as if data was not fragmented.

- **Replication independence** – relations or tables and fragments of relations or tables can be represented at the physical level by multiple, distinct stored copies or replicas at distinct sites; replicas are transparent to the user.

- **Distributed query processing** – local computer and input–output activity occur at multiple sites, with data communications between the sites; both local and global optimisation of query processing are supported (that is, the system finds the cheapest way to answer a query that involves accessing several databases).

- **Distributed transaction management** – single transactions are able to execute code at multiple sites, causing updates at multiple sites.

- **Hardware independence** – distributed database systems are able to run on different kinds of hardware with all machines participating as equal partners where appropriate.

- **Operating system independence** – distributed database systems are able to run under different operating systems.

- **Network independence** – distributed database systems are able to work with different communications networks.

- **Database independence** – distributed database systems are able to be built of different kinds of databases, provided they have the same interfaces.

If you consider those 12 objectives, you may think that they are difficult to achieve. It could well be that, for many years to come, most distributed data systems will consist of a number of individual databases federated in such a way that, to the end-user only, they appear as a single system.

TOP-DOWN FRAGMENTATION AND PARTITIONING

The development of a set of local logical schemas from a global logical schema involves using the techniques of fragmentation and partitioning. Fragmentation is the splitting of a table (or relation) into fragments, each of which represents a distinct subset of the data required at one or more specific sites. Partitioning then involves combining fragments so that all the fragments required at a particular site are grouped into a partition.

Fragmentation can be vertical, horizontal or hybrid. Vertical fragmentation involves assigning each column of the table to one (and only one) fragment. There is one exception

Figure 13.1 An example of vertical fragmentation

payroll_ number	surname	first_name	birth_date	salary	department	grade
AY334	Watson	Barbara	1952-12-06	20340	Finance	4
AY478	Wilson	John	1953-07-03	13436	Production	5
BZ987	Smith	Joe	1964-02-24	35625	HQ	1
CA446	Jones	Phil	1974-05-05	27750	Production	2
CX137	Rogers	Jenny	1970-01-10	27750	Finance	2
DJ777	Phillips	Henry	1974-05-05	22570	Finance	3
EX115	Thompson	Brian	1979-06-11	21785	Production	3
FJ678	Harrison	Roger	1988-04-27	14300	Finance	4
FL233	Smith	Jane	1989-08-25	12725	Production	5

payroll_ number	birth_date	salary
AY334	1952-12-06	20340
AY478	1953-07-03	13436
BZ987	1964-02-24	35625
CA446	1974-05-05	27750
CX137	1970-01-10	27750
DJ777	1974-05-05	22570
EX115	1979-06-11	21785
FJ678	1988-04-27	14300
FL233	1989-08-25	12725

payroll_ number	surname	first_name	department	grade
AY334	Watson	Barbara	Finance	4
AY478	Wilson	John	Production	5
BZ987	Smith	Joe	HQ	1
CA446	Jones	Phil	Production	2
CX137	Rogers	Jenny	Finance	2
DJ777	Phillips	Henry	Finance	3
EX115	Thompson	Brian	Production	3
FJ678	Harrison	Roger	Finance	4
FL233	Smith	Jane	Production	5

to this: the primary key column(s) must appear in each fragment so that the original table can be reconstituted from the fragments. Horizontal fragmentation involves the assignment of the rows of the table to one (and only one) fragment. Hybrid fragmentation is a combination of the vertical and horizontal fragmentation where a vertical fragment is further fragmented horizontally or a horizontal fragment is further fragmented vertically.

Figure 13.1 shows an example of vertical fragmentation. At the top is a table of personnel data. Beneath are two tables, each being a vertical fragment from the first table. The fragment on the left has the **birth_date** and **salary** columns while the fragment on the right has the remaining columns.

In Figure 13.2, the larger vertical fragment is further fragmented horizontally so that there is a fragment for each department. The end result is, therefore, a hybrid fragmentation.

Any fragmentation must be lossless and disjoint. Lossless means that no data must be lost. Recombining the fragments provides all the data. Disjoint means that each data value (other than the primary key values in the case of vertical fragmentation) appears in only one fragment. The fragments shown in Figure 13.2 meet these criteria.

All of these fragments can be grouped into a single partition to be allocated to the database that is local to the human resources department. This partition happens to be equivalent to the original table, but that is coincidence.

Each of the departmental horizontal fragments can form partitions that are allocated to the departmental databases. This implies that some of the data is replicated. The replication is of complete fragments, not individual data values.

The aim of fragmentation and partitioning, and any associated decisions about replication, is to organise data so that it is placed closest to where it needs to be used.

BOTTOM-UP INTEGRATION

The techniques of fragmentation and partitioning for the top-down decomposition of a global logical schema to create a number of local logical schemas are well documented. They are included in most texts that cover distributed data and distributed databases. Unfortunately there is no commonly agreed process for integrating a number of local logical schemas into a single global logical schema. The task is the equivalent of developing a corporate data model by joining project or area models, which was discussed in Chapter 4. You will recall that this approach to the development of a corporate data model was rejected because of its high failure rate.

The development of a global logical schema through the direct combination of a number of local logical schemas is equally likely to fail. The formats used for common data items may well be different in the disparate local schemas; for example a date may be held as text using the **CHARACTER VARYING** datatype in one system and using a **DATE** datatype in another system. Columns with the same name in two local schemas can represent entirely different concepts; for example a column named **description** in the **PRODUCT** table in one system may hold the names by which the products are known, whereas the

Figure 13.2 An example of hybrid fragmentation

payroll_number	first_name	surname	birth_date	salary	department	grade
AY334	Barbara	Watson	1952-12-06	20340	Finance	4
AY478	John	Wilson	1953-07-03	13436	Production	5
BZ987	Joe	Smith	1964-02-24	35625	HQ	1
CA446	Phil	Jones	1974-05-05	27750	Production	2
CX137	Jenny	Rogers	1970-01-10	27750	Finance	2
DJ777	Henry	Phillips	1974-05-05	22570	Finance	3
EX115	Brian	Thompson	1979-06-11	21785	Production	3
FJ678	Roger	Harrison	1988-04-27	14300	Finance	4
FL233	Jane	Smith	1989-08-25	12725	Production	5

payroll_number	birth_date	salary
AY334	1952-12-06	20340
AY478	1953-07-03	13436
BZ987	1964-02-24	35625
CA446	1974-05-05	27750
CX137	1970-01-10	27750
DJ777	1974-05-05	22570
EX115	1979-06-11	21785
FJ678	1988-04-27	14300
FL233	1989-08-25	12725

payroll_number	surname	first_name	department	grade
BZ987	Smith	Joe	HQ	1

payroll_number	surname	first_name	department	grade
AY334	Watson	Barbara	Finance	4
CX137	Rogers	Jenny	Finance	2
DJ777	Phillips	Henry	Finance	3
FJ678	Harrison	Roger	Finance	4

payroll_number	surname	first_name	department	grade
AY478	Wilson	John	Production	5
CA446	Jones	Phil	Production	2
EX115	Thompson	Brian	Production	3
FL233	Smith	Jane	Production	5

PRODUCT table in another system may have two columns, **designation** and **description**, where **designation** holds the formal names of the products and the **description** column holds additional information that amplifies the designation where necessary. Columns with entirely different names can represent identical concepts; for example columns named **sex** and **gender** in different systems may both have the same valid values – 'Male', 'Female' or 'Unknown'. Identification of these common concepts could be made more difficult through differences in coding. For example the concepts 'Male', 'Female' and 'Unknown' may be coded as M, F and U in one system, as 0, 1 and 99 in another system and as 1, 2 and 0 in yet a third system. To make matters worse, these codings might not even be documented. The identification of all these issues is normally only achieved by getting together subject-matter experts from the business and database experts for each of the databases in question so that they can talk through the issues in great detail. Even then some problems can be overlooked.

The situation can be eased if there is a common understanding of the global data requirements that the global logical schema is to represent. Then it is a case of identifying how each of the individual data requirements is handled in each of the local logical schemas and arranging a mapping to a common representation of the requirement in the global logical schema. An integration project of this kind is more likely to succeed if there is an existing data management initiative and a corporate data model within the organisation.

THE MANAGEMENT OF REPLICATION

When looking at the concepts of fragmentation and partitioning, we saw that some or all of the data may be replicated in a distributed data system. Replication is duplication of data and one of the fundamental principles of database design is that duplication of data should be avoided. This is what the normalisation process we saw in Chapter 2 is about – the removal of duplication to avoid update anomalies. Replication, however, is acceptable because it is managed duplication; replication implies that we have management procedures in place to ensure that the collective distributed database remains consistent.

Replication may be:

- full or partial;
- synchronous or asynchronous;
- subject to master–slave or update-anywhere updating.

Full replication is where the entire body of data, including all updates, is copied to every database instance within the distributed system. In partial replication, only data that it is deemed necessary to hold at a site is copied to the database supporting that site.

Synchronous replication is where all the copies of the data are held in a strictly consistent state. Any update at any one site is copied to all the other sites that require it and all sites, including the originating site, commit that update to their databases simultaneously. If any one site cannot commit the data to its database then no site, including the originating site, is allowed to do so. In asynchronous replication, the individual databases are allowed to become inconsistent for a time with the intention that all sites become consistent eventually. The time that databases are inconsistent may be very short, fractions of a second say, but in an environment where data is being constantly updated the databases may never actually be totally consistent. The time delays and the degree of consistency are largely dependent on the capacity, quality and reliability of the network that connects the sites.

Master–slave updating is where one site, the master, has control of all updating. Any site that wishes to update data informs the master, which then propagates the update to every site, including the site that originated the update. All sites then commit the update to their database. Update-anywhere is a form of updating that does away with the reliance on a central site, the master. Each site is now aware of the location of all the replicas and passes updates to sites with replicas as necessary. Both master–slave and update-anywhere updating can be used with either synchronous or asynchronous replication.

SUMMARY

This chapter started by considering the rationale for distributing data and then looked at the techniques of fragmentation and partitioning that are important when undertaking a top-down distribution of data. This was followed by a discussion of bottom-up integration. The chapter finished by discussing replication, which is important to both top-down distribution and bottom-up integration.

14 BUSINESS INTELLIGENCE

Business intelligence is the name that has been given to the set of 'techniques' that is used to transform raw data into information that can be used to inform high-level decision making. This set of techniques enables decision makers to take historical, current or predictive views of the business. The techniques include data warehousing, data mining and online analytical processing (OLAP).

DATA WAREHOUSING

A data warehouse is not just a large collection of data. At its simplest it is a copy of transactional data – that is, the data created in the operational systems used by the enterprise. This copied data is specifically structured to make it easy for the data to be queried and analysed. Senior management can use this copied data to monitor the progress of the business and, hence, to make strategic decisions that affect the future of the business.

Although at its heart a data warehouse holds copies of transactional data, to make it easier to analyse and query that data, a data warehouse also holds some aggregated or summarised data – copied data that has been processed in some way. Most data warehouses also hold a considerable amount of human-readable metadata to help management and other users understand the data in the warehouse.

Figure 14.1 shows a typical architecture for a data warehouse. On the left are the operational systems used by a supermarket chain: for example the electronic point-of-sale (EPOS) systems visible at the checkouts, the stock-ordering systems and the human resources systems. The data is copied to the data warehouse using extraction, translation and loading (ETL) processes, where the data is copied from the operational systems (extraction), converted from the structure and formats of the operational systems to the structure and formats of the data warehouse (translation) and then written to the data warehouse (loading). The translation process might include cleaning of the data if there is any doubt as to its quality. This cleaning might, for example, include the substitution of statistically determined values for missing data.

Figure 14.1 A typical data warehouse architecture

The data warehouse contains data that is:

- **subject-oriented** – the data warehouse contains copies of data that are organised so that all the data relating to the same event or other subject of interest is associated with each other;
- **time-variant** – the data is arranged so changes over time can be identified;
- **non-volatile** – once data is in the data warehouse it is never updated or deleted;
- **integrated** – the data in the data warehouse is from most or all of the enterprise's operational systems and is structured so that it is seen as a single collection of data.

For a supermarket, the data warehouse could record that a customer – who may or may not have a loyalty card and may or may not, therefore, be identifiable – bought two 200g tins of brand X baked beans, one 415g tin of brand Y cream of tomato soup, one own-brand uncut white loaf and other items as they passed through a particular checkout in a particular store at a particular time on a particular day.

This data can then be used to, amongst other things:

- compare sales between stores;
- compare sales of own-brand products against branded products;
- identify purchasing patterns for particular days of the week or times of day;
- identify relationships between product purchases – for example it has been reported that a supermarket chain discovered that beer is more often bought by those who buy disposable nappies than by those who do not buy disposable nappies.

On the right of Figure 14.1 are a number of smaller collections of data known as data marts, each of which has a copied subset of the data in the enterprise data warehouse that is subject or business-area specific. The main difference between a data mart and the enterprise data warehouse from which the data mart has drawn its data is the reduced scope of the data held by the data mart, although each data mart may hold more or less aggregated or summarised data than is held in the enterprise data warehouse.

Since the data in a data warehouse or a data mart is a historical copy of transactional data and is not going to be updated, there is no need to worry about update anomalies. There is, therefore, no requirement for the data to be normalised. This allows the data to be structured in a way that makes it easy to query.

THE MULTIDIMENSIONAL MODEL OF DATA

Conceptually, users of data warehouses find it easy to visualise the data as a 'cube' of three, four or even five or more dimensions (cubes with more than three dimensions are sometimes known as 'hypercubes'). If a company sells products at stores and the company's performance is measured over time, the associated data can be visualised as in Figure 14.2; that is, as a cube with three dimensions (a **Product** dimension, a **Store** dimension and a **Time** dimension).

Figure 14.2 A multidimensional data model

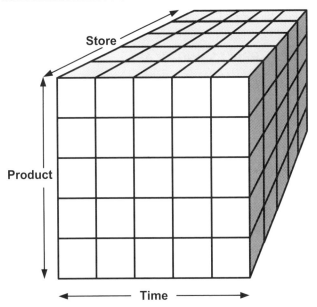

The conceptual visualisation of data in this way is referred to as the multidimensional model of data. The points (cells) within the cube are where the measurements for the particular combinations of product, store and time are stored. This way the value of the sales of a particular product (200g tin of brand X baked beans) at a particular store (Store 315) over a particular time (2–3pm on Friday 18 January 2013) can be directly seen. Summing along the store dimension gives the value of all of the sales of 200g tins of brand X baked beans at all of the company's stores during that hour. Summing along the product dimension gives the value of the sales of all the products sold at that store during that hour. Summing along the time dimension gives the value of the sales of 200g tins of brand X baked beans at that store over the extended time period (month, year and so on).

Once structured in this way the data can be:

- used with standard reporting tools;
- queried using OLAP (online analytical processing) techniques;
- subject to data mining.

STANDARD REPORTING TOOLS

Reporting tools, for example, can provide the simple sales information over the store, period or time dimensions as described above. These tools easily support questions of the 'who …?' and 'what …?' variety, such as 'which store had the greatest value of sales in December 2012?' and 'what was our best-selling product in December 2012?'

ONLINE ANALYTICAL PROCESSING (OLAP)

The term 'online analytical processing' (OLAP) has been applied to a range of techniques that can be used by senior managers and knowledge workers to query historical, summarised multidimensional data. The term is used in contrast to 'online transactional processing' (OLTP), where front-line staff are interacting with databases in the course of day-to-day operations. The data associated with OLTP is current, up to date and, probably, relational.

OLAP techniques provide the ability to answer more sophisticated questions than those provided by the standard reporting tools, such as 'what if …?' and 'why …?' A typical question would be 'what will happen to our sales figures if we withdraw 200g tins of brand X baked beans from our product range?' The OLAP techniques are based around four basic operations that can be applied to a multidimensional cube of data: slice, dice, roll-up and drill-down.

The slice operation provides a sub-cube of data by selecting a subset of one of the dimensions. Slicing along the store dimension provides a sub-cube that contains data for a single store or a group of stores (for example Store 315 or all the stores in the northern region, but showing the values for each product in the product range at each time period in the time range). Slicing along the product dimension provides a sub-cube that contains data for a single product or a category of products (for example 200g tins of brand X baked beans or all canned goods, but showing the values for each store at each time period in the time range). Slicing along the time dimension provides a sub-cube that contains data for a single time period (for example 2–3pm on Friday 18 January 2013 or the whole of the first quarter 2013, but showing the values for each product in the product range sold at each store). Slicing purely selects a subset of the data that was available in the original cube without changing any of the values.

The dice operation provides a sub-cube of data by selecting a subset of two or more of the dimensions. The resultant sub-cube may, for example, contain data for a single store for a limited product range over a limited time period (for example the value of sales of each product within the tinned goods category at Store 315 during January 2013). As with the slice operation, dicing purely selects a subset of the data that was available in the original cube without changing any of the values.

The roll-up (or aggregation) operation provides a new cube of data with the values along one or more dimensions aggregated; for example rolling up along the product dimension gives a cube showing the total values for the sales for all products in each store in each time period. Unlike the slicing and dicing operations, the roll-up operation calculates new values.

The drill-down (or de-aggregation) operation provides a new cube of data with a more detailed view of the data along one or more dimensions. When drilling down, the new cube is not formed from the existing cube of data (as it is for slice, dice and roll-up operations) but is formed from more detailed data; the assumption is that the original cube was showing aggregated data and more detailed data is held in the data warehouse. For example, if we have a cell showing, as a single value, the value of all the sales for tinned goods in all the stores in the northern region on Friday 18 January 2013, we can drill down to look at the sales by individual store, for each individual product or for each hour of the day, or for any combination of these three.

DATA MINING

Data mining is the application of advanced statistical and other techniques against the large volumes of data held in a data warehouse to discover previously unknown patterns in the data that may be of interest to the business. The patterns are discovered by identifying the underlying rules and features in the data. Data mining is sometimes known as knowledge discovery in databases (KDD). The techniques used in data mining include, amongst others, statistical techniques, cluster analysis and neural networks.

Statistical techniques can be used in a number of different ways. They can be applied to remove any erroneous or irrelevant data before any further analysis is carried out. Sampling techniques could be used to reduce the amount of data that has to be analysed. Other statistical techniques may be used to identify classes within data, for example to find common shopping times and common purchases, or to find associations within sets of data, for example discovering where products are commonly bought together. An example of using the a-priori algorithm, a statistical technique to discover associations, is given in Appendix F.

Cluster analysis is the process of finding clusters or subsets of data so that the data in the cluster (or subset) shares some common property. For example, cluster analysis could be used to generate a profile of people who responded to a previous mailing campaign. This profile can then be used to predict future responses, enabling future mailings to be directed to gain the best response.

Neural networks are the computer equivalent of a biological nervous system. Each neural network is a network of processing elements called neurons. Neural networks are useful in data mining because they 'learn' as they analyse data. Once a neural network has been trained, it can be seen as an 'expert' in the category of data that it has been trained to analyse. A neural network is seen as a black box that takes a number of inputs and provides an output. The neurons in a network are arranged in layers; there are at least an input layer and an output layer, but there may well also be a number of intermediate layers that are hidden. Examples of the use of neural networks include the prediction of stock prices and the prediction of the risk of cancer.

A RELATIONAL SCHEMA FOR A DATA WAREHOUSE

While there are database management systems on the market that are based on the multidimensional model of data, it is possible to emulate the multidimensional view of data using a relational database management system. Our three-dimensional cube (product, store and time) could be represented using the star schema shown in Figure 14.3.

Figure 14.3 A typical relational schema for a data warehouse

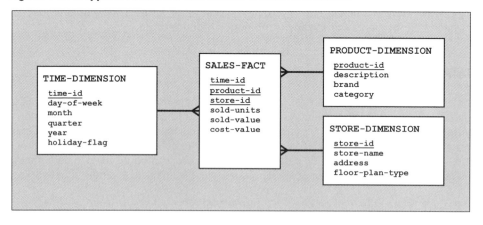

At the centre of the star is a single fact table – in this case the **SALES-FACT** table. This fact table has a many-to-one relationship with each of the dimension tables, **STORE-DIMENSION**, **PRODUCT-DIMENSION** and **TIME-DIMENSION**.

In this schema the fact table contains the daily sales totals, i.e. the units sold, the cost value and the sale value, for each product in each store. This is as a result of a decision that was made following an analysis of the likely queries that may be made of the data.

If it is likely that a user may at some time in the future wish to analyse the distribution of sales throughout a day, the time dimension table needs an additional column (say 'hour'). Decisions about the granularity of the dimensions of the data warehouse are, therefore, very important. Users can only drill down to the lowest level of granularity at which data is stored. Once data has been stored in the data warehouse with the granularity of the time dimension being set as a day, it is impossible to determine the pattern of sales at different times during the day.

There are a number of things to note about this schema. The primary key of the fact table is the combination of the foreign keys that reference the dimension tables. The only non-key columns of the fact table are all numerical. This is important because they are to be subject to statistical analysis. The dimension tables are not normalised – there is a lot of repetition of data. Additionally, the **TIME-DIMENSION** table has a column called **holiday-flag**. This enables users to query the data to see what effect holidays have on the sales. The other columns in the time-dimension table allow for analyses that compare sales on Mondays against sales on, say, Tuesdays, January sales against March sales, first quarter sales against third quarter sales, and sales on May Day Bank Holiday 2012 against May Day Bank Holiday 2013. The **STORE-DIMENSION** table has a **floor-plan-type** column. This allows analyses that look at the extent to which different store layouts may influence sales. Why are the fruit and vegetables by the entrance and the in-store bakeries diagonally opposite the entrance in most supermarkets?

There are possible variations on the star schema such as the snowflake schema and the galaxy schema.

Figure 14.4 provides an example of a snowflake schema. Such a schema introduces a degree of normalisation into the dimensions but this makes it more difficult to query.

Figure 14.5 provides an example of a galaxy schema. This is a schema where two or more fact tables share one or more of the dimensions.

Figure 14.4 A snowflake schema

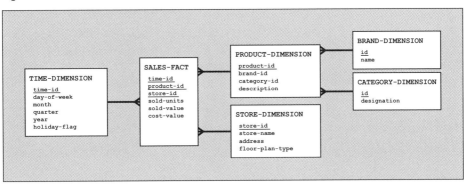

The latest versions of SQL have introduced support for OLAP operations with a relational schema such as a **GROUP BY ROLLUP** facility.

Figure 14.5 A galaxy schema

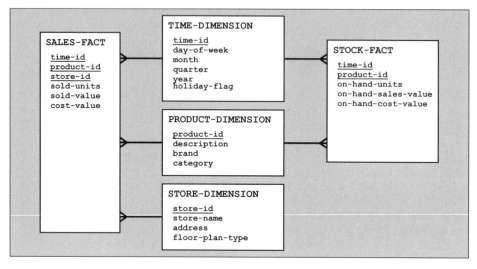

SUMMARY

This chapter has provided an overview of the key 'techniques' that are used to provide business intelligence including data warehousing, data mining and online analytical processing (OLAP). The multidimensional data model and its representation in a relational database were also introduced.

15   OBJECT ORIENTATION

This chapter introduces object orientation, a programming paradigm, and then discusses in detail two approaches to handling objects in databases: the specification of an Object Definition Language from the Object Data Management Group and the extensions to SQL to make it 'object-relational'.

WHAT IS OBJECT ORIENTATION?

Object orientation is a programming paradigm where the world is seen as a collection of objects that exhibit both state and behaviour. The state of an object at any one time is the aggregation of the values of the object's attributes. The behaviour is the set of messages to which the object can respond. Objects respond to messages by executing methods, short pieces of program code.

Objects are grouped into classes. So, for example, within an object oriented program to manage human resources there could be an **Employee** class with attributes of *payrollNumber*, *title*, *surname*, *otherNames*, *birthDate*, *salary* and so on. One of the objects of this class has the state 'CX137, Mrs, Rogers, Jennifer Alyson, 10 January 1970, 27750'. This object also has an object identifier that is used by the system to uniquely identify the object. The object identifier is totally independent of the values of its attributes, is system generated and is hidden from the user. This means that object orientation has no equivalent of the primary key concept of the relational model of data.

Examples of the sort of messages that instances of the **Employee** class may respond to are:

- 'What is your surname?', where the answer is generated by a method that reads the value of the *surname* attribute;
- 'What is your full name?', where the answer is generated by a method that concatenates the values of the *title*, *otherNames* and *surname* attributes;
- 'What is your age?', where the answer is generated by a method that calculates the difference between the current date and the value of the *birthDate* attribute;
- 'Change surname to (new surname)';
- 'Change salary to (new salary)'.

THE FUNDAMENTAL CONCEPTS OF OBJECT ORIENTATION

There are four fundamental concepts underlying the object orientation programming paradigm. These are:

- encapsulation (or data hiding);
- inheritance;
- polymorphism;
- aggregation.

Encapsulation is the hiding of the implementation of an object's data structure and methods from the user. The only way that an object can interact with other objects is through the passing of messages. It is not possible to directly query the attributes of an object to find their value. We cannot, for instance, query the **salary** attribute of the 'Jenny Rogers' object of the **Employee** class and get the result '27750', but we can send the message 'What is your salary?' to that object. On receipt of that message the appropriate method is executed and a message is returned which says 'My salary is 27750'. The principle of encapsulation goes further in that we should not even need to know that objects of the **Employee** class have a **salary** attribute. The encapsulation principle can best be explained by considering an object of the **Cube** class within a system to handle geometric shapes. This object may respond to the message 'What is the length of one of your edges?' with the answer '3m' and to the message 'What is your volume?' with the answer '27m³', but we do not know whether objects of the **Cube** class have an **edgeLength** attribute and respond to the 'What is your volume?' message by calculating the cube of the value of that **edgeLength** attribute or if they have a **volume** attribute and respond to the 'What is the length of one of your edges?' message by calculating the cube root of the value of the **volume** attribute. Furthermore, we should not care. Provided we know the messages that an object responds to, we know all that we need to know to be able to use that object in a program.

Inheritance is the ability of one object class to reuse the data structures and methods of another class without reimplementing them. For example, the **Cube** class can inherit the properties of the **RectangularSolid** class which, in turn, can inherit the properties of the **RegularSolid** class. Objects of the **Sphere** class can also inherit the properties of the **RegularSolid** class. All objects of the **RegularSolid** class can respond to the 'What is your volume?' message. This means that all objects of the **RectangularSolid** class (which includes all objects of the **Cube** class) and of the **Sphere** class can also respond to that same message.

Polymorphism is where different objects in different classes respond to the same message by executing different methods. For example, objects of the **Cube** class can respond to the 'What is your volume?' message by cubing the value of the **edgeLength** attribute, objects of the **RectangularSolid** class can respond to the 'What is your volume?' message by multiplying together the values of the **length**, **breadth** and **height** attributes, while objects of the **Sphere** class can respond to the 'What is your volume?' message by cubing the value of the **radius** attribute, then multiplying the result by the constant $4\pi/3$.

Aggregation, which is sometimes also known as containment, is the ability to group objects to make more complex or composite objects. For example, an object of the

Department class may hold a reference (the object identifier) to an object of the **Set** class, where each element of that set is itself a reference to an object of the **Employee** class; a department contains all of its employees.

OBJECT ORIENTED DATABASES

It is important that persistent storage of objects is available in any information system that hosts object oriented application programs. Some object oriented programming environments do provide persistent storage, but it is then closely coupled to the application programs themselves. There are, however, some object oriented database management systems available on the market, but they tend to be used in fairly specialised environments, such as computer-aided design and manufacturing (CAD/CAM) and geographic information systems (GIS). Those products that are available, although following generally accepted object oriented principles, have been developed using different approaches, such as the extension of an existing object oriented programming language or the development of class libraries using an object oriented programming language, and use different syntaxes for the data definition and data manipulation languages. There are no commonly accepted standards (yet) for object oriented databases.

The Object Data Management Group (ODMG) has, however, developed a formal specification for object oriented databases. This specification includes a data definition language called Object Definition Language (ODL) and a query language called Object Query Language (OQL). There is not a single manipulation language; the manipulation of the objects needs to be programmed in an object oriented programming language such as C++ or Java. Figure 15.1 shows a partial conceptual data model, which includes additional notation to show the unique identifiers for each entity type that is described in Appendix A. Figure 15.2 shows the ODL schema definitions to implement the model in Figure 15.1.

Figure 15.1 A partial conceptual data model

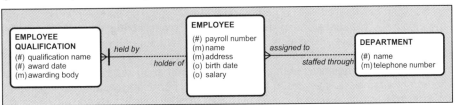

The **extent** is a name that is given to all the instances of this class within the particular database. This name is used by the OQL in its queries. The **keys** are not keys in the relational sense but are, in fact, uniqueness constraints. Remember that the equivalent in the object oriented paradigm of the relational model's primary key is the system-generated object identifier, which is hidden from the user. Note that the ODL key declarations can include relationships as well as attributes – *held_by* is part of the key of *Employee_Qualification*.

Figure 15.2 The ODL schema definitions for the partial conceptual data model

```
class Employee
(  extent employees
   keys payroll_number, (name, address) )
{
   attribute string payroll_number,
   attribute string name,
   attribute Address address,
   attribute date birth_date,
   attribute Payment salary,
   relationship set<Employee_Qualification> holder_of inverse Employee_Qualification::held_by,
   relationship Department assigned_to inverse Department::staffed_through,
   Payment calculate_monthly_payment()
};

class Employee_Qualification
(  extent employees_qualifications
   keys (held_by, name, award_date) )
{
   attribute string name,
   attribute date award_date,
   attribute Organisation awarding_body,
   relationship Employee held_by inverse Employee::holder_of
};

class Department
(  extent departments
   keys name )
{
   attribute string name,
   attribute string telephone_number,
   relationship set<Employee> staffed_through inverse Employee::assigned_to
};
```

Each attribute is declared with a name and a literal type. The *payroll_number* attribute of the *Employee* class uses one of the built-in literal types, **string**, whereas the *address* attribute of the *Employee* class uses a user-defined structured literal type, **Address**.

Each relationship is declared with both a forward and an inverse traversal path in the definition of each class involved in the relationship. For example, the relationship that each **EMPLOYEE** may be *holder of* one or more **EMPLOYEE QUALIFICATIONS** and each **EMPLOYEE QUALIFICATION** must be *held by* one and only one **EMPLOYEE** is represented by the following declaration in the *Employee* class:

> **relationship** *set<Employee_Qualification> holder_of*
> **inverse** *Employee_Qualification::held_by*

and also by the following declaration in the *Employee_Qualification* class:

> **relationship** *Employee held_by*
> **inverse** *Employee::holder_of*

The first of these declarations says that there is a relationship between *Employee* and *Employee_Qualification* called *holder_of* such that each instance of the *Employee* class may reference a set literal type whose elements are references to the instances of the *Employee_Qualification* class that represent the qualifications held by that employee (the forward traversal path), and to see that relationship from the other way you need to look at the specification of the *held_by* relationship in the *Employee_Qualification* class (the inverse traversal path). There can be zero, one or many elements in a set, so there may be zero, one or many qualifications recorded for each employee.

The second of these declarations says that there is a relationship between *Employee_Qualification* and *Employee* called *held_by* such that each instance of the *Employee_Qualification* class may reference an instance of the *Employee* class that represents the holder of this qualification (the forward traversal path), and to see that relationship from the other way you need to look at the specification of the *holder_of* relationship in the *Employee* class (the inverse traversal path). There can be only one employee holding each employee qualification.

Although *set* is used in these declarations for the 'many' relationships, it is not the only collection literal type that can be used. A *set* has no duplicates. If duplicates are possible, a *bag* collection type can be used. The elements of *sets* and *bags* are unordered. If there is an implied order in the 'many', a *list* collection type may be used.

Methods, such as the method to calculate the monthly payment from the annual salary, can also be specified. Only the method signature is included in the ODL specification; the methods themselves have to be implemented in another object oriented programming language. In the case of the *calculate_monthly_payment()* method, the result that is returned is of the **Payment** user-defined structured literal type.

Note that there is no explicit specification for optionality (mandatory or optional) for relationships. If it is required, optionality has to be handled through the use of methods.

OBJECT-RELATIONAL DATABASES

In the latest versions of SQL, published since 1999, the scope has been extended to include some object-like facilities. Databases using these extended facilities are often called object-relational databases. These object-relational facilities include user-defined structured types and collection types such as **MULTISETS** ('multiset' is another name for a 'bag' – a set where duplicates are allowed) and **ARRAYS.**

Figure 15.3 shows the declarations for two structured types, **st_address** and **st_qualification**. (The **st_** is not necessary; it is just used as a device to distinguish a structured type from other database items with similar names.) The **st_address** structured type has five attributes (**name_or_number**, **street**, **area**, **town**, **post_code**); the **st_qualification** structured type has three attributes (**qualification_name**, **award_date**, **awarding_body**).

Figure 15.3 Structured type declarations

```
CREATE TYPE st_address
( name_or_number        VARCHAR(30),
  street                VARCHAR(30),
  area                  VARCHAR(30),
  town                  VARCHAR(30),
  post_code             VARCHAR(8)
);


CREATE TYPE st_qualification
( qualification_name    VARCHAR(30),
  award_date            DATE        ,
  awarding_body         VARCHAR(30)
);
```

Figure 15.4 shows the **CREATE TABLE** statements that are needed to implement the conceptual data model shown in Figure 15.1 using these structured types. The structured types are used in the declarations of two columns in the **employee** table. The **address** column is declared with the **st_address** structured type as its datatype – complete addresses are held as values in a single column. The **qualifications** column is declared with a **MULTISET** as its datatype, with each element of the **MULTISET** being of the **st_qualification** structured type – the complete details of the employee's qualifications (zero, one or many) are held as a single value and there is no longer any requirement for a separate **employee_qualification** table.

Figure 15.4 Table declarations using structured types and collections

```
CREATE TABLE department
( name                  VARCHAR(25)           NOT NULL,
  telephone_number      VARCHAR(15)           NOT NULL,
  PRIMARY KEY name
);

CREATE TABLE employee
( payroll_number        CHAR(5)               NOT NULL,
  name                  VARCHAR(50)           NOT NULL,
  address               st_address            NOT NULL,
  birth_date            DATE                        ,
  salary                INTEGER                     ,
  qualifications        st_qualification MULTISET   ,
  assigned_to_department_name VARCHAR(25)     NOT NULL,
  PRIMARY KEY payroll_number,
  FOREIGN KEY assigned_to_department_name REFERENCES department
);
```

Structured types are objects and so may have methods and may exist in inheritance hierarchies. In Figure 15.4 we see structured types being used as the datatype for a column. Structured types may, however, also be used as the specification for a table and, where inheritance is involved, this ability can be used to directly implement entity subtypes, something not previously possible. Figure 15.5 shows a revised conceptual data model that now includes two subtypes of **EMPLOYEE, PART-TIME EMPLOYEE** and **FULL-TIME EMPLOYEE**.

Figure 15.5 Revised partial conceptual data model with entity subtypes

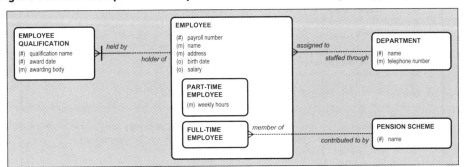

Figure 15.6 shows the **CREATE TYPE** statements needed to implement this revised conceptual data model using tables based on the structured types. The **st_address** and **st_qualification** structured types are unchanged. The **st_employee** type is very similar to the previous employee table with two very important differences. First, there are no constraints (**NOT NULL, PRIMARY KEY** and so on); constraints are applied to tables, not to types. Second, the attribute that will become the column that provides the foreign key to the department table has a different name and is of a **REF** datatype. This is explained when we see how the tables are created. The fact that **st_part_time_employee** and **st_full_time_employee** are both subtypes of **st_employee** is shown by the declaration that they are both **UNDER st_employee**.

Figure 15.7 shows the **CREATE TABLE** statements that use these structured types. The **employee** table has eight columns, seven from the structured type (**payroll_number, name, address, birth_date, salary, qualifications** and **assigned_to_department_ref**) and an additional column called **row_id**. This additional column holds a system-generated value of the **REF** type – the object identifier. It is also declared as the primary key. The **CREATE TABLE** statement for the **employee** table also includes the **NOT NULL** and **FOREIGN KEY** constraints.

The **part_time_employee** and **full_time_employee** tables are declared as being **UNDER employee**, i.e. as subtables of the **employee** table. The **part_time_employee** table now has nine columns, the eight columns inherited from the employee table and the additional **weekly_hours** column. All details of employees are automatically stored in the appropriate table, in the **part_time_employee** table for part-time employees and in the **full_time_employee** table for full-time employees. A query seeking the name and address of all the full-time employees reads the **full_time_employee** table. A query seeking the name and address of all employees reads the **full_time_employee**

Figure 15.6 Creating structured types

```
CREATE TYPE st_address
( name_or_number                    VARCHAR(30),
  street                            VARCHAR(30),
  area                              VARCHAR(30),
  town                              VARCHAR(30),
  post_code                         VARCHAR(8)
);

CREATE TYPE st_qualification
( qualification_name                VARCHAR(30),
  award_date                        DATE     ,
  awarding_body                     VARCHAR(30)
);

CREATE TYPE st_employee
( payroll_number                    CHAR(5),
  name                              VARCHAR(50),
  address                           st_address,
  birth_date                        DATE,
  salary                            INTEGER,
  qualifications                    st_qualification MULTISET,
  assigned_to_department_ref        REF(st_department) SCOPE department
);

CREATE TYPE st_part_time_employee
    UNDER st_employee AS
( weekly_hours                      DECIMAL(5,2)
);

CREATE TYPE st_full_time_employee
    UNDER st_employee AS
( member_of_pension_scheme_ref      REF(st_pension_scheme) SCOPE pension_scheme
);

CREATE TYPE st_pension_scheme
( name                              VARCHAR(40)
);

CREATE TYPE st_department
( name                              VARCHAR(25),
  telephone_number                  VARCHAR(15)
);
```

table for the names and addresses of all the full-time employees, the **part_time_ employee** table for the names and addresses of all the part-time employees, and the **employee** table for those employees who are neither full-time employees nor part-time employees (there should not be any of these). Thus inheritance is managed 'under the covers' by the database management system.

SUMMARY

This chapter provided an overview of the object oriented programming paradigm and then looked at the specification of the Object Definition Language from the Object Data Management Group and the extensions to the SQL standard that make SQL 'object-relational'.

Figure 15.7 Creating tables based on the structured types

```
CREATE TABLE department
    OF st_department
( REF IS row_id SYSTEM GENERATED,
  PRIMARY KEY (row_id)
  name WITH OPTIONS NOT NULL,
  telephone_number WITH OPTIONS NOT NULL
) ;

CREATE TABLE pension_scheme
    OF st_pension_scheme
( REF IS row_id SYSTEM GENERATED,
  PRIMARY KEY (row_id),
  name WITH OPTIONS NOT NULL
) ;

CREATE TABLE employee
    OF st_employee
( REF IS row_id SYSTEM GENERATED,
  PRIMARY KEY (row_id),
  payroll_number WITH OPTIONS NOT NULL,
  name WITH OPTIONS NOT NULL,
  address WITH OPTIONS NOT NULL,
  assigned_to_department_ref WITH OPTIONS NOT NULL,
  FOREIGN KEY assigned_to_department_ref REFERENCES department
) ;

CREATE TABLE part_time_employee
    OF st_part_time_employee
    UNDER employee
( weekly_hours WITH OPTIONS NOT NULL
) ;

CREATE TABLE full_time_employee
    OF st_full_time_employee
    UNDER employee
( FOREIGN KEY member_of_pension_scheme_ref REFERENCES pension_scheme
) ;
```

16 MULTIMEDIA

This chapter introduces the characteristics of multimedia and then goes on to address two approaches for handling multimedia with databases: storing the multimedia outside the database and providing a reference to the multimedia, and storing the multimedia within the database. There is also a brief mention of special packages for multimedia.

WHAT IS MULTIMEDIA?

When we have discussed data so far we have generally been referring to data that comprises short character strings (names and so on), numbers and dates. This is often called structured data. Not all data is structured however. There is another category of data that is sometimes called multimedia data and sometimes called unstructured data. This data includes line figures such as charts, graphs and illustrations; photographs and other pixellated images that are seen as pictures by the human eye; and digitised audio and video.

Storing and retrieving multimedia data presents a number of challenges because of its nature:

- Multimedia data is usually complex.

- Multimedia data is usually large.

- Multimedia data may have many possible representations; for example a photograph may be in JPG, PNG, GIF or BMP format.

There is often a requirement to store multimedia data with structured data. For example the human resources department might want to store a photograph of each employee as part of their employee record or there may be a requirement to hold word-processed summaries of meetings with data recording the dates, locations, subjects and attendees of those meetings.

STORING MULTIMEDIA OUTSIDE A DATABASE

The multimedia data may be stored external to the structured database, with only a reference to the multimedia stored within the database. In this way it is possible to call up the record for an individual employee and for the application program to automatically retrieve and display the employee's photograph or, similarly, to automatically retrieve the summary of a meeting by querying the database using the subject and the date. When the multimedia data is stored externally like this, it is only partially under the control of the database management system. Users could access the multimedia data without using the database management system at all.

When storing multimedia data externally to the database, a reference to the location of the multimedia data needs to be stored in the database. Until recently the only way to do this was to store the reference as a path reference, for example the photograph of Jenny Rogers may be referenced as 'c:\hr_docs\photos\cx137jrogers.gif'. The photograph is still accessible to any user who knows its location and could be replaced with a photograph that is more up to date without needing to access the database, provided the new photograph is given the same name as the old photograph and is stored in the same location. If the photograph is deleted or moved, the now inaccurate reference could remain in the database. A well-intentioned attempt to 'tidy up' the directory structure on a hard disk could cause havoc with direct references of this sort.

The latest versions of the SQL standard have yet another new datatype that helps to overcome the problems when multimedia data is stored externally. This is the **DATALINK** datatype. A column declared as being of the type **DATALINK** has values that are expressed as a URL, for example 'file:///localhost/c:/hr_docs/photos/cx137jrogers. gif'. One advantage of this is that the multimedia data may be held remotely from the database server, perhaps close to where the data is used, to reduce the overall network traffic. A **DATALINK** column may be declared with special properties that, in association with some additional datalinker software, allow there to be some control of the external multimedia data. One property ensures that the multimedia file cannot be renamed or deleted; another property denies access to the multimedia file other than as a result of querying the database; and a third property ensures that if the **DATALINK** reference is deleted from the database, an appropriate action is carried out and either the multimedia file is deleted or control is passed back to the normal file-management system.

STORING MULTIMEDIA INSIDE A DATABASE

Alternatively the multimedia data can be stored within the database, which means that access to the data is fully under the control of the database management system.

With recent releases of the SQL standard there are two new datatypes that enable the internal storage of multimedia data: the **BINARY LARGE OBJECT** (also known as **BLOB**) and the **CHARACTER LARGE OBJECT** (also known as **CLOB**). With the **BLOB** datatype, the multimedia data is stored as a meaningless stream of bits and it is impossible to query the multimedia data itself. To retrieve the photographs of all the fair-haired employees, it would necessary to have the colour of each employee's hair recorded as structured data; there is no pattern in the bit stream that can be used to determine whether the subjects of the photographs have fair, or any other colour, hair. With the **CLOB** datatype, the multimedia data is stored as a stream of text characters. There can, therefore, be limited querying of the multimedia data. Note that most word-processing software stores documents in a proprietary format and these word-processed documents need to be stored using the **BLOB** datatype and not the **CLOB** datatype. The text of the document can be stored using a **CLOB**, but the formatting of the document is lost. One way to store a document as text (so that it can be stored using the **CLOB** datatype) is to format the document using the HyperText Markup Language (HTML), which is discussed when we look at web technology.

STORING MULTIMEDIA USING SPECIAL PACKAGES

Another way of handling multimedia data is to use a specially designed 'package'. The ISO/IEC 13249 series of standards has created a number of standard packages that make use of the SQL structured type feature to support the handling of multimedia data, particularly for full-text documents, still images and spatial data.

The Full-Text package (ISO/IEC 13249-2, 2003) provides methods for recording and querying large streams of text. The querying can test whether the text contains a pattern (where the pattern can be a word or a phrase, can contain wildcard characters, can include Boolean (AND or OR) conditions, can test for the proximity of words or phrases, can test for a synonym of a given word, can test for words based on a given stem) or a combination of patterns.

The Still-Image package (ISO/IEC 13249-5, 2003) provides methods for the recording and the manipulation of images such as photographs, with the images either being stored internally, as a **BLOB**, or externally, referenced by a **DATALINK** value. The manipulation methods allow the image to be resized, scaled, rotated and displayed as a thumbnail.

The Spatial package (ISO/IEC 13249-3, 2011) provides methods for the recording and management of spatial data (points, lines and areas) within given spatial frames of reference (latitude and longitude, national grids and so on). The principal use of this package is for geospatial and mapping applications, but its use is not restricted to this area.

SUMMARY

This chapter has looked at multimedia and approaches for handling multimedia with databases. The direct references and the **DATALINK** datatype for the handling of multimedia that is stored outside the database were discussed, as was the storage of the multimedia inside the database using the **BINARY LARGE OBJECT** and the **CHARACTER LARGE OBJECT** datatypes. The Full-Text, Still-Image and Spatial packages specified in ISO/IEC 13249 were introduced.

17 WEB TECHNOLOGY

This chapter looks at data and web technology. We introduce the concept of the web and its associated technologies, HTML and XML. We then look at some approaches to link databases and web technology. We also look into dealing with the large quantities of data generated by the web, introducing the subjects of Big Data and NoSQL databases along the way. We conclude by introducing the concept of the semantic web.

THE INTERNET AND THE WEB

The internet is a global federation of interconnected networks that can be used for the passing of email messages between users and for conferencing services. The internet also hosts the web, a global network of information resources. Web users 'browse' information using application programs called web browsers such as Microsoft Internet Explorer, Mozilla Firefox and Safari. The information resources are stored as documents written using the HyperText Markup Language (HTML).

HTML is a general-purpose display language derived from the Standard Generalised Markup Language (SGML). SGML provides a grammar for specifying formats based on standard markup notations ('markup' is the name given to the concept of combining text with extra information about the text). The markup information is provided as plain-text 'tags' so that documents formatted using SGML, or any of its derivatives, can be read both by machines and by humans.

HTML documents are held on computers known as web servers. To enable the HTML documents to be found there is a uniform naming scheme used within the web, with each document given its own unique name, known as a Uniform Resource Identifier (URI). The documents are delivered to the browsers from the servers using a standard protocol such as HyperText Transfer Protocol (HTTP).

Because it is relatively simple to design HTML documents and because web technology is easy to use, many organisations are employing the same technology to manage their business. If this technology is used exclusively within a business (i.e. it is not open to outside users) it is known as an intranet; if the technology is used to exclusively deal with a company's external customers or associates, it is sometimes known as an extranet.

HTML is purely concerned with the way that an information resource, such as a document, is presented by a web browser. It is not concerned with the meaning of the information contained in the document. Another markup language based on SGML is used for that purpose. That language is known as the eXtensible Markup Language (XML). XML is only concerned with the definition and structure of the information in the document, having no tags to specify presentation. Further descriptions of both HTML and XML, including some discussion of problems associated with the use of XML, are provided in Appendix G.

THE ARCHITECTURE OF THE WEB

The user interface for the web is a browser (the client) that uses a network (the internet, an intranet or an extranet) to access a web server as shown in Figure 17.1. This is known as a two-tier architecture. The role of the web server is to provide the information requested by the web browser. Web browsers are designed to read HTML documents that are, by their very nature, static. Using HTML alone it is very difficult to keep the information in the documents up to date, especially if that information is changing rapidly.

Figure 17.1 The two-tier architecture

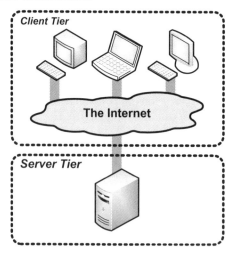

What is required for web technology to be used more dynamically is for databases to be added into this architecture. The web pages can then be created dynamically using data from the database or the database can then store as data the information that the user has input into a web browser. Adding a database server (the database management system and the actual database) gives us the three-tier architecture shown in Figure 17.2.

It is the middle tier that does most of the work, extracting data from the database and inserting it into HTML pages or vice versa.

This three-tier architecture is conceptual. For many web applications, handling tens of thousands of requests an hour, it is possible to mount the web server and the database management system on a single machine. For the more popular websites, handling far

Figure 17.2 The three-tier architecture

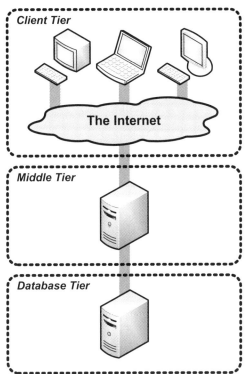

more requests, it makes sense to install the web server and the database management system on different machines. Indeed, both the web server and the database server may even be installed onto separate clusters of machines, allowing for faster and more scalable applications.

XML AND DATABASES

XML is principally a mechanism for transferring data; on receipt, an XML document can be parsed to retrieve and present the data to a user at the receiving site. However, it may be that we need to store the data from the XML document in a database at the receiver site. That data may then be used to compose another XML document for transfer to yet a different site. It is important, therefore, to recognise the requirement for the transfer of data from XML documents to databases and also the requirement to create XML documents from data in databases.

There are a number of databases on the market that store data in XML format. These are known as native XML databases (or NXDs). In a native XML database, the standard unit of storage is the XML document. As a technology, native XML databases are in their infancy and, apart from XQuery, there are no standards commonly accepted by all the vendors.

A native XML database is not the only option, however, for the storage of data contained in an XML document. XML documents or elements of XML documents could, for instance, be stored in relational database columns that have been declared as either **CHARACTER VARYING** or **CLOB** datatypes. The whole XML document may be stored in a single column or decomposed so that the elements are stored as individual data values. Additional support for the handling of XML documents is recently available because the SQL standard now includes a part known as SQL/XML. This new part introduces an **XML** datatype that can be used in the same way as any other datatype, i.e. as a datatype for a column, as a variable or as a parameter for a function. SQL/XML also introduces facilities that provide for the composition of XML using data extracted from a relational database and, conversely, for the storage of data extracted from an XML document in a relational database. These facilities are described in more detail in Appendix H.

XML documents may be composed from existing data selected from a database, they may be received as a result of a business-to-business (B2B) transaction or they may contain original data created using an XML editor. Although XML was initially developed with the limited but important job of transferring data within a web environment so that the meaning of the content was known, XML is now often regarded as the way to solve all IT problems. It is almost impossible to avoid new suggestions for the use of XML. In many cases these new uses are over-sold.

OTHER WAYS TO LINK DATABASES INTO WEB TECHNOLOGY

We have seen that XML documents can be created by querying a relational database and, conversely, that information can be extracted from an XML document and inserted into a relational database. Furthermore, it is possible to extract the information from an XML document and insert it in an HTML page ready for display. However, XML is not the only option available when we need to interact with a database from a web browser.

It is possible, for example, to embed programs in HTML documents using a scripting language such as JavaScript or PHP. Scripting languages allow the user to input information and provide facilities for database connectivity. The popular Google search engine (www.google.co.uk), for example, has JavaScript functions embedded in its web pages.

There are also a number of interface specifications that can be used to transfer information between web browsers or web servers and databases. Some of these are proprietary while others are openly available specifications. An example of an openly available specification is the Common Gateway Interface (CGI). Using CGI a web server can pass requests for data generated at a web browser to a database and then pass the database output back to the web browser. The Java Database Connectivity (JDBC) specification is another openly available specification that allows Java, a programming language commonly used to develop web-based applications, to access and manipulate data stored in relational databases.

An important group of techniques that are popular at the time of writing are known collectively as Ajax, which stands for Asynchronous JavaScript and XML. Despite the name, the use of XML is not required, with an alternative format for data interchange known as JavaScript Object Notation (JSON) often used instead, and the requests do not need to be asynchronous.

DEALING WITH THE LARGE QUANTITIES OF DATA GENERATED OVER THE WEB

As mentioned above, one advantage of the three-tier architecture is that it allows for scalability when very large quantities of data need to be handled. Unfortunately, SQL databases do not scale easily, so there has been a move to alternative storage models for data. Collectively, databases built around these alternative storage models have become known as NoSQL databases, where this can mean 'NotOnlySQL' or 'NeverSQL' depending on the alternative storage model being considered.

NoSQL databases are often discussed alongside the concept of Big Data, data that can be defined by some combination of the following five characteristics:

- **Volume** – where the amount of data is sufficiently large so as to require special considerations.
- **Variety** – where the data consists of multiple types of data potentially from multiple sources; this variety can be combinations of:
  - **structured data** – tables, objects and so on for which the metadata is well defined;
  - **semi-structured data** – documents and so forth for which the metadata is contained internally, for example XML or JSON documents;
  - **unstructured data** – photographs, video, binary data and so on.
- **Velocity** – where the data is produced at high rates and operating on 'stale' data is not valuable.
- **Value** – where the data has perceived or quantifiable benefit to the enterprise or organisation using it.
- **Veracity** – where the correctness of the data can be assessed.

To accommodate Big Data we require databases that are flexible so that they can easily accommodate new data types. We also need databases that are not disrupted by content structure changes from third-party data providers. Unfortunately, in addition to not scaling well for large volumes of data, the rigidly defined, schema-based approach used by SQL databases makes it very difficult, if not impossible, to quickly incorporate new types of data. SQL databases are also not a good fit for unstructured and semi-structured data. Hence NoSQL databases are replacing SQL databases in the database server tier.

NoSQL databases have replaced the ACID principles associated with traditional databases (see Chapter 8) with CAP principles, where CAP stands for:

- **Consistency** – where all clients always have the same view of the data;
- **Availability** – where each client can always read and write data;
- **Partition-tolerance** – where the system works well despite physical network partitions.

You can only ever meet two out of these three principles.

There are over 150 NoSQL databases available. They all achieve performance gains by doing away with some (or all) of the restrictions traditionally associated with conventional databases, such as read–write consistency, in exchange for scalability and distributed processing. NoSQL databases can be categorised under four main headings:

- key-value store;
- document store;
- extensible record (or wide-column) store;
- graph database.

A key-value store is where the data can be stored in a schema-less way with the 'key-value' relationship consisting of a key, normally a string, and a value, which is the actual data of interest. The value itself can be stored using a datatype of a programming language or as an object.

A document store is a key-value store where the values are the native documents, such as Microsoft Office (MS Word, MS Excel and so on), PDF, XML or JSON documents. While every row in a table in an SQL database will have the same sequence of columns, each document could have data items that are completely different. An example of a JSON document is shown in Figure 17.3. Whole documents can be retrieved based on their 'key' but, in addition, document stores should provide an ability to retrieve a document based on its content.

Like SQL databases, extensible record stores, or wide-column stores, have 'tables' (called 'Super Column Families') which contain columns (called 'Super Columns'). However, each of the columns contains a mix of 'attributes', similar to key-value stores. This is shown in Figure 17.4. The most common NoSQL databases, such as Hadoop, are extensible record stores.

A graph database consists of interconnected elements with an undetermined number of interconnections. These can be used for data representing concepts such as social relationships, public transport links, road maps or network topologies.

Figure 17.3 Example of a JSON document

```
{
    "orderNumber": 201366784425,
    "customer": {
    "firstName": "James",
    "lastName": "Munro",
    "address": {
       "houseNumber": "35",
       "street": "Main Street",
       "town": "Westchester",
       "postCode": "WT7 5QR"
       },
    },
    "items": [
       {
          "isbn": "1-902527-23-0",
          "discount": 3.60,
          "amount": 27.39
       },
       {
          "isbn": "0-323-19445-7",
          "amount": 15.99
       }
    ],
    "value": 43.38
}
```

THE SEMANTIC WEB

The vision for the future of the web is what is known as the semantic web: a system that enables the computers at the heart of the web to 'understand' and respond to complex requests from users based on their meaning, or the context of the request. To achieve this, the information sources, for example the HTML pages, must be semantically structured.

According to the World Wide Web Consortium (W3C), the body responsible for standards for the web, 'The Semantic Web provides a common framework that allows data to be shared and reused across application, enterprise, and community boundaries.'

To make this happen we need to be able to categorise all 'things of interest', and the relationships between them, in such a way that the categorisation can be understood by a computer. To achieve this we are in the world of taxonomies (systems for naming and organising things into groups that share similar characteristics) and ontologies (specifications of concrete or abstract things, and the relationships among them, in a prescribed domain of knowledge).

Technologies such as the Resource Description Framework (RDF), the Web Ontology Language (OWL) and, even, XML are used to provide these categorisations.

Figure 17.4 Conceptual view of an extensible record store

Super Column Families : Customers

RowID : 1050201

Super Column : Name
First Name : James
Last Name : Munro

Super Column : Address
House Number : 35
Street : Main Street
Town : Westchester
Post Code : WT7 5QR

Super Column : Order Track
Last Order : 201366784425
Value : £43.38

RowID : 1050374

Super Column : Name
First Name : Jacqueline
Last Name : Overend

Super Column : Address
Apartment Number : 22A
Building Name : Jupiter Mansions
Street : Jupiter Street
Town : Cunningham
Post Code : CN3 6AA

Super Column : Order Track
Last Order : 201366784437
Value : £53.99

Super Column Families : Orders

RowID : 6372031

Super Column : Order
Number : 201366784425
Date : 27-01-2013

Super Column : Items
ISBN : 1-902527-23-0

Super Column : Amounts
Discount : £3.60
Amount : £27.39

RowID : 6373745

Super Column : Order
Number : 201366784425
Date : 27-01-2013

Super Column : Items
ISBN : 0-323-19445-7

Super Column : Amounts
Amount : £15.99

RowID : 6374427

Super Column : Order
Number : 201366784437
Date : 03-02-2013

Super Column : Items
ISBN : 1-60427-192-2

Super Column : Amounts
Amount : £53.99

RDF is similar to conceptual data modelling: it is concerned with making statements about things. These statements take the form of subject-predicate-object expressions, known as triples in RDF. For example, we can represent the idea that 'Scotch whisky is made in Scotland' in RDF as the triple: a subject denoting 'Scotch whisky', a predicate denoting 'is made in', and an object denoting 'Scotland'.

The subject of an RDF triple, a resource, is usually a Uniform Resource Identifier (URI). The predicate, another resource representing a relationship, is always a URI. The object, yet another resource, is also usually a URI. Subjects and objects may be blank nodes, which represent anonymous resources.

The URIs used in RDF denote, and can be used to access, actual data on the World Wide Web.

Despite its name, OWL is actually a family of knowledge representation languages that use formal semantics in the authoring of ontologies. These languages allow the specification of concepts within a domain, such as classes and their instances, subclasses, properties and operations.

An example of an ontology expressed using RDF and OWL is FOAF, an acronym of Friend of a Friend. This ontology describes people, their activities and their relations to other people and objects. Anyone can use FOAF to describe themself. FOAF allows groups of people to describe social networks without the need for a centralised database.

SUMMARY

This chapter has looked at data and web technology. We looked at the architecture of the web and then discussed the use of HTML and XML documents. We followed this by looking briefly at some other approaches to link databases and web technology. We concluded by looking at two current topics: dealing with the large quantities of data generated by the web, which introduced the subjects of Big Data and NoSQL databases, and the sematic web.

APPENDICES

The Appendices provide a range of supporting material.

Appendix A – Comparison of Data Modelling Notations – looks at some alternatives to the data modelling notation used throughout the book.

Appendix B – Hierarchical and Network Databases – looks at two popular pre-relational database models and their implementations.

Appendix C – Generic Data Models – looks at why data models become generic (or abstract) and the advantages and disadvantages of using generic data models as the basis for database design.

Appendix D – An Example of a Data Naming Convention – provides a complete example of a data naming convention.

Appendix E – Metadata Models – looks at the data models that underpin data dictionaries and repositories.

Appendix F – A Data Mining Example – provides a worked example of just one of the many data mining techniques that are available.

Appendix G – HTML and XML – looks in more detail at these two key 'technologies' used with web technology.

Appendix H – XML and Relational Databases – looks at the support for XML provided in the SQL standard.

Appendix I – Techniques and Skills for Data Management – looks at the techniques and skills needed for data administration, database administration and repository administration.

Appendix J – International Standards for Data Management – provides a brief introduction to some of the main International Standards that data managers will find useful.

Appendix K – Bibliography – provides a list of list of useful reading, some of which has been helpful in the preparation of this book.

APPENDIX A
COMPARISON OF DATA MODELLING NOTATIONS

This appendix compares five notations that are in common use for data modelling, with the same business scenario drawn in each notation. The notations are:

- the Ellis–Barker notation – see Figure A.1 and Figure A.2;
- the Chen entity-relationship notation – see Figure A.3;
- the Information Engineering notation – see Figure A.4;
- the IDEF1X notation – see Figure A.5;
- the UML notation for object class diagrams – see Figure A.6.

THE ELLIS–BARKER NOTATION

Figure A.1 shows a data model drawn using my preferred notation. This notation does not have a formal name, but I am calling it the Ellis–Barker notation because it was developed in the early 1980s by Harry Ellis and Richard Barker when they were working for CACI, an IT services company. Richard Barker then took the notation and its related methodology into the development of Oracle's CASE tool. It is this notation that he describes in his book *CASE*METHOD: Entity Relationship Modelling* (Barker, 1990). It is also used by David Hay in his book *Data Model Patterns: Conventions of Thought* (Hay, 1996).

The beauty of this notation is that it is easy to read. Harry Ellis and Richard Barker set out to develop a notation that unambiguously and accurately portrayed the data requirements yet at the same time reduced the number of interactions that the analyst would require with the users. I have used this notation with many who have never seen a data model before; they find the concepts easy to grasp and are soon able to describe the data requirements that led to the model being discussed.

The model in Figure A.1 represents the data requirements associated with the handling of orders. Some of the orders are 'call-off' orders, i.e. there are 'framework orders' in place and the customer submits orders for the products or services, the call-off orders, as required. There may also be normal orders, i.e. orders that are not called off from a framework arrangement. Hence, to allow for the recording of the call-off orders being associated with a framework order, each **ORDER** may be *part of* one and only one other **ORDER**.

Figure A.1 A data model in Ellis–Barker notation

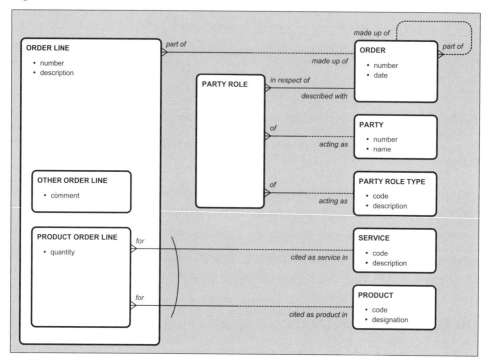

Parties, persons or organisations, can play different roles associated with an order. They may be the customer who placed the order, the consignee of the goods or services as they are delivered, the department to which the invoice is to be sent or the staff member who is responsible for ensuring that the order is completed. Hence, each **ORDER** must be described with one or more **PARTY ROLES**, where each **PARTY ROLE** must be of one and only one **PARTY** and each **PARTY ROLE** must be described by one and only one **PARTY ROLE TYPE**.

The details of the order, the products or services being ordered or other comments, are included as 'order lines'. Hence each **ORDER** may be made up of one or more **ORDER LINES**. Each of these **ORDER LINES** must be either a **PRODUCT ORDER LINE**, a specification of a product or service being ordered, or an **OTHER ORDER LINE**, to enable a comment to be added to an order. Furthermore, each **PRODUCT ORDER LINE** must be for one and only one **PRODUCT** OR must be for one and only one **SERVICE**.

There are a number of variations that can be used with this notation. The attributes can be omitted from the model diagram to aid readability. Attributes can be annotated with (#), to indicate it is part of the unique identifier, with (m), if it is mandatory for a value to exist, or (o), if values are optional. For a complete indication of unique identification, those relationships that are part of a unique identifier, sometimes called identifying relationships, are annotated with a bar across the relationship line. These additional annotations are shown in Figure A.2.

Figure A.2 Ellis–Barker data model with attribute annotation and unique identifiers

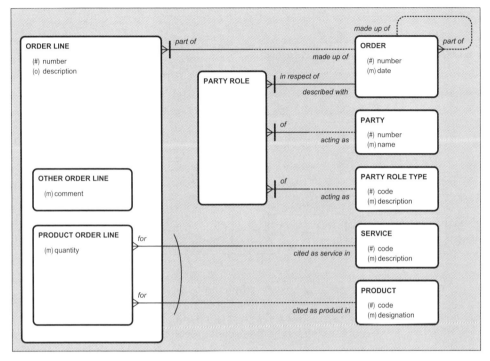

The unique identifiers for the entities shown in Figure A.2 are:

- for **ORDER** – the **number** attribute;
- for **ORDER LINE** – the combination of the **number** attribute and the <u>must be</u> *part of* <u>one and only one</u> **ORDER** relationship;
- for **PRODUCT** – the **code** attribute;
- for **SERVICE** – the **code** attribute;
- for **PARTY** – the **number** attribute;
- for **PARTY ROLE TYPE** – the **code** attribute;
- for **PARTY ROLE** – the combination of the <u>must be</u> *in respect of* <u>one and only one</u> **ORDER** relationship, the <u>must be</u> *of* <u>one and only one</u> **PARTY** relationship, and the <u>must be</u> *described by* <u>one and only one</u> **PARTY ROLE TYPE** relationship.

THE CHEN NOTATION

The Chen notation in Figure A.3 was the original entity-relationship modelling notation proposed by Peter Chen in his paper *The Entity-Relationship Model: Toward a Unified View of Data* (Chen, 1976) and the notation, with some refinements, is still in use today in a number of environments.

Figure A.3 A data model in Chen notation

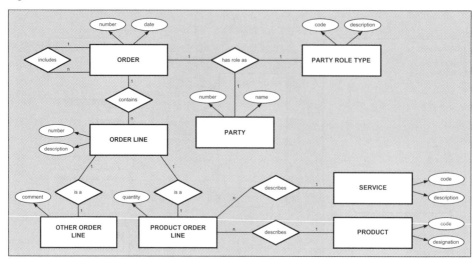

Entity types are represented by boxes, relationships by diamonds and attributes by ellipses attached to the entity type boxes. Relationships can be 'n-ary', in that more than two entity types may be related by a single relationship. Hence the **PARTY ROLE** entity type of Figure A.1 is represented by the 'has role as' relationship in this notation.

There are no equivalents of the exclusive arc or entity subtyping. The supertype–subtype hierarchy is simulated by the two 'is a' relationships, but these do not fully cover the concept because they do not document the fact that the subtypes are mutually exclusive.

THE INFORMATION ENGINEERING NOTATION

Figure A.4 shows the same business area drawn using the Information Engineering data modelling notation. Information Engineering was developed by James Martin and Clive Finkelstein in the late 1970s. It was very popular in the UK, Europe and USA in the 1980s and 1990s, where it had extensive CASE tool support. The methodology had a number of techniques that looked at data (its structure and how it changed over time) and processes and provided some cross-checking to ensure that there is a correlation between data and process.

The relationship notation is as precise as that used in the Ellis–Barker notation, but more symbols are used to impart the same message. A crow's foot with a bar across its base means 'one or more', while a crow's foot with a circle at its base means 'zero, one or more'. The absence of a crow's foot with two bars means 'one and only one' and the absence of a crow's foot with a circle and a single bar means 'zero or one'. So from Figure A.4, the relationship between **PARTY** and **PARTY ROLE** is read as 'each **PARTY** *is quoted in* <u>zero, one or more</u> **PARTY ROLES**' and 'each **PARTY ROLE** *references* <u>one and only</u>

Figure A.4 A data model in Information Engineering notation

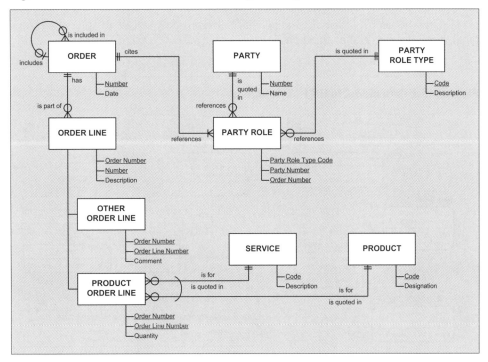

<u>one</u> **PARTY**' and the recursive relationship on **ORDER** reads as 'each **ORDER** *includes* <u>zero,</u> <u>one or more</u> **ORDERS**' and 'each **ORDER** *is included in* <u>zero or one</u> **ORDER**'.

Attributes can be included on the diagram. They are listed outside the entity type box as shown, with the unique identifiers (primary keys) being underlined. Exclusive arcs and entity subtypes are supported. The subtypes are shown separately from the supertype but connected to it by a line. There is no special notation for this line and it is possible for the subtypes to become visually separated from their supertype. Because the subtypes are external to the supertype, it is possible to include more than one set of subtypes on the same diagram. For example, a **PERSON** entity type could be subtyped into **MALE PERSON** and **FEMALE PERSON** and at the same time could also be subtyped into **EMPLOYEE** and **CUSTOMER**. This ability to support multiple subtyping hierarchies is not possible in the Ellis–Barker notation where the subtypes are located within the supertype 'box'.

THE IDEF1X NOTATION

IDEF1X, shown in Figure A.5, is one of the family of ICAM Definition Languages (IDEF). ICAM is short for Integrated Computer-Aided Manufacturing, an initiative managed by the US Air Force. IDEF1X is a data modelling language – there was an IDEF1, an information modelling language, but this was extended and renamed as IDEF1X. Amongst the other IDEF languages are IDEF0, a functional modelling language; IDEF2, a dynamics modelling language; and IDEF3, a process or workflow modelling language. IDEF1X is now a US Federal standard and the language has become very widely used both within the US and internationally. IDEF1X is a very rich notation encompassing many different facets of the basic entity type (called an entity in IDEF1X and not an entity type), attribute and relationship concepts.

Figure A.5 A data model in IDEF1X notation

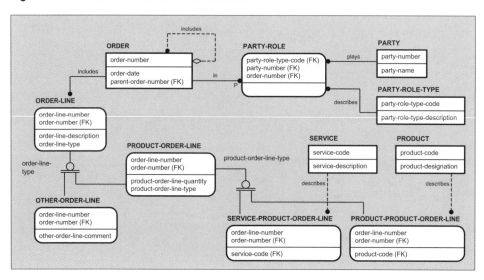

For example, within the language there are two different types of entity: independent and dependent. An independent entity is one that does not depend on any other for its identification and is shown on an IDEF1X diagram using a box with square corners. A dependent entity, therefore, is one that depends on one or more other entities for its identification and is shown on an IDEF1X diagram using a box with rounded corners. The entities **ORDER**, **PRODUCT**, **SERVICE**, **PARTY** and **PARTY-ROLE-TYPE** are independent entities; the entities **ORDER-LINE** (and its subtypes) and **PARTY-ROLE** are dependent entities.

In a full IDEF1X diagram, both types of entity have their attributes listed in two groups. The attributes above the separation line in the entity box are the 'key attributes' (or the 'primary key attributes' – the attributes that form the primary key columns in the equivalent table in an SQL implementation), while the attributes below the line are the non-key attributes. All attributes, key and non-key, that are part of a foreign key are marked with '(FK)'. Note the rule that all attribute names (except for those that are part of a foreign key) must be unique within the model, which means that the entity name often has to be added to the attribute name to ensure this uniqueness. Foreign key attributes can retain their original names or can be renamed when in their foreign key role.

The relationship notation is very complex. A solid line represents an identifying relationship (a relationship where all the primary key attributes of the parent entity become part of the primary key of the child entity) and a dotted line represents a non-identifying relationship. A 'blob' on the end of the relationship line is almost the equivalent of a crow's foot in the Ellis–Barker and Information Engineering notations – it represents the end of the relationship, that is at the child end of the relationship (the 'foreign key end'). Unannotated, the 'blob' represents 'zero or more'; annotated with a 'P' (for positive), it represents 'one or more'; annotated with a 'Z' (for zero), it represents 'zero or one'; annotated with a number, for example '2', it represents 'exactly 2'. An open diamond at the parent end (the 'primary key end') of a non-identifying relationship indicates that the parent entity is optional, for example not every **ORDER** is included in another **ORDER**.

As with Information Engineering, subtypes are shown external to their supertype but there is a specific notation to indicate the subtypes. A subtype is known as a 'category entity' in IDEF1X and the combination of a supertype and its subtypes is known as a category or generalisation hierarchy. There is, however, a specific notation for a category hierarchy. This is a circle over two bars for a complete hierarchy (where each instance of the supertype has an equivalent instance of one of the subtypes) and a circle over a single bar for an incomplete hierarchy. (An incomplete hierarchy does not meet our rule for subtypes given in Chapter 2 that every instance of the supertype must also be an instance of one of the subtypes as well as the subtypes being mutually exclusive.) The name of the attribute in the supertype that is to act as the 'category discriminator' is alongside the category-hierarchy notation. Because the subtypes are shown external to the supertype, multiple subtyping hierarchies can be used.

There is no equivalent of the exclusive arc in IDEF1X, which means that mutually exclusive relationships must be shown using subtyping. Hence we have the subtypes **PRODUCT–PRODUCT–ORDER–LINE** and **SERVICE–PRODUCT–ORDER–LINE** of **PRODUCT–ORDER–LINE**, which play no role other than to relate **PRODUCT–ORDER–LINE** with **PRODUCT** and **SERVICE** respectively.

> **Aside:** Once he had seen the notation I use, an American friend of mine employed as a data modeller on a multinational project resorted to annotating one of his IDEF1X models with 'These two relationships are mutually exclusive' to get over the proliferation of unnecessary subtypes throughout the model.

Because the IDEF1X notation is very rich, it is not very easy for those not involved in data modelling to understand the model. This becomes even less easy, the greater the number of entities on the model. An IDEF1X model is more an expression of a logical schema than a conceptual data model that documents a business area's information requirements. The information requirements are documented, but they are swamped by a mass of detail that is really there so that the design of the database can be automated. It is sometimes difficult 'to see the wood for the trees'.

THE UML CLASS DIAGRAM NOTATION

The Unified Modeling Language (UML) is a set of modelling notations for object oriented analysis and design. It is not a method because each of the model types stands alone – there is no overall process in UML to tie the separate models together. There are some processes, such as the Rational Unified Process, that use UML notations but they are not part of UML. Central to all object oriented analysis and design methods is the modelling of object classes. This is very similar to data modelling and UML class diagrams are increasingly replacing data models in software development.

Each object class is represented by a box that is split into three separate sections. The top section contains the name of the class. The middle section lists the attributes of the class. Each attribute may be annotated with its type (string, integer, date and so on) and with a default value (but no default values are shown in Figure A.6). The bottom section contains the operations of the class – the processes that a class knows how to carry out. As we are only interested in data (that is, attributes), no operations are shown in Figure A.6.

Figure A.6 A UML class diagram

The 'multiplicity' of each relationship (called associations in UML) is shown using textual annotations as opposed to the crow's foot or similar notation. The black diamond represents composition. An **ORDER** (a **SINGLE ORDER** on our class diagram) is composed of a number of **ORDER LINES**, representing the items being ordered. An **ORDER LINE** has no relevance without its parent order and cannot be transferred between orders.

There is a standard notation, the white arrowhead, for the subclass concept. **PRODUCT ORDER LINE** and **OTHER ORDER LINE** are subclasses of **ORDER LINE**. Note that early versions of UML had no equivalent of the recursive relationship so the *part of – made up of* relationship on order is achieved by subclassing **ORDER** into **COMPOSITE ORDER** and **SINGLE ORDER**.

Although there is no direct equivalent of the exclusive arc, there is the ability to annotate the model with additional constraints (shown in brackets, { }) and general notes.

There is no equivalent of the unique identification or primary key concepts. This is because within an object oriented system, each object (an instance of an object class) is identified within the system by a system-generated identifier that is hidden from the user of the system.

Despite their popularity with IT professionals, UML class diagrams, like IDEF1X models, are often found to be difficult to understand by those not involved in data or object modelling.

COMPARISON OF THE NOTATIONS

Figure A.7 shows for comparison the different relationship notations used in the Ellis–Barker, Information Engineering, IDEF1X and UML notations. Figure A.8 provides an overall comparison of the notations.

Figure A.7 Comparison of the relationship notations

You will see that IDEF1X gets more ticks than any of the other notations in Figure A.8. One of those is because it provides the ability to use multiple subtyping hierarchies but this is a facility that I believe should not be available. Every time I have seen multiple subtyping hierarchies used, I have seen confusion and errors. The discipline provided by the Ellis–Barker notation, that there can only be a single subtyping hierarchy for any one entity type, is a sound discipline.

Figure A.8 Comparison of the overall data model notations

	'Ellis/Barker'	Chen	Information Engineering	IDEF1X	UML
Dependent/independent entities	✗	✗	✗	✓	✗
Entity subtyping	✓	✗	✓	✓	✓
Multiple subtyping hierarchies	✗	✗	✓	✓	✓
Exclusive arcs	✓	✗	✓	✗	?
Identifying relationships	?	✗	✗	✓	✗
'n-ary' relationships	✗	✓	✗	✗	✗
'Many over time' relationships	✗	✗	✗	✗	✗

There are two question marks. Although UML does not have an explicit exclusive arc, the mutual exclusivity of relationships (associations) can be documented using the additional constraint concept. The Ellis–Barker notation can have relationships annotated to indicate that they are identifying relationships but most data modellers do not make use of this notation.

You will see that none of the notations distinguishes what I have called 'many over time' relationships. 'Many' relationships can cover three separate circumstances and it would be useful for the notations to distinguish between them. These three circumstances are:

- Many instances of the 'child' entity type are associated with the 'parent' entity type at the same time, but there is no implied sequence associated with those instances; for example the personal computers installed in an open-plan office.

- Many instances of the 'child' entity type are associated with the 'parent' entity type at the same time, but there is a sequence associated with those instances; for example the lines within an order (they are displayed in sequence down the page on a printed order).

- Only one instance of the 'child' entity type is associated with the 'parent' entity type at any one time, but there may be many instances of the 'child' entity type over time; for example a person can only have one current British passport, but may have held many passports in the past and records need to be kept of those previous passports.

APPENDIX B
HIERARCHICAL AND NETWORK DATABASES

For the majority of the discussions in this book we have been considering the relational model of data, first proposed by Edgar F. Codd (1970), when talking about the way that data is structured in databases. In the relational model, data is logically stored in relations, which are sets of tuples, with each tuple being a set of attribute-value pairs. In the physical embodiment of this model, with database management systems based on the SQL database language, the data is logically considered to be stored in tables.

Although it is the most common logical construct for storing data in databases, the table is not the only logical construct. Other models of data include:

- the hierarchical model;
- the network model;
- the multidimensional model;
- the object oriented model.

Both the multidimensional model of data and the object oriented model were discussed in Chapters 14 and 15 respectively. The hierarchical model of data and the network model of data are discussed in this appendix. Both these models predate the relational model of data, which was proposed by Edgar Codd to counter the shortcomings of these two models.

To provide a comparison, Figure B.1 shows a conceptual data model that will be developed into the hierarchical and network schemas and Figure B.2 shows some specimen data arranged as if it was stored in a relational database.

HIERARCHICAL DATABASES

The hierarchical model of data formed the basis for a number of early database management systems, the most prominent being IBM's Information Management System (IMS). IMS was first released in 1968 and is still in use today in many legacy mainframe-hosted applications where it is used for accounting and inventory control.

Figure B.3 shows an example of a schema diagram for a hierarchical database. The schema in Figure B.3 has only one hierarchy, but there could be many hierarchies in a single database. Each hierarchy comprises a number of record types, with each record type comprising a number of field types. Each hierarchy has a root record type. In Figure B.3 the root is the **DEPARTMENT** record type, which has two field types or data items: **DNAME**, the name of the department, and **DTELNUMBER**, the telephone number of the department.

Figure B.1 Conceptual data model used in comparison

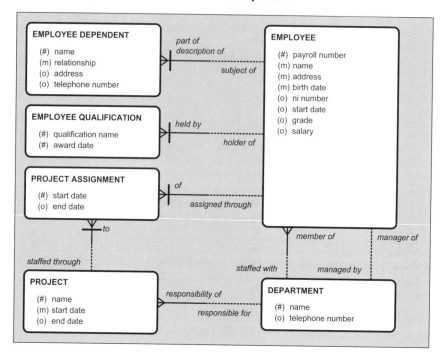

Figure B.2 Relational database occurrences

employee

payroll_ number	name	address	birth_date	ni_number	start_date	grade	salary	member_of_ department_name
AY334	Barbara Watson	3 Richmond ..	1952-12-06	XU996543B	1994-06-03	4	20340	Finance
AY478	John Wilson	55 Aberfan ..	1953-07-03	YA775421C	1972-12-05	5	13436	Production
BZ987	Joe Smith	The Manor ..	1964-02-24	ZR564439A	2003-09-01	1	35625	HQ
CA446	Phil Jones	37 Short ..	1974-05-05	BC906671A	1998-02-07	2	27750	Production
CX137	Jenny Rogers	37 Rushmore ..	1970-01-10	YC223456A	1995-01-03	2	27750	Finance
DJ777	Henry Phillips	33/2 Long ..	1974-05-05	SS677845D	1992-09-03	3	22570	Finance
EX115	Brian Thompson	29 Mayland ..	1979-06-11	JN905067C	1997-10-10	3	21785	Production
FJ678	Roger Harrison	9 Collier ..	1988-04-27	BH878754A	2004-11-05	4	14300	Finance
FL233	Jane Smith	99 Rushmore ..	1989-08-25	HL778923B	2006-12-08	5	12725	Production

employee_qualification

payroll_ number	qualification_ name	award_date
CX137	Dip FM	1998-09
CX137	ACCA	2003-10-20
CX137	First Aid	2005-04-30

employee_dependent

payroll_ number	name	relationship	address	telephone_ number
CX137	Mr John Rodgers	Husband	37 Rush ..	01377 376427
CX137	Miss A L Rogers	Daughter	Flat 4 ..	01451 276810

department

name	telephone_ number	managed_ by
HQ	NULL	NULL
Finance	ext 452	CX137
Production	ext 664	CA446

project

name	start_date	end_date	responsibility_of_ department name
Venus	2007-01-08	2007-03-23	Production
Patriot	2007-01-29	NULL	Production

project_assignment

of_employee_ payroll_number	to_project_ name	start_date	end_date
AY478	Venus	2007-01-08	2007-03-23
EX115	Venus	2007-01-08	2007-01-26
EX115	Patriot	2007-01-29	2007-04-13
FL233	Patriot	2007-02-05	2007-04-13

Each hierarchy has a number of one-to-many parent–child relationship types. There may be zero, one or more child-record instances for each instance of a parent record. In Figure B.3 these are (**DEPARTMENT**, **EMPLOYEE**), (**DEPARTMENT**, **DEPTMANAGER**), (**DEPARTMENT**, **PROJECT**), (**EMPLOYEE**, **EMPQUALIFICATION**), (**EMPLOYEE**, **DEPENDENT**) and (**PROJECT**, **PROJASSIGNMENT**). Instead of the relationships between a parent-record type and its child-record types being represented by the foreign key mechanism as in a relational database, in a hierarchical database these relationships are represented by the parent–child links themselves. Despite this, you may note that there are some data items that look like 'foreign keys' within the schema, for example **PAYROLLNO** from **EMPLOYEE** appears as **EPAYROLLNO** in **PROJASSIGNMENT** and as **MGRPAYROLLNO** in **DEPTMANAGER**. These are there to cope with the fact that our conceptual model in Figure B.1 is not purely hierarchical. The management of the integrity of the values of these data items would need to be managed by the application code.

Figure B.3 Hierarchical database schema

Figure B.4 provides an example of the data definition statements required to implement the schema from Figure B.3, with some of the more detailed syntax omitted. Note that the **DEPARTMENT** record type is specifically declared as being the root of the hierarchy. All the other record types are declared with the name of the record type that is their parent and with their sequence under the parent – **EMPLOYEE** is the first child of **DEPARTMENT**, **DEPTMANAGER** is the second child of **DEPARTMENT** and so on. Also most record types have an order by clause specifying how the records, the instances of the record type, are to be ordered. This ordering, both of the child record types under their parent and of the individual records of a record type, is fundamental to the management of the data within a hierarchical database.

Figure B.5 shows how the data shown in Figure B.2 is stored as records within the hierarchical database, declared using the statements in Figure B.4.

Figure B.4 Data definition statements for a hierarchical database

```
SCHEMA NAME = EMPLOYEEMANAGEMENT

RECORD
        NAME = DEPARTMENT
        TYPE = ROOT OF HIERARCHY
        DATA ITEMS  =
                DNAME                   CHARACTER 25
                DTELNUMBER              CHARACTER 15
        KEY = DNAME
        ORDER BY DNAME

RECORD
        NAME = EMPLOYEE
        PARENT = DEPARTMENT
        CHILD NUMBER = 1
        DATA ITEMS  =
                PAYROLLNO               CHARACTER 5
                ENAME                   CHARACTER 30
                EADDRESS                CHARACTER 180
                BDATE                   CHARACTER 9
                NINUMBER                CHARACTER 9
                SDATE                   CHARACTER 9
                GRADE                   CHARACTER 2
                SALARY                  INTEGER
        KEY = PAYROLLNO
        ORDER BY ENAME

RECORD
        NAME = PROJECT
        PARENT = DEPARTMENT
        CHILD NUMBER = 2
        DATA ITEMS  =
                PNAME                   CHARACTER 25
                PSTARTDATE              CHARACTER 9
                PENDDATE                CHARACTER 9
        KEY = PNAME
        ORDER BY PSTARTDATE

RECORD
        NAME = DEPTMANAGER
        PARENT = DEPARTMENT
        CHILD NUMBER = 3
        DATA ITEMS  =
                MGRPAYROLLNO            CHARACTER 5
                MGRSTARTDATE            CHARACTER 9
        KEY = MGRPAYROLLNO
        ORDER BY MGRSTARTDATE

RECORD
        NAME = EMPQUALIFICATION
        PARENT = EMPLOYEE
        CHILD NUMBER = 1
        DATA ITEMS  =
                QNAME                   CHARACTER 25
                QAWARDDATE              CHARACTER 9
        ORDER BY QAWARDDATE

RECORD
        NAME = DEPENDENT
        PARENT = EMPLOYEE
        CHILD NUMBER = 2
        DATA ITEMS  =
                DEPNAME                 CHARACTER 30
                RELATIONSHIP            CHARACTER 12
                DEPADDRESS              CHARACTER 180
                DEPTELNUMBER            CHARACTER 25
        ORDER BY RELATIONSHIP

RECORD
        NAME = PROJASSIGNMENT
        PARENT = PROJECT
        CHILD NUMBER = 1
        DATA ITEMS  =
                EPAYROLLNO              CHARACTER 5
                PROJASSSTARTDATE        CHARACTER 9
                PROJASSENDDATE          CHARACTER 9
```

Figure B.5 Hierarchical database occurrences

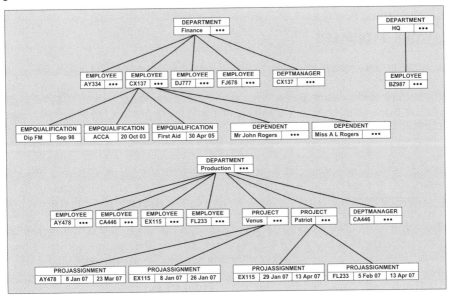

In a hierarchical database, the records may be stored sequentially, reading the hierarchical trees from top to bottom and left to right. The resulting sequence is shown in Figure B.6.

Figure B.6 Hierarchical database records in sequence

DEPARTMENT	Finance
EMPLOYEE	AY334
EMPLOYEE	CX137
EMPQUALIFICATION	Dip FM - Sep 98
EMPQUALIFICATION	ACCA - 20 Oct 03
EMPQUALIFICATION	First Aid - 30 Apr 05
DEPENDENT	Mr John Rogers
DEPENDENT	Miss A L Rogers
EMPLOYEE	DJ777
EMPLOYEE	FJ678
DEPTMANAGER	CX137
DEPARTMENT	HQ
EMPLOYEE	BZ987
DEPARTMENT	Production
EMPLOYEE	AY478
EMPLOYEE	CA446
EMPLOYEE	EX115
EMPLOYEE	FL233
PROJECT	Venus
PROJASSIGNMENT	AY478 - 8 Jan 07
PROJASSIGNMENT	EX115 - 8 Jan 07
PROJECT	Patriot
PROJASSIGNMENT	EX115 - 29 Jan 07
PROJASSIGNMENT	FL233 - 5 Feb 07
DEPTMANAGER	CA446

187

Alternatively the records may be linked using pointers, extra fields that contain data that identifies the location of the related record.

NETWORK DATABASES

Like its predecessor, the hierarchical model of data, the network model of data formed the basis for a number of pre-relational database management systems. The model was based on the recommendations of the Conference on Data Systems Languages (CODASYL) Data Base Task Group, published in 1971. The most prominent product based on the network model was the Integrated Database Management System (IDMS) from Cullinet Software, Inc (now part of Computer Associates). Many IDMS implementations are still in use today.

Figure B.7 shows an example of a schema diagram for a network database. The main difference between the hierarchical model of data and the network model of data is that in the network model, a record type can have more than one parent, whereas in the hierarchical model each record type is limited to only one parent. The 'links' between record types are known as sets. Each set has an owner record type (the parent, with only one occurrence allowed) and a member record type (the children, with zero, one or more occurrences). In Figure B.7 the **WORKS-IN** set has the **DEPARTMENT** record type as its owner and the **EMPLOYEE** record type as its member, while the **IS-MANAGED-BY** set has the **EMPLOYEE** record type as its owner and the **DEPARTMENT** record type as its member. The arrowhead is the equivalent of a crow's foot in an entity-relationship conceptual data model.

Figure B.7 Network database schema

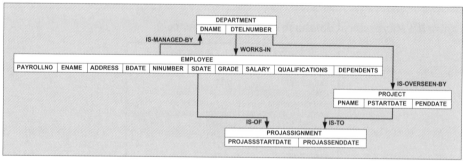

There are two other points to note. First, repeating groups, which in the relational model we remove in the move to first normal form, can be used in the network model, so the **EMPLOYEE** record type has two field types with plural names, **QUALIFICATIONS** and **DEPENDENTS**. Second, there are no foreign keys specified in the schema; the relationships between instances of the record types are specified in the sets. Foreign keys can, however, be specified in the network model if needed. One situation where they are probably needed is to implement a recursive relationship; most implementations of the network model do not support the concept of a set with both its owner and its member being of the same record type.

Figure B.8 Data definition statements for a network database

```
SCHEMA NAME IS EMPLOYEEMANAGEMENT

RECORD NAME IS DEPARTMENT
    DUPLICATES ARE NOT ALLOWED FOR DNAME
        02    DNAME              PIC X(25)
        02    DTELNUMBER         PIC X(15)

RECORD NAME IS  EMPLOYEE
    DUPLICATES ARE NOT ALLOWED FOR PAYROLLNO
        02    PAYROLLNO          PIC X(5)
        02    ENAME              PIC X(30)
        02    ADDRESS            PIC X(180)
        02    BDATE              PIC X(6)
        02    NINUMBER           PIC X(9)
        02    SDATE              PIC X(6)
        02    GRADE              PIC X(2)
        02    SALARY             PIC 99999
        02    QUALIFICATIONS
              03    QNAME        PIC X(25)
              03    QAWARDDATE   PIC X(6)
        02    DEPENDENTS
              03    DEPNAME      PIC X(30)
              03    RELATIONSHIP PIC X(12)
              03    DEPADDRESS   PIC X(180)
              03    DEPTELNUMBER PIC X(25)

RECORD NAME IS  PROJECT
    DUPLICATES ARE NOT ALLOWED FOR PNAME
        02    PNAME              PIC X(25)
        02    PSTARTDATE         PIC X(6)
        02    PENDDATE           PIC X(6)

RECORD NAME IS  PROJASSIGNMENT
        02    PROJASSSTARTDATE   PIC X(6)
        02    PROJASSENDDATE     PIC X(6)

SET NAME IS  WORKS-IN
    OWNER IS DEPARTMENT
    MEMBER IS EMPLOYEE

SET NAME IS  IS-MANAGED-BY
    OWNER IS EMPLOYEE
    MEMBER IS DEPARTMENT

SET NAME IS  IS-OVERSEEN-BY
    OWNER IS DEPARTMENT
    MEMBER IS PROJECT

SET NAME IS  IS-TO
    OWNER IS PROJECT
    MEMBER IS PROJASSIGNMENT

SET NAME IS  IS-OF
    OWNER IS EMPLOYEE
    MEMBER IS PROJASSIGNMENT
```

Figure B.8 shows the data definition statements required to implement the network schema shown in Figure B.7. Again some of the more detailed syntax is omitted. The full network data definition statements include many that provide details of how the database is mapped to the physical storage.

There are definitions for both the records and the sets. The fields of the records are annotated with level numbers and the use of level numbers indicates repeating groups. The **QUALIFICATIONS** repeating group has two fields, **QNAME** and **QAWARDDATE**, and the **DEPENDENTS** repeating group has four fields, **DEPNAME**, **RELATIONSHIP**, **DEPADDRESS** and **DEPTELNUMBER**.

Figure B.9 Network database occurrences

Figure B.9 shows how the example data is stored in a network database. The sets are maintained by a series of pointers. The **DEPARTMENT** record instance for the Finance Department is the owner of one of the **WORKS-IN** sets and has a pointer that points to the first member in the set, the **EMPLOYEE** record for the employee whose payroll number is AY334. This in turn points to the next **EMPLOYEE** record in the set and so on. The last **EMPLOYEE** record in the set has a pointer that points back to the owner record, the **FINANCE** department.

APPENDIX C
GENERIC DATA MODELS

What has become known as 'generic data modelling' is, to all intents and purposes, data modelling using all the conventional procedures and techniques of data modelling but where the current business rules are not allowed to affect the shape of the model itself. Instead the model is adapted to treat such business rules as part of the subject matter being modelled. This provides longer-term stability to the model and to any databases whose design is informed by the model.

The main difference between 'traditional' data models and generic data models is that the latter are characterised by entity types that are more abstract or generic than in a traditional data model. For example, in a model for a commercial business there could be a **PARTY** entity type instead of separate **CUSTOMER**, **SUPPLIER** and **SUBCONTRACTOR** entity types. Generic data models are also characterised by the inclusion of more 'type' entity types. These are entity types, such as **ASSOCIATION TYPE**, that allow for the recording in the database of the semantic definition of other data.

There are, however, other differences between traditional data models and generic data models, principally:

- There is generally a smaller number of entity types in a generic data model than in a traditional data model, making it easier to understand (although its relevance to the business may be less obvious).

- Roles played by instances of entity types and associations between entity types are represented in a generic data model by new entity types (and associated relationships) and not by relationships alone.

- As a consequence of using abstract entity types, for which 'real-world identifiers' are often not available, identifiers in a generic data model have to be artificial. These identifiers have to be managed to be unique. Such artificial identifiers are often called surrogate keys.

Generic data models can be developed for use at both the project and the corporate level. At the project level the resulting database is more robust than if it had been developed from a 'traditional' data model, leading to the likelihood that the overall lifetime cost of the project is reduced. It is, however, at the corporate level that generic data models provide the greatest benefit. They enable different business viewpoints of data to be accommodated within the same data model. They also enable the easy accommodation of new business viewpoints as the business develops. Additionally, because they generally have fewer entity types, they are more manageable and easier to understand.

Figure C.1 shows some of the stages on the continuum from generic to specific. The more generic the model, the more high level the names of the entity types. The ultimate generic model has an entity type called **THING**.

Figure C.1 The generic to specific continuum

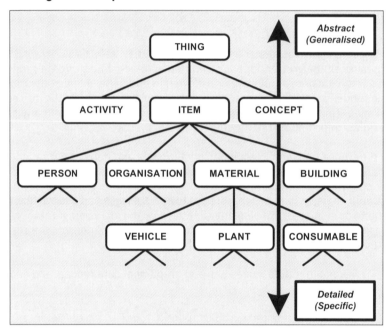

The more abstract or generic the data model, the greater its stability and the wider its perspective. This leads to a more stable database design, providing greater 'future-proofing'.

In its document *Developing High Quality Data Models*, the European Process Industries STEP Technical Liaison Executive (EPISTLE) has set out to describe how to develop data models that will:

- meet the data requirement;
- be clear and unambiguous to all (not just the authors);
- be stable in the face of changing data requirements;
- be flexible in the face of changing business practices;
- be reusable by others;
- be consistent with other models covering the same scope;
- be able to reconcile conflicting data models.

Aside: The content of this EPISTLE publication was written by Matthew West who described himself as the 'thought leader' for data management in Shell International Limited, which he worked for. He was developing these ideas at the same time that I was responsible for data management in the British Army. Unbeknown to each other, we were following an almost identical path in the development of our approach to data management. The EPISTLE work has been taken forward into an international standard – ISO 15926-2:2003 (*Industrial automation systems and integration – Integration of life-cycle data for process plants including oil and gas production facilities – Part 2: Data model*).

In this work, six principles that will lead to the development of high-quality data models have been identified. These are:

- Candidate attributes should be treated as representing relationships to other entity types.

- Entity types should have a local identifier within a database or exchange file. These should be artificial and managed to ensure uniqueness. Relationships should not be used as part of the local identifier.

- Activities, associations and event-effects should be represented by entity types (not relationships or attributes).

- Relationships (in the entity-relationship sense) should only be used to express the involvement of entity types with activities or associations.

- Entity types should represent, and be named after, the underlying nature of the object, not the role it plays in a particular context.

- Entity types should be part of a subtype–supertype hierarchy in order to define a universal context for the model.

What EPISTLE calls a 'high-quality data model' is a generic data model. They also use the term 'flexible design'. They have identified a number of advantages and disadvantages of developing data models such as this, which they have encapsulated in a diagram similar to Figure C.2.

All gains have to be paid for and the inherent flexibility gained by 'genericity' invokes a performance penalty.

Information systems that have their database design informed by generic data models have the following advantages:

- **Reduced maintenance costs.** Traditional designs tend to encapsulate the current business processes. As procedures change, information systems require maintenance to enable them to handle the revised procedures. Systems designed to be flexible from the outset do not incur this maintenance cost.

- **Reduced enhancement costs.** Similarly the costs involved in adding extra functionality are reduced if the system is designed to be flexible.

Figure C.2 The cost-balance of flexible design

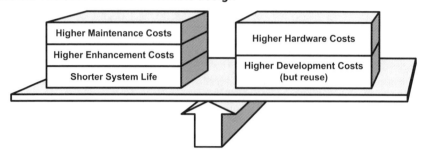

- **Longer system life.** The maintenance and enhancement costs associated with traditional designs can become prohibitive, leading to a premature requirement to replace the system.

- **Design reuse.** Being designed to cover a wide scope and to be inherently flexible to change in business procedures, any single generic data model, its resulting database design and the software used to address that database design can be used in many different systems. This reduces, over time, the need for some data analysis and a considerable amount of database and software design.

Aside: It is not the intention to claim that the use of a generic data model totally removes the need for data analysis. Any project reusing an existing generic data model should still analyse its data requirements to ensure that they can be met by the chosen generic data model.

On the other hand, information systems that have their database design informed by generic data models have the following disadvantages:

- **High development costs.** Initially, at least, the use of a generic data model as the basis of a database design for an information system leads to higher development costs than if a traditional data model is used. These higher development costs come about partly through the unfamiliarity of the developers with the concepts embodied in the model and partly from the fact that there is little tool support available for such development. These costs, however, are offset over time by the ability to reuse tested software components.

- **High hardware costs.** Flexible designs based on generic data models require more powerful hardware to achieve performance comparable to more traditional designs. These costs, over time, are offset by the continuing reduction in the cost of hardware.

APPENDIX D
AN EXAMPLE OF A DATA NAMING CONVENTION

This data naming convention is based on a convention developed for a client. A similar naming convention is described by Michael Brackett in his book Data Sharing: Using a Common Data Architecture, *published by John Wiley & Sons in 1994.*

INTRODUCTION

1. The purpose of applying a data naming standard to the naming of all data objects (entity types, attributes, domains and relationships in conceptual data models, and tables and columns in the logical schemas for SQL databases) is to ensure that all data objects have consistent, unique and meaningful names.

2. The parts of this data naming standard are:
   a. concepts used in naming (paragraphs 3 to 13);
   b. the naming of entity types in a conceptual data model (paragraphs 14 to 21);
   c. the naming of domains in a conceptual data model (paragraphs 22 to 25);
   d. the naming of attributes in a conceptual data model (paragraphs 26 to 30);
   e. the naming of relationships in a conceptual data model (paragraphs 31 to 33);
   f. the naming of tables in an SQL logical schema (paragraph 34);
   g. the naming of columns in an SQL logical schema (paragraphs 35 to 37);
   h. rules for abbreviations in data names (paragraphs 38 to 39);
   i. restricted terms (paragraph 40 and Tables D.1 to D.4);
   j. the naming of attributes: a formal description (paragraphs 41 to 46 and Table D.5).

CONCEPTS USED IN NAMING

3. Each data object must have one, and only one, primary data name.

4. The primary data name for a conceptual data model data object must be the real-world name, fully spelled out, not codified or abbreviated. Such names must not be subject to any length restrictions.

5. The primary data name for an SQL database logical schema data object should be derived from an associated conceptual data model data object. Such names may be subject to length restrictions and may, therefore, need to be abbreviated. Abbreviation of these names should be avoided wherever possible. Any abbreviation should follow the rules set out in paragraphs 38 and 39.

6. The primary data name for each data object (a conceptual data model data object or an SQL database logical schema data object) must uniquely identify that data object within the common data architecture.

7. The primary data name must provide consistency throughout the common data architecture. Restrictions are placed upon the use of some terms as described in paragraph 40.

8. The primary data name must unambiguously represent the underlying content and meaning of the data and not the way that the data is used or processed.

9. The primary data name must be meaningful to, and understood by, the business.

10. The primary data name must represent any variations in content or meaning of the data.

11. The primary data name must be complete, with the components of the name progressing from the general to the specific.

12. The primary data name must represent the conceptual or logical structure of data objects within the common data architecture.

13. All other names are secondary data names; each secondary data name must be cross-referenced to the relevant primary data name.

THE NAMING OF ENTITY TYPES IN A CONCEPTUAL DATA MODEL

14. Each entity type is named with a singular noun or noun phrase, with the name representing a single instance of the entity type.

   Examples are:

   VEHICLE

   PURCHASE ORDER

15. Entity type names are normally shown in **BOLD SMALL CAPITALS** in textual descriptions.

16. Uniqueness of entity type names within the common data architecture is to be achieved as follows:

   a. Each entity type name is to be unique within the conceptual data model that includes the entity type.

   b. The concatenation of the name of the conceptual data model with the entity type name provides a unique name for each entity type within the common data architecture.

17. Abbreviations are not used in entity type names.

18. Entity subtypes can be named following one of two conventions. All subtypes of an immediate supertype are to be named using the same convention. The conventions are as follows:

    a.   Entity subtype names comprise the immediate supertype entity name prefixed with an adjective to define the subtype.

        Examples are:

            VEHICLE OPERATION is a subtype of **OPERATION**

            MAINTENANCE VEHICLE OPERATION is a subtype of **VEHICLE OPERATION**

    b.   Entity subtype names identify independent concepts.

        Examples are:

            FACILITY is a subtype of **RESOURCE**

            ORGANISATION is a subtype of **PARTY**

19. Entity types that 'characterise' another entity type are to have names that comprise the name of the entity type being characterised, now acting as an adjectival phrase, suffixed by a noun that represents the nature of the characterisation.

        Examples are:

            RESOURCE STATUS characterises **RESOURCE**

            EMPLOYEE QUALIFICATION characterises **EMPLOYEE**

20. Entity types that provide a categorisation or classification for instances of another entity type are to have names that comprise the name of the entity type whose instances are being categorised, now acting as an adjectival phrase, suffixed by one of the words category, class or type as appropriate.

        Examples are:

            INDIVIDUAL SKILL CATEGORY categorises **INDIVIDUAL SKILL**

            EQUIPMENT TYPE categorises **EQUIPMENT**

            VEHICLE CLASS categorises **VEHICLE**

[Note: A distinction can be drawn between the use of the suffix **CATEGORY** on the one hand and the use of the suffixes **CLASS** and **TYPE** on the other. **CLASS** and **TYPE** refer to 'business' categorisations where system users may need to add new classes or types as part of normal operations. **CATEGORY** refers to categorisations that are to be kept under strict control. These categorisations may have been modelled as domains for attribute values had it been possible to identify at the time of modelling a full and final set of values that would never change.]

21. Entity types that represent a relationship (or association) between two entity types can be named following one of two conventions as follows:

    a.   The name represents the essence of the association formed from the rules above.

Examples are:

> **FACILITY VEHICLE CAPABILITY** provides an association between **FACILITY** and **VEHICLE**

> **ASSET STRUCTURE ELEMENT** provides a recursive association on **ASSET**

b. The names of the two entity types being associated are concatenated and suffixed by the word association. In the special case of a recursive association, the associated entity name is only used once.

Examples are:

> **OPERATION RESOURCE ASSOCIATION** provides an association between **OPERATION** and **RESOURCE**

> **PARTY ASSOCIATION** provides a recursive association on **PARTY**

The style of subparagraph (a) above is preferred to that in subparagraph (b) above. If the style of subparagraph (b) is used, it is normally because this entity type represents a generic association and an additional categorisation entity type (for example **PARTY ASSOCIATION CATEGORY**) is required.

THE NAMING OF DOMAINS IN A CONCEPTUAL DATA MODEL

22. Each domain is named with a singular noun or noun phrase, with the name representing the concept that the values of the domain collectively represent.

> Examples are:

> **WEIGHT**

> **CONTROLLED NAME**

23. Domain names are normally shown in **BOLD SMALL CAPITALS** in textual descriptions.

24. Uniqueness of domain names within the common data architecture is to be achieved as follows:

a. For domains intended to be used across the common data architecture (i.e. where the same domain may be used within more than one conceptual data model), the domain name is to be unique.

b. For domains to be used in a single conceptual data model, each domain is to be named with a name that is unique within that conceptual data model. The concatenation of the name of the conceptual data model with the domain name provides a unique name for that domain within the common data architecture.

25. Abbreviations are not used in domain names.

THE NAMING OF ATTRIBUTES IN A CONCEPTUAL DATA MODEL

26. Each attribute is named with a singular noun or noun phrase, with the name representing the meaning of the value to be recorded. The name of the entity type of the attribute is not included in the name of the attribute but is used with the attribute name when referring to the attribute conversationally.

Examples are:

designation (in **EQUIPMENT TYPE**, conversationally **EQUIPMENT TYPE designation**)

last service date (in **EQUIPMENT**, conversationally **EQUIPMENT last service date**)

international standard book number (in **PUBLICATION**, conversationally **PUBLICATION international standard book number**)

27. Attribute names are normally shown in **bold lower case** in textual descriptions.

28. Uniqueness of attribute names within the common data architecture is to be achieved as follows:

    a. Attribute names are to be unique within the entity type to which they belong. This is known as the 'short attribute name'.

    b. The concatenation of the name of the entity type to which the attribute belongs with the short attribute name provides a unique name for each attribute within the conceptual data model. This is known as the 'full attribute name'.

    c. The concatenation of the name of the conceptual data model with the full attribute name provides a unique name for each attribute within the common data architecture.

29. Abbreviations are not used in attribute names.

30. A more formal description of the naming of attributes is included in paragraphs 41 to 46.

THE NAMING OF RELATIONSHIPS IN A CONCEPTUAL DATA MODEL

31. Each relationship is named using two sentences of the following forms:

Each **VEHICLE** must be *within* one and only one **VEHICLE CLASS**.

Each **VEHICLE CLASS** may be *classification for* one or more **VEHICLES**.

where:

• in the first sentence:

must be represents the fact that the entity type **VEHICLE** has mandatory participation with respect to this relationship, represented by a solid line on a conceptual data model diagram.

within is the link phrase associated with the entity type **VEHICLE**.

one and only one represents the fact that only one instance of the entity type **VEHICLE CLASS** can be associated with any one instance of the entity type **VEHICLE** through this relationship, represented by the absence of a crow's foot on a conceptual data model diagram.

- and in the second sentence:

may be represents the fact that the entity type **VEHICLE CLASS** has optional participation with respect to this relationship, represented by a dashed line on a conceptual data model diagram.

classification for is the link phrase associated with the entity type **VEHICLE CLASS**.

one or more represents the fact that many instances of the entity type **VEHICLE** can be associated with only one instance of the entity type **VEHICLE CLASS** through this relationship, represented by a crow's foot on a conceptual data model diagram.

32. Uniqueness of relationship names within the common data architecture is to be achieved as follows:

    a. Relationship names are to be unique within a conceptual data model.

    b. The concatenation of the name of the conceptual data model with the relationship name provides a unique name for each relationship within the common data architecture.

33. Abbreviations are not used in relationship names.

THE NAMING OF TABLES IN AN SQL LOGICAL SCHEMA

34. All tables are named with singular nouns or noun phrases in upper case, with the name representing a single instance of the concept recorded by a single row of the table; the underscore character is used as the separator in names consisting of a phrase of more than one word.

    Examples are:

    VEHICLE

    PURCHASE_ORDER

THE NAMING OF COLUMNS IN AN SQL LOGICAL SCHEMA

35. Except in the particular cases described in paragraphs 36 and 37, all columns are named with singular nouns or noun phrases in lower camel case, with the name representing the value recorded at the row–column intersection in the table. The name of the table is not included in the name of the column, but is used with the column name when referring to the column conversationally.

Examples are:

designation (in **EQUIPMENT_TYPE**, conversationally **EQUIPMENT_TYPE.designation**)

lastServiceDate (in **EQUIPMENT**, conversationally **EQUIPMENT.lastServiceDate**)

isbn (in **PUBLICATION**, conversationally **PUBLICATION.isbn**)

36. Columns declared as a single-column primary key of a table using the **IDENTITY** or **AUTONUMBER** datatype are named '**ID**'.

37. Columns declared as a foreign key are named with a composite name comprising seven elements. The first element is the opening square bracket character ([). The second element is a role name in lower camel case. This is generally derived from the associated link phrase of the conceptual relationship instantiated by the foreign key. The third element is the point (.) character. The fourth element is the name of the referenced table. The fifth element is the point (.) character. The sixth element is the name of the column in the referenced table referenced by this foreign key column. The seventh element is the closing square bracket character (]).

Examples are:

[partOf.EQUIPMENT_TYPE.ID]

[withinOrOtherwiseAssociatedWith.FACILITY.ID]

RULES FOR ABBREVIATIONS IN DATA NAMES

38. The abbreviation of data names is deprecated but, if necessary, the names of SQL logical schema data objects (tables and columns) may be abbreviated. Names of conceptual data model data objects (entity types, domains, attributes and relationships) are not to be abbreviated.

39. The priority for selecting abbreviations is as follows:

    a. standard abbreviations in use within the 'business' areas of XYZ plc;

    b. abbreviations in common use within the United Kingdom;

    c. abbreviations in common use internationally;

    d. abbreviations contained in the Shorter Oxford English Dictionary, 5th Edition, published 26 September 2002, ISBN 0198605757;

    e. abbreviations formed by the removal of all vowels from the word being abbreviated, except where the initial letter of the word is a vowel.

RESTRICTED TERMS

40. To aid consistency in naming, a number of terms have restricted meanings. These are described in Tables D.1 to D.4.

Table D.1 Restricted terms used in the naming of entity types

Term	Restricted meaning
CATEGORY	This is used as a suffix in the name of a 'categorisation' entity type (i.e. an entity type that provides a categorisation or classification for instances of another entity type) where the 'categorisation' entity type is included in the model principally for data management purposes (to allow a level of flexibility in a set of valid values for a business domain concept), as opposed to business purposes, and the instances of the 'categorisation' entity type need to be centrally managed.
CLASS	This is used as a suffix in the name of a 'categorisation' entity type (i.e. an entity type that provides a categorisation or classification for instances of another entity type) where the 'categorisation' entity type is included in the model to represent a real-world business concept, such as providing a specification for a subset of the instances of the entity type being categorised, and the word 'class' is in common business use in this context, for example **VEHICLE CLASS** categorising **VEHICLE**. In all other cases, the word **TYPE** is preferred for this role.
TYPE	This is used as a suffix in the name of a 'categorisation' entity type (i.e. an entity type that provides a categorisation or classification for instances of another entity type) where the 'categorisation' entity type is included in the model to represent a real-world business concept, such as providing a specification for a subset of the instances of the entity type being categorised, for example **EQUIPMENT TYPE** categorising **EQUIPMENT**.
DETAIL	This is used as a suffix in the name of a 'characterisation' entity type (i.e. an entity type that provides further description or clarification for instances of another entity type) where the 'characterisation' entity type provides information about a component part or an element of the entity type being characterised, for example **SKILL SET DETAIL** characterising **SKILL SET**.

Table D.2 Restricted terms used in the naming of domains

Term	Restricted meaning
CODE	This is used to indicate that this domain is an enumerated domain that has three or more valid values.
INDICATOR	This is used to indicate that this domain is an enumerated domain that has exactly two valid values. These valid values are generally the Boolean values 'True' and 'False', but indicators are not restricted to the Boolean values.

Table D.3 Restricted terms used in the naming of attributes

Term	Restricted meaning
code	This is used to indicate that the attribute takes its values from an enumerated domain that has three or more valid values.
description	This is used to provide further clarification of the label or name of the entity type instance. Attributes with description in their name will almost invariably take values from the **GENERAL DESCRIPTIVE TEXT** domain.
indicator	An indication that the attribute takes its values from an enumerated domain that has exactly two valid values. These valid values are generally the Boolean values 'True' and 'False', but indicators are not restricted to the Boolean values.
label	This is used to name a concept where it is felt necessary to maintain data management control over the values of the attribute. Attributes with label in their name will almost invariably take values from the **CONTROLLED LABEL** domain or from another domain that is a specialisation of the **CONTROLLED LABEL** domain.
name	This is used to name a concept where there is no requirement to control the values of the attribute. Attributes with name in their name will almost invariably take values from the **BUSINESS NAME** domain or from another domain that is a specialisation of the **BUSINESS NAME** domain.
number	This is used where it is necessary to provide some form of identification for some or all of the instances of the entity type. Real-world examples are employee numbers and vehicle registration numbers. Despite their name, such 'numbers' generally include alphabetic and other non-numeric characters and it is meaningless to carry out arithmetic operations on the values (even if they are all numeric). Attributes with number in their name will have domains unique to themselves, such as the **INTERNATIONAL STANDARD BOOK NUMBER** domain.

Table D.4 Restricted terms used in the naming of relationships

Term	Restricted meaning
may be	This represents the fact that the referencing entity type has optional participation with respect to this relationship. (This is represented by a dashed line on a conceptual data model diagram.)

(Continued)

Table D.4 (Continued)

Term	Restricted meaning
must be	This represents the fact that the referencing entity type has mandatory participation with respect to this relationship. (This is represented by a solid line on a conceptual data model diagram.)
one and only one	This represents the fact that only one instance of the referenced entity type can be associated with any one instance of the referencing entity type through this relationship. (This is represented by the absence of a 'crow's foot' on a conceptual data model diagram.)
one or more	This represents the fact that many instances of the referenced entity type can be associated with any one instance of the referencing entity type through this relationship. (This is represented by a 'crow's foot' on a conceptual data model diagram.)

THE NAMING OF ATTRIBUTES: A FORMAL DESCRIPTION

41. As described in paragraph 28b, a 'full attribute name' consists of the concatenation of the entity type name and the 'short attribute name', where the latter is the unique name of the attribute within the entity type.

42. There are a number of formal approaches to the naming of attributes but most see a 'full attribute name' broken down into three components. These components can be given different names within different approaches to naming, but a common classification identifies these components as:

   - a **prime term**, which is mandatory;

   - a **modifier term**, which is optional;

   - a **class term**, which is mandatory.

43. The prime term identifies the context for the attribute, i.e. the set of things that this attribute can be used to describe. This is, effectively, the name of the entity type that includes the attribute.

44. The class term identifies the class (category or type) of the information that the attribute provides about the context.

45. The optional modifier term is used to discriminate between different attributes providing information of the same class for the same context or to provide some further specification or clarification to the attribute name.

46. Table D.5 provides examples to illustrate the use of these concepts.

Table D.5 Examples of formal attribute names

Full attribute name	Terms		
	Prime	Modifier	Class
PERSON family name	PERSON	family	name
VEHICLE CATEGORY label	VEHICLE CATEGORY	(–)	label
STOCK HOLDING unit of measure	STOCK HOLDING	(–)	unit of measure
ASSIGNMENT start date	ASSIGNMENT	start	date
ASSIGNMENT end date	ASSIGNMENT	end	date

APPENDIX E
METADATA MODELS

INTRODUCTION

Data dictionaries and repositories are specialised information systems used by data managers and those involved in software development, as are the range of systems known as Computer-Aided Software Engineering (CASE) tools. The use of these systems and tools is described in Chapter 11 but, like every other information system, they need a database to store their persistent data. The persistent data that is stored in these specialised information systems is metadata. The models specifying the design of these databases are often known as metadata models.

METADATA MODEL TO RECORD CONCEPTUAL DATA MODELS

Figure E.1 shows a metadata model to support the concepts of conceptual data modelling. It has three major entity types – **ENTITY TYPE**, **ATTRIBUTE** and **DOMAIN**.

To handle the exclusive arc concept there are the **RELATIONSHIP END GROUP** and **RELATIONSHIP END** entity types in the model. A **RELATIONSHIP END GROUP** links one or more **RELATIONSHIP ENDS** to their host **ENTITY TYPE** such that these **RELATIONSHIP ENDS** within the **RELATIONSHIP END GROUP** are mutually exclusive. The two **RELATIONSHIP ENDS** at each end of a relationship are associated through the relationship where each **RELATIONSHIP END** must be *paired with* one and only one **RELATIONSHIP END**. Since exclusive arcs are rare, in most cases there is only one **RELATIONSHIP END** in a **RELATIONSHIP END GROUP**.

In the conceptual data model snippet at Figure E.2, there are four **RELATIONSHIP ENDS** (labelled A, B, C and D) and three **RELATIONSHIP END GROUPS**. The first of these **RELATIONSHIP END GROUPS** is the combination of the **RELATIONSHIP ENDS** A and B; the second is the **RELATIONSHIP END** C on its own; and the third is the **RELATIONSHIP END** D on its own.

Unique identifiers are explicitly handled in this model. Each **ENTITY TYPE** may be *with instances identified by* one or more **UNIQUE IDENTIFIERS**. Furthermore, each **UNIQUE IDENTIFIER** must be *comprised of* one or more **UNIQUE IDENTIFIER ELEMENTS**. Since the instances of an entity type can be uniquely identified by the values of one or more attributes or by one or more related entity instances, the model shows that each **UNIQUE IDENTIFIER ELEMENT** must be *role of* one or more **ATTRIBUTES** or *role of* one or more **RELATIONSHIP ENDS**.

The valid value and valid operation entity types are included such that each **VALID VALUE** must be *for* one and only one **DOMAIN** and each **VALID OPERATION** must be *for* one and only

Figure E.1 A metadata model describing conceptual data model concepts

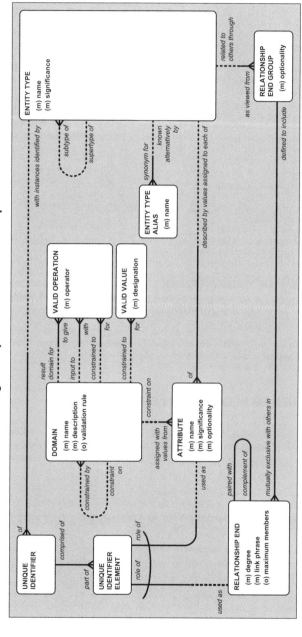

Figure E.2 A conceptual data model snippet

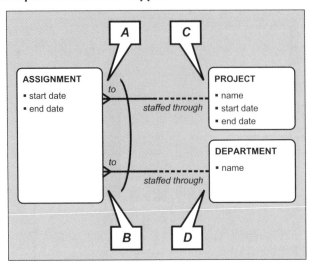

one **DOMAIN**. Additionally, **VALID OPERATION** has two other relationships such that each **VALID OPERATION** must be *with* one and only one **DOMAIN** and each **VALID OPERATION** must be *to give* one and only one **DOMAIN**. For example, a **VALID OPERATION** may be defined for a 'Date' **DOMAIN** (the *for* **DOMAIN**) that adds (the operation held by the *operator* attribute) a number of days (the *with* **DOMAIN** is 'day time interval') to give a result that is another date (the *to give* **DOMAIN** is also 'Date').

METADATA MODEL TO RECORD SQL LOGICAL SCHEMAS

Figure E.3 shows a metadata model covering the concepts involved in the logical schema for an SQL-based relational database. It enables the tables and columns in many different databases to be recorded. The uniqueness, referential and general constraints that may be declared for those tables and columns can also be recorded.

METADATA MODEL TO SUPPORT THE MAPPING OF CONCEPTS

Figure E.4 shows how the two separate metadata models may be combined to provide the capability of recording how two or more conceptual data models relate to each other or how physical SQL implementations match the conceptual data models from which they are derived.

The mapping structure allows one or more elements of one conceptual data model to be mapped to one or more elements in another conceptual data model (for example a many-to-many relationship in the first model is equivalent to two one-to-many relationships and an entity type in the second model). One or more elements of an SQL schema can be mapped to one or more elements in its conceptual data model (for example an entity

Figure E.3 A metadata model describing physical SQL database concepts

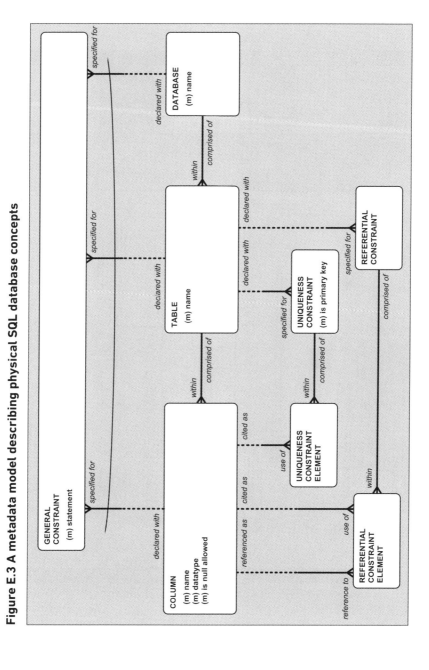

Figure E.4 A metadata model showing mapping between elements

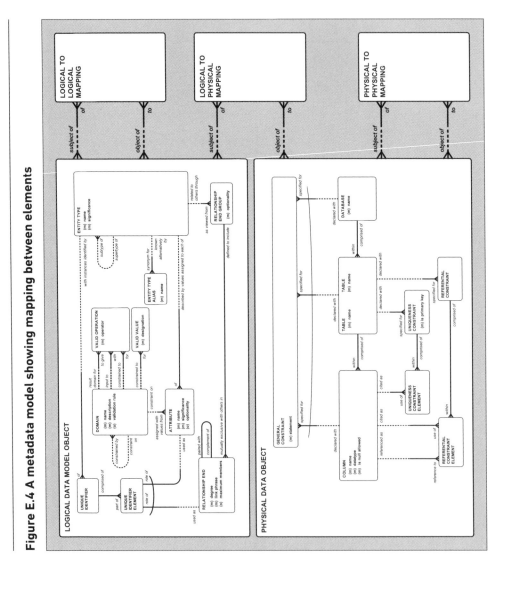

supertype and its two entity subtypes are implemented in one system by a single table with a number of constraints and in another system by three tables with two referential constraints and a general constraint to make those two referential constraints mutually exclusive at the 'supertype' end). The entity types **LOGICAL TO LOGICAL MAPPING**, **LOGICAL TO PHYSICAL MAPPING** and **PHYSICAL TO PHYSICAL MAPPING** shown in Figure E.4 are high-level entity types – the detail required to actually achieve the mapping is more complex.

THE INCLUSION OF PROCESSES

It is often useful to also map the logical and physical data structures to their equivalents associated with the processing of data – the process model, the programs and the modules in the applications. An early example of the application of this is the Data Dictionary System (DDS) developed by ICL Ltd (now Fujitsu Services Limited). This was originally released in 1976. It was the first commercially available data dictionary system to support both analysis of the business area and the design and development of the information system to support that business area. The structure of the DDS is shown in Figure E.5.

Figure E.5 The ICL Data Dictionary System

The left-hand side of the DDS provides for the documentation of the processes and applications; the right-hand side covers the data model and the database structure. The top half is labelled as the 'Real World' and covers the process and conceptual data models; the bottom half is labelled as the 'Computer World' and covers the applications and database structures.

APPENDIX F
A DATA MINING EXAMPLE

INTRODUCTION

This example uses just one statistical technique, the a-priori algorithm. This algorithm is used to find association rules in data. It uses data that appears more than a certain percentage of the time, the 'support threshold'.

THE SCENARIO

A supermarket chain wishes to determine whether customers opt for either 'own-label' products or branded products.

Raw data is available for each customer's purchases, recording the quantities of each product bought during each supermarket visit. The data from 500 such visits will be investigated.

The support threshold is 15 per cent.

Step 1

The raw data is scanned to determine the frequency of each product category bought during a visit. The results satisfying the support threshold are shown in Table F.1

Table F.1 A-priori algorithm: Step 1 results

Product category	Count
Branded bread	286
Own-label bread	238
Own-label breakfast cereals	225
Branded breakfast cereals	192
Eggs	178
Potatoes	160

Step 2

The raw data is scanned again to determine the frequency of each pair of product categories bought during a visit. The results satisfying the support threshold are shown in Table F.2.

Table F.2 A-priori algorithm: Step 2 results

Product category pairs	Count
Branded breakfast cereals and branded bread	160
Own-label breakfast cereals and own-label bread	155
Eggs and branded bread	94
Eggs and own-label breakfast cereals	93
Potatoes and branded bread	83
Eggs and branded breakfast cereals	80
Eggs and own-label bread	78
Potatoes and own-label bread	77

Step 3

For each result in Step 2, the confidence level for the association rules for the pairs of product categories is calculated using the count figures from Steps 1 and 2. The results are shown in Table F.3.

Table F.3 A-priori algorithm: Step 3 results

Product category pairs	Association rules	Confidence
Branded breakfast cereals and branded bread	If branded breakfast cereals are bought then branded bread is also bought	160/192 = 83%
	If branded bread is bought then branded breakfast cereals are also bought	160/286 = 56%
Own-label breakfast cereals and own-label bread	If own-label breakfast cereals are bought then own-label bread is also bought	155/225 = 69%
	If own-label bread is bought then own-label breakfast cereals are also bought	155/238 = 65%
Eggs and branded bread	If eggs are bought then branded bread is also bought	94/178 = 53%
	If branded bread is bought then eggs are also bought	94/286 = 33%
Eggs and own-label breakfast cereals	If eggs are bought then own-label breakfast cereals are also bought	93/178 = 52%
	If own-label breakfast cereals are bought then eggs are also bought	93/225 = 41%
Potatoes and branded bread	If potatoes are bought then branded bread is also bought	83/160 = 52%
	If branded bread is bought then potatoes are also bought	83/286 = 29%
Eggs and branded breakfast cereals	If eggs are bought then branded breakfast cereals are also bought	80/178 = 45%
	If branded breakfast cereals are bought then eggs are also bought	80/192 = 42%
Eggs and own-label bread	If eggs are bought then own-label bread is also bought	78/178 = 44%
	If own-label bread is bought then eggs are also bought	78/238 = 33%
Potatoes and own-label bread	If potatoes are bought then own-label bread is also bought	77/160 = 48%
	If own-label bread is bought then potatoes are also bought	77/238 = 32%

Step 4

The raw data is scanned again to determine the frequency of each triple of product categories bought during a visit. The results satisfying the support threshold are shown in Table F.4.

Table F.4 A-priori algorithm: Step 4 results

Product category triples	Count
Branded breakfast cereals, eggs and branded bread	80
Own-label breakfast cereals, eggs and own-label bread	78

Step 5

For each result in Step 4, the confidence level for the association rules for the triples of product categories is calculated using the count figures from Steps 1, 2 and 4. The results are shown in Table F.5.

Step 6

The raw data is scanned again to determine the frequency of each quadruple of items bought during a visit. The results satisfying the support threshold are shown in Table F.6.

Table F.5 A-priori algorithm: Step 5 results

Product category triples	Association rules	Confidence
Branded breakfast cereals, eggs and branded bread	If branded breakfast cereals are bought then eggs and branded bread are also bought	80/192 = 42%
	If eggs are bought then branded breakfast cereals and branded bread are also bought	80/178 = 45%
	If branded bread is bought then eggs and branded breakfast cereals are also bought	80/286 = 28%
	If branded breakfast cereals and eggs are bought then branded bread is also bought	80/80 = 100%
	If branded breakfast cereals and branded bread are bought then eggs are also bought	80/160 = 50%
	If eggs and branded bread are bought then branded breakfast cereals are also bought	80/94 = 85%
Own-label breakfast cereals, eggs and own-label bread	If own-label breakfast cereals are bought then eggs and own-label bread are also bought	78/225 = 35%
	If eggs are bought then own-label breakfast cereals and own-label bread are also bought	78/178 = 44%
	If own-label bread is bought then own-label breakfast cereals and eggs are also bought	78/238 = 33%
	If own-label breakfast cereals and eggs are bought then own-label bread is also bought	78/93 = 84%
	If own-label breakfast cereals and own-label bread are bought then eggs are also bought	78/155 = 50%
	If eggs and own-label bread are bought then own-label breakfast cereals are also bought	78/78 = 100%

Table F.6 A-priori algorithm: Step 6 results

Product category quadruples	Count

Since there are no results that satisfy the support threshold, the process stops.

CONCLUSIONS

The following association rules are significant:

- If branded breakfast cereals are bought then branded bread is also bought (83%).
- If own-label breakfast cereals are bought then own-label bread is also bought (69%).
- If branded breakfast cereals and eggs are bought then branded bread is also bought (100%).
- If eggs and branded bread are bought then branded breakfast cereals are also bought (85%).
- If own-label breakfast cereals and eggs are bought then own-label bread is also bought (84%).
- If eggs and own-label bread are bought then own-label breakfast cereals are also bought (100%).

These significant association rules suggest that customers consistently purchase own-label or branded goods.

INTRODUCTION

As described in Chapter 17, both HyperText Markup Language (HTML) and eXtensible Markup Language (XML) are derived from the Standard Generalised Markup Language (SGML). In SGML, extra information is provided by means of 'tags', enabling SGML documents to be read by both machines and humans.

HTML

The tags provided within an HTML document are purely concerned with the way that the information in the document is presented (rendered, to use the technical term) by a web browser. HTML tags can be used to achieve a number of effects. As well as enabling basic text formatting, HTML tags can specify links, known as hypertext links, to other information both within the document and in other documents. They can also be used to call for the display of images stored externally to the HTML document. Program code created in a scripting language such as JavaScript or PHP can also be hosted within HTML documents, along with some limited features that allow data to be input to feed the scripting-language programs.

In an HTML document, the tags are enclosed in 'angle brackets' and in most cases are used in pairs, an opening tag and a complementary closing tag. The whole document is enclosed within a pair of tags that indicate that this is an HTML document; the opening tag is <html> and the closing tag </html>, the '/' being used in markup languages to indicate a closing tag. The document consists of two sections: a header, enclosed within the <head> and </head> tags, and a main body, enclosed within the <body> and </body> tags. The header provides information about the document to the browser while the body contains the information to be displayed.

Figure G.1 shows a document formatted using HTML and Figure G.2 shows the result of rendering this document using a web browser, Mozilla Firefox.

The header of the document in Figure G.1 contains two elements. The title element is mandatory and the text enclosed within the <title> and </title> tags is displayed in the title bar of the browser when the document is rendered, as can be seen in Figure G.2. The second element is an example of a metadata element. In this case the metadata element identifies me as the author of the document. Metadata elements are not displayed.

Figure G.1 An example of an HTML document

```
<html>
  <head>
    <title> Display of Fig G.1 </title>
    <meta name="author" content="Keith Gordon">
  </head>
  <body>
    <p align="right"><a name="top"></a>This is the top.
       <a href="#bottom">Click here</a> to move to the bottom.</p>
    <h1>  Principles of Data Management </h1>
    <h2>  Facilitating Information Sharing </h2>
    <p>This book is called <em>Principles of Data Management</em> but it is really
       about having the policies and procedures in place within an organization
       so that the various information systems that the organization uses to
       support its activities can provide high quality information to their users,
       even if that information did not originate in the information system that the
       user is currently using.<br><br>For this to happen the organization's information
       systems must be able to share information.<br><br>This book is aimed at three
       audiences:<ul> <li><strong>Data management practitioners</strong>, already
       committed to data management but need more information.<li><strong>IT/IS managers
       </strong>, who need to understand the involvement required and the implications
       of implementing data management.<li><strong>Business managers</strong>, who need
       to understand why data management is important to a business.</ul></p>
    <p>You can review a <a href="booksummary.htm">summary of each chapter of
       the book</a> or see <a href="dataandinformation.jpg">an example of a
       diagram from the book</a><br><br>This book is published by the
       <a href="http://www.bcs.org">BCS, The Chartered Institute for IT</a></p>
    <p><img src="bcslogo.jpg" width="60" height="75" border="0" align="middle" /></p>
    <p align="right"><a name="bottom"></a>This is the bottom.
       <a href="#top">Click here</a> to move to the top.</p>
  </body>
</html>
```

The body of the document contains seven elements. These are five paragraphs, enclosed by <p> and </p> tags, and two headings. The first heading is at the highest heading level, enclosed by <h1> and </h1> tags, and the other heading is at the second-highest heading level, enclosed by <h2> and </h2> tags. HTML provides six levels of headings.

The main body of the text is contained in the first paragraph after the headings. The title of the book, Principles of Data Management, is enclosed by emphasis tags, the <em> and </em> tags. Most browsers render emphasis as italics; the same effect could be achieved by enclosing the title in <i> and </i> tags. Line breaks are forced in the paragraph by using <br> tags, for which there are no corresponding closing tags. This first paragraph ends with a list enclosed by <ul> and </ul> tags. This is an unordered list, so the items in the list are preceded by bullet points. If this had been an ordered list, using <ol> and </ol> tags, each item in the list would have been preceded by a number. The start of each list item is denoted by a <li> tag; there are no closing list item tags. The first few words of each list item are enclosed in <strong> and </strong> tags, which most browsers render as bold text; the same effect can be achieved by using <b> and </b> tags.

The next paragraph provides the user with hyperlinks to another document, an image and a website. Each of these hyperlinks is enclosed within <a> and </a> tags. The text between these tags is normally rendered in a different colour and underlined, the common representation for a hyperlink. Most regular users of web browsers understand that they need to click on this link with their mouse to move to the resource referenced

Figure G.2 The HTML document rendered in Mozilla Firefox

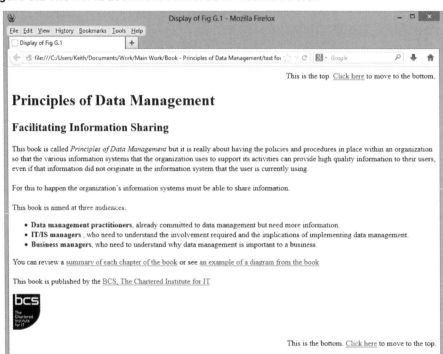

by the link. The opening tag of each of these pairs of <a> and </a> tags has a single attribute that provides the hyperlink reference for the resource that the browser is to open if this link is selected. The first opening <a> tag has a reference attribute, href="booksummary.htm", that is the name of an HTML document that is co-located with the current document (no path information is provided, so it is assumed to be in the same location as the current document). The second opening <a> tag has a reference attribute, href="dataandinformation.jpg", that is the name of a JPEG image that is also co-located with the current document. This image is displayed as a complete page by the web browser. The final opening <a> tag of this paragraph has a reference attribute, href="http://www.bcs.org", that is the URI of the BCS website.

The next paragraph is an instruction to display the image contained in the "bcslogo.jpg" file within the page.

The first and last paragraphs are similar to each other and are there to provide navigation within the document. They are both aligned to the right of the page using the align attribute in the opening <p> tag and they both contain two sets of <a> and </a> tags to enable the in-document navigation. The first set of <a> and </a> tags in the first paragraph provides an anchor point in the document, called "top". The second set of <a> and </a> tags in the last paragraph contains the hyperlink reference, 'href="#top"', to enable navigation to that anchor point in the document. The other sets of <a> and </a> tags in these two paragraphs provide for navigation in the opposite direction to the bottom of the document. The example document is relatively short and these navigation anchor points and references are not really needed. They are included here to show how navigation may be provided within a large document.

HTML is purely concerned with the way that an information resource such as a document is presented by a web browser. It is not concerned with the meaning of the information contained in the document.

XML

XML is concerned with the definition and structure of the information in the document. XML has no tags to specify presentation.

Figure G.3 An example of an XML document

```
<?xml version = "1.0"?>
<department>
  <department-name>Finance</department-name>
  <department-telephone>452</department-telephone>
  <department-manager>CX137</department-manager>
  <department-staff>
    <employee>
      <staff-no>AY334</staff-no>
      <first-name>Barbara</first-name>
      <last-name>Watson</last-name>
      <birth-date>12 June 1952</birth-date>
      <start-date>3 June 1994</start-date>
    </employee>
    <employee>
      <staff-no>CX137</staff-no>
      <first-name>Jenny</first-name>
      <last-name>Rogers</last-name>
      <birth-date>10 January 1970</birth-date>
      <start-date>3 January 1995</start-date>
      <qualifications>
        <qualification>
          <qualification-name>Dip FM</qualification-name>
          <qualification-award-date>September 1998</qualification-award-date>
        </qualification>
        <qualification>
          <qualification-name>ACCA</qualification-name>
          <qualification-award-date>2 October 2003</qualification-award-date>
        </qualification>
        <qualification>
          <qualification-name>First Aid</qualification-name>
          <qualification-award-date>30 April 2005</qualification-award-date>
          <qualification-expiry-date>29 April 2008</qualification-expiry-date>
        </qualification>
      </qualifications>
    </employee>
    <employee>
      <staff-no>DJ777</staff-no>
      <first-name>Henry</first-name>
      <last-name>Phillips</last-name>
      <birth-date>5 May 1974</birth-date>
      <start-date>3 September 1992</start-date>
    </employee>
    <employee>
      <staff-no>FL233</staff-no>
      <first-name>Jane</first-name>
      <last-name>Smith</last-name>
      <birth-date>25 August 1989</birth-date>
      <start-date>8 December 2006</start-date>
    </employee>
  </department-staff>
</department>
</xml>
```

Figure G.3 shows an example of an XML document that provides details of the Finance department and its staff. Each item of data is known as an element and is enclosed within tags that describe the meaning of the data. For example, the element that is the name of a qualification is enclosed within <qualification-name> and </qualification-name> tags. Elements can be grouped. The name and award date of a qualification are both within a larger 'qualification' element, enclosed within <qualification> and </qualification> tags, and, in turn, a number of qualifications are listed within an even larger 'qualifications' element, enclosed within <qualifications> and </qualifications> tags.

XML documents have an inverted tree structure. At the top is a single root element, the 'department' element in this case. The tree structure for our document is shown in Figure G.4.

Figure G.4 The tree structure of the XML document

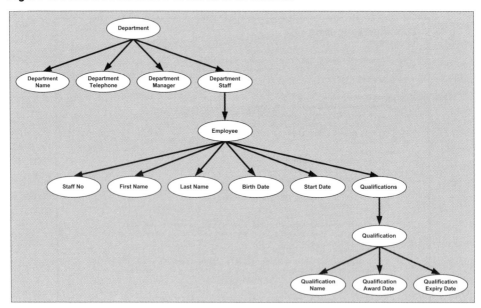

A valid XML document meets a number of technical criteria, the most important ones being:

- There is a single root element.
- Start tags and end tags match exactly.
- There are no overlapping elements; each node in the tree has only one parent.

An XML document can easily be read by a human being, especially if it is well laid out. The XML document shown in this appendix has each element on a new line and indentation is used to illustrate the nesting of elements. However, a valid XML document can be laid out in any way. At the extreme there may be no new lines or spaces at all, although these documents are less easy for a human to read. An XML document is also machine-readable, providing the machine that is reading the document understands the tags.

In HTML the tags are all standardised and included in a specification published by the World Wide Web Consortium (W3C); there is no equivalent standard for XML. The data enclosed by the <last-name> and </last-name> tags in our example could just as easily have been enclosed by <lastname> and </lastname> tags, <family-name> and </family-name> tags, or <surname> and </surname> tags (and no doubt you can think of other possible tags that could be used here). The number of possible tags that can be used in an XML document is, therefore, infinite; the definition of tags is uncontrolled. The lack of standard tags for XML is a problem. XML provides a very effective way to transfer data but the XML structure to be used for that transfer of data has to be defined in the same way that a structure, or schema, has to be defined for a relational database. Both sending and receiving parties, be they machines or humans, have to use the same elements, with those elements specified with the same enclosing tags, and the meaning of the content of those elements being unambiguously defined. Without common element definitions, data cannot be transferred. If XML is to be used within an enterprise or between enterprises, there has to be the same commitment to data definition as would be needed for common database designs for the sharing of data between databases. The set of allowed elements needs to be defined and the structure, the way that elements can be nested within each other, also needs to be specified. For example, 'qualifications' can be within 'employee', 'qualification' can be within 'qualifications', and 'qualification-name' can be within 'qualification'. There have been a number of initiatives within particular industries to develop standard XML formats for the exchange of data between companies within that industry, but these initiatives are not co-ordinated. You can, therefore, end up with different formats for the same concept in different industries.

There are other problems with XML. First, it can generate documents that are very verbose to get over some quite simple data; this verbosity can inflate transmission and storage costs. Second, there are no datatypes in XML; everything is a character string. Third, all XML structures are hierarchical in nature. This is a step backwards – hierarchical databases were replaced by network databases and then by relational databases because it is extremely difficult to represent the full complexity of data relationships using a hierarchical model alone. See Appendix B for an overview of hierarchical and network databases.

To document XML definitions and in an attempt to overcome some of these problems, the overall XML architecture includes a number of other components:

- Document Type Definition (DTD) is a specification of the rules a group of XML documents must follow to be valid; for example the elements that are allowed within a document are specified. One problem with DTDs is that they are expressed in a language that is not XML.

- XML Schema Definition (XSD) is another way to specify the rules for a group of XML documents. An XSD is specified using an XML schema language and allows for more detailed constraints on a document's logical structure than can be achieved with a DTD.

- eXtensible Stylesheet Language (XSL) is the standard for describing presentation rules that apply to XML documents. The format of XML data can be converted into HTML so that it can be displayed using a web browser.

- XSL Transformations (XSLT) is a specification that describes how to transform XML documents from one format to another.

- XLink is a specification that describes how to define links between XML documents.

- XPointer is a specification that describes how to specify a particular element within a document as the target of a link.

- XPath makes it possible to refer to individual parts of an XML document to provide access to XML data from elsewhere.

- XQuery is a query language for XML. It is analogous to SQL in relational databases but it can only be used to read data, not to manipulate it. XQuery provides the ability to navigate, select, combine, transform, sort and aggregate XML data.

APPENDIX H
XML AND RELATIONAL DATABASES

INTRODUCTION

As described in Chapter 17, the latest SQL standard includes a new part known as SQL/XML. This part introduces an **XML** datatype and facilities that provide for the composition of **XML** using data extracted from a relational database and, conversely, for the storage of data extracted from an XML document in a relational database. The **XML** datatype can be used in the same way as any other datatype, i.e. as a datatype for a column, as a variable or as a parameter for a function.

REPRESENTING DATA FROM A DATABASE AS XML

The facilities that enable data to be extracted and then represented as XML offer a range of alternatives. The specimen data stored in the relational database tables shown in Figure H.1 are used to demonstrate these facilities.

Figure H.1 Specimen data for XML representation examples

department

name	telephone_number	managed_by
HQ	NULL	NULL
Finance	ext 452	CX137
Production	ext 664	CA446

employee

payroll_number	surname	forename	birth_date	start_date	department
AY334	Watson	Barbara	1952-12-06	1994-06-03	Finance
CX137	Rogers	Jenny	1970-01-10	1995-01-03	Finance
DJ777	Phillips	Henry	1974-05-05	1992-09-03	Finance
FJ678	Harrison	Roger	1988-04-27	2004-11-05	Finance

employee_qualification

payroll_number	name	award_date	expiry_date
CX137	Dip FM	1998-09	NULL
CX137	ACCA	2003-10-20	NULL
CX137	First Aid	2005-04-30	2008-04-29

One option is to output the complete contents of a table or a schema into a standard XML structure using a simple mapping. There are two possible approaches to this. The first of these approaches provides a structure that is a valid XML document. Figure H.2 shows the XML obtained when outputting the contents of the **employee** table using this approach.

The XML shown in Figure H.2 is a valid XML document because the XML is in the form of a true hierarchy, having a single root element. In this case the root element is called 'employee', the name being automatically derived from the name of the table. There are a series of elements, called 'row', for each row in the table. Within each 'row' element there is an element for each column in the table, with the element name also being automatically derived from the column names.

Figure H.2 The employee table represented as a valid XML document

```
<employee>
  <row>
    <payroll_number>AY334</payroll_number>
    <surname>Watson</surname>
    <forename>Barbara</forename>
    <birth_date>1952-12-06</birth_date>
    <start_date>1994-06-03</start_date>
    <department>Finance</department>
  </row>
  <row>
    <payroll_number>CX137</payroll_number>
    <surname>Rogers</surname>
    <forename>Jenny</forename>
    <birth_date>1970-01-10</birth_date>
    <start_date>1995-01-03</start_date>
    <department>Finance</department>
  </row>
  <row>
    <payroll_number>DJ777</payroll_number>
    <surname>Phillips</surname>
    <forename>Henry</forename>
    <birth_date>1974-05-05</birth_date>
    <start_date>1992-09-03</start_date>
    <department>Finance</department>
  </row>
  <row>
    <payroll_number>FJ678</payroll_number>
    <surname>Harrison</surname>
    <forename>Roger</forename>
    <birth_date>1988-04-27</birth_date>
    <start_date>2004-11-05</start_date>
    <department>Finance</department>
  </row>
</employee>
```

The alternative approach provides XML elements without the root element. Figure H.3 shows the XML obtained when outputting the contents of the **employee** table using this alternative approach.

Figure H.3 The employee table represented as XML without a root element

```
<employee>
    <payroll_number>AY334</payroll_number>
    <surname>Watson</surname>
    <forename>Barbara</forename>
    <birth_date>1952-12-06</birth_date>
    <start_date>1994-06-03</start_date>
    <department>Finance</department>
</employee>
<employee>
    <payroll_number>CX137</payroll_number>
    <surname>Rogers</surname>
    <forename>Jenny</forename>
    <birth_date>1970-01-10</birth_date>
    <start_date>1995-01-03</start_date>
    <department>Finance</department>
</employee>
<employee>
    <payroll_number>DJ777</payroll_number>
    <surname>Phillips</surname>
    <forename>Henry</forename>
    <birth_date>1974-05-05</birth_date>
    <start_date>1992-09-03</start_date>
    <department>Finance</department>
</employee>
<employee>
    <payroll_number>FJ678</payroll_number>
    <surname>Harrison</surname>
    <forename>Roger</forename>
    <birth_date>1988-04-27</birth_date>
    <start_date>2004-11-05</start_date>
    <department>Finance</department>
</employee>
```

The XML shown in Figure H.3 has a series of elements, each named after the table name, with one element for each row of the table, but it lacks a root element. As before, within each row element there is an element for each column in the table, with the element name automatically derived from the column names. This output could be made into a valid XML document by simply adding a root element. This could be done automatically by the database management system.

It is also possible to create an XML document that contains data selected from one or more tables. This is achieved by using special SQL functions, known as XML publishing functions, within an SQL **SELECT** query. For example, the query shown in Figure H.4 can be used to produce the XML document similar to that shown in Figure H.5 (which is a copy of Figure G.3) from the data in Figure H.1.

Figure H.4 An example SQL query to create an XML document

```
SELECT
   XMLELEMENT (NAME department,
     XMLELEMENT (NAME department-name, department.name),
     XMLELEMENT (NAME department-telephone, department.telephone_number),
     XMLELEMENT (NAME department-manager, department.managed_by),
     XMLELEMENT (NAME department-staff,
       (SELECT
          XMLAGG (XMLELEMENT (NAME employee,
            XMLELEMENT (NAME staff-no, employee.payroll_number),
            XMLELEMENT (NAME first-name, employee.forename),
            XMLELEMENT (NAME last-name, employee.surname),
            XMLELEMENT (NAME birth-date, employee.birth_date),
            XMLELEMENT (NAME start-date, employee.start_date),
            XMLELEMENT (NAME qualifications,
              (SELECT
                 XMLAGG (XMLELEMENT (NAME qualification,
                   XMLFOREST (employee_qualification.name AS qualification-name,
                              employee_qualification.award_date AS qualification-award-date,
                              employee_qualification.expiry_date AS qualification-expiry-date)
               FROM employee_qualification
               WHERE employee.payroll_number = employee_qualification.payroll_number)
        FROM employee
        WHERE department.name = employee.department))))))))
   AS department-details
FROM department
WHERE department.name = 'Finance';
```

The query uses the three publishing functions **XMLELEMENT**, **XMLAGG** and **XMLFOREST**, all of which return XML structures of the **XML** datatype.

The **XMLELEMENT** function has two arguments. The first of these is the name that is to be given to the XML element that is produced and the second is the data that is to form that element. In Figure H.5 the first use of **XMLELEMENT** provides the department root element (the first argument is **NAME department**) and has as its second argument the specification of the hierarchy of elements that forms the rest of the document. The second use of **XMLELEMENT** provides the first element within the root element. This provides the name of the department (the first argument is **NAME department-name**) and has as its second argument the name of the column (**department.name**) from which the data is to be obtained. The second argument for the **XMLELEMENT** function can be any valid SQL expression, so it can even be an SQL **SELECT** sub-query. This is shown in the fifth use of the **XMLELEMENT** function.

The **XMLAGG** function takes a single argument, the specification of an element, and returns XML that is a series of these elements. The 'department-staff' element is an aggregation of a number of 'employee' elements, where each employee has a 'staff-no', 'first-name', 'last-name' and so on, and the 'qualifications' element is an aggregation of a number of 'qualification' elements.

Each 'qualification' element is created using the **XMLFOREST** function. This function produces a 'forest' of elements (remember, an element is logically a hierarchical 'tree' even if it only has one node) where each argument specifies one of these elements. The 'qualification' element uses data from the **name** column, the **award_date** column and the **expiry_date** column of the **employee_qualification** table, but these are renamed

Figure H.5 An example of an XML document

```xml
<?xml version = "1.0"?>
<department>
  <department-name>Finance</department-name>
  <department-telephone>452</department-telephone>
  <department-manager>CX137</department-manager>
  <department-staff>
    <employee>
      <staff-no>AY334</staff-no>
      <first-name>Barbara</first-name>
      <last-name>Watson</last-name>
      <birth-date>12 June 1952</birth-date>
      <start-date>3 June 1994</start-date>
    </employee>
    <employee>
      <staff-no>CX137</staff-no>
      <first-name>Jenny</first-name>
      <last-name>Rogers</last-name>
      <birth-date>10 January 1970</birth-date>
      <start-date>3 January 1995</start-date>
      <qualifications>
        <qualification>
          <qualification-name>Dip FM</qualification-name>
          <qualification-award-date>September 1998</qualification-award-date>
        </qualification>
        <qualification>
          <qualification-name>ACCA</qualification-name>
          <qualification-award-date>2 October 2003</qualification-award-date>
        </qualification>
        <qualification>
          <qualification-name>First Aid</qualification-name>
          <qualification-award-date>30 April 2005</qualification-award-date>
          <qualification-expiry-date>29 April 2008</qualification-expiry-date>
        </qualification>
      </qualifications>
    </employee>
    <employee>
      <staff-no>DJ777</staff-no>
      <first-name>Henry</first-name>
      <last-name>Phillips</last-name>
      <birth-date>5 May 1974</birth-date>
      <start-date>3 September 1992</start-date>
    </employee>
    <employee>
      <staff-no>FL233</staff-no>
      <first-name>Jane</first-name>
      <last-name>Smith</last-name>
      <birth-date>25 August 1989</birth-date>
      <start-date>8 December 2006</start-date>
    </employee>
  </department-staff>
</department>
</xml>
```

as 'qualification-name', 'qualification-award-date' and 'qualification-expiry-date' respectively.

We have already seen that the XML values returned by the **XMLELEMENT**, **XMLAGG** and **XMLFOREST** publishing functions are of the **XML** datatype. This is a datatype that is only known to the database management system. These values can, however, be converted to character strings using another SQL/XML function, the **XMLSERIALISE** function.

EXTRACTING RELATIONAL DATA FROM AN XML DOCUMENT

Just as there are a number of alternative approaches to extracting data from a relational database and publishing it as XML, there are also a number of approaches that can be used to take data from an XML document and place it in a relational database.

One approach is to use the concept of shredding, where the content of the XML document is decomposed and stored in tables created using the XML structure. For example, the XML document in Figure H.5 can be shredded back into the structure in Figure H.1 (although it yields only one row, the 'Finance' row, in the **department** table). Alternatively an XML document can be shredded into a single table, known as an 'edge' table. Figure H.6 shows the edge table created from the document in Figure H.5. This edge table can then be used to populate other database tables.

There is also a function known as the **XMLTABLE** function. This function produces a virtual SQL table containing data derived from XML values. There are two arguments for this function. The first is the specification, expressed using XQuery, of the XML values that are used to provide the data for the virtual table. The second argument is a set of column definitions for the virtual table. The names of these columns may match the names of the relevant XML elements, in which case the column is automatically populated with data from that element. If the column names and the XML element names do not match, an XQuery expression has to be used to identify the source XML element for that column. Figure H.7 shows an example query using **XMLTABLE** and Figure H.8 shows the virtual table produced as a result of executing that query.

The data in this table can then be manipulated using SQL in the same way that the data in any other SQL table can be manipulated.

Figure H.6 An edge table created by shredding an XML document

parent_id	child_id	node_name	content
null	1	department	null
1	2	department-name	Finance
1	3	department-telephone	452
1	4	department-manager	CX137
1	5	department-staff	null
5	6	employee	null
6	7	staff-no	AY334
6	8	first-name	Barbara
6	9	last-name	Watson
6	10	birth-date	12 June 1952
6	11	start-date	3 June 1994
5	12	employee	null
12	13	staff-no	CX137
12	14	first-name	Jenny
12	15	last-name	Rogers
12	16	birth-date	10 January 1970
12	17	start-date	3 January 1995
12	18	qualifications	null
18	19	qualification	null
19	20	qualification-name	Dip FM
19	21	qualification-award-date	September 1998
18	22	qualification	null
22	23	qualification-name	ACCA
22	24	qualification-award-date	2 October 2003
18	25	qualification	null
25	26	qualification-name	First Aid
25	27	qualification-award-date	30 April 2005
25	28	qualification-expiry-date	29 April 2008
5	29	employee	null
29	30	staff-no	DJ777
29	31	first-name	Henry
29	32	last-name	Phillips
29	33	birth-date	5 May 1974
29	34	start-date	3 September 1992
5	35	employee	null
35	36	staff-no	FL233
35	37	first-name	Jane
35	38	last-name	Smith
35	39	birth-date	25 August 1989
35	40	start-date	8 December 2006

Figure H.7 A query on an XML document

```
SELECT payroll_number, surname
FROM XMLTABLE (
   'doc("file:///C:/query/finance_department.xml")//department-staff'
   COLUMNS payroll_number CHAR(5) PATH 'employee/staff-no',
           surname VARCHAR(25) PATH 'employee/last-name',
           birth_date DATE PATH 'employee/birth-date')
WHERE birth_date < '1973-01-01';
```

Figure H.8 The result of the query on an XML document

payroll_number	surname
AY334	Watson
CX137	Rogers

APPENDIX I
TECHNIQUES AND SKILLS FOR DATA MANAGEMENT

TECHNIQUES AND SKILLS FOR DATA ADMINISTRATION

Data administration is often situated in a highly technical environment. Data administrators need to be able to communicate with skilled IT or IS technicians but they also need to be able to communicate with business-oriented managers and end-users. The ideal data administrator should have knowledge, experience and expertise in a variety of areas relating both to the organisation and to the IT or IS environment. The skills that are required by a data administrator are shown in Figure I.1.

Figure I.1 The data administration skill set

An understanding of the organisation is essential. The data administrator needs an in-depth knowledge of:

* the structure of the organisation;
* the products or services developed or sold by the organisation;
* the major competitors of the organisation;

- the business strategy of the organisation;
- the internal politics within the organisation;
- the management practices and procedures;
- the relationship between different departments within the organisation;
- the relationship between different companies in a group.

An understanding of data analysis and modelling, database design and administration and, of course, data dictionaries or repositories is extremely useful, but the level of expertise required is dependent on the tools and techniques in use. If the data management staff are responsible for the development of methodologies or for the use of software tools, this also impacts upon the level of technical expertise required.

Communication is a fundamental skill, as a data administrator needs to talk to personnel throughout the organisation at all levels. The data administrator needs to be able to promote data management, interview staff at all levels in order to understand the need for data, make formal presentations, write clear and concise reports and be comfortable in all communication activities. Good negotiating skills are also essential as there are many issues concerning the use of data to be resolved.

To be able to understand complex and often ill-defined problems, and to resolve them, is an essential skill of a data administrator. So it is useful for the data administrator to be a lateral thinker, able to take a number of differing views, put them together and produce an innovative practical solution.

Unfortunately not many organisations are able to recruit skilled data engineers with good communication and negotiating skills who are brilliant lateral thinkers and have a detailed knowledge of the organisation. If I was asked to rate these four areas in order of importance when seeking a recruit for data administration, the order would be:

- business knowledge;
- interpersonal skills;
- lateral thinking;
- data engineering knowledge.

The deep understanding of the business required by a data administrator can only be acquired through experience over a long time, which implies that data administrators should be appointed from within the organisation. Good interpersonal skills and lateral thinking are inherent; some people have them, others do not. Knowledge of data analysis, data modelling, database design and administration and data dictionaries or repositories can be taught quite easily once someone is in post. It should not, therefore, be an essential prerequisite for appointment as a data administrator. The post-appointment teaching required may be delivered in-house or through formal courses.

TECHNIQUES AND SKILLS FOR DATABASE ADMINISTRATION

The skills required by a database administrator are very different from those required by a data administrator. The good database administrator is an information technology professional who has:

- a detailed product knowledge of the database management systems in use within the enterprise;
- the ability to pay attention to detail;
- the ability to be diplomatic.

Database administrators are normally trained to work with one or more specific database management systems. Indeed most of the major database management system vendors, such as Oracle, Microsoft (with SQL Server) and IBM (with DB2) now offer certification for database administrators. While certification is helpful because it indicates that the database administrator has gone through a formal training programme so that they know the facilities provided by the product and the product-specific procedures for the database administration tasks, certification is not necessarily an indication of ability. The deep product knowledge that enables the database administrator to cope with an unexpected situation can only come from experience.

The personal skills required of a database administrator are the ability to pay attention to detail and diplomacy. The first of these is because there is a lot of detail involved in the administration of a database. Carrying out tasks in the right order at the right time is vital, as is the maintenance of meticulous records. Diplomacy is required because the database administrator needs to deal with questions and requests from business management and end-users, and these requests may sometimes be difficult, if not impossible, to fulfil.

In the case of the database administrator, technical skills and knowledge should take precedence over personal skills. The fundamental duties involve getting the best out of the database management systems in use in the organisation.

TECHNIQUES AND SKILLS FOR REPOSITORY ADMINISTRATION

Since there is similarity between the two roles, the techniques and skills required by the repository administrator are very similar to those required by the database administrator. The repository administrator is an IT professional, trained to work with the specific repository software that is in use. Again attention to detail is required. The main difference is that, whereas the database administrator needs to interact with business management and end-users, the repository administrator is principally interacting with data administrators.

APPENDIX J
INTERNATIONAL STANDARDS FOR DATA MANAGEMENT

There are a number of International Standards published by the International Organization for Standardization (ISO), sometimes in collaboration with the International Electrotechnical Commission (IEC), that are of interest to data managers. They include the following:

ISO/IEC TR 10032 – *Information technology – Reference model of data management*

This technical report establishes a framework for co-ordinating the development of existing and future standards for the management of persistent data in IT systems. It defines common terminology and concepts pertinent to all data held within IT systems. Such concepts are used to define more specifically the services provided by particular data management components, such as database management systems or data dictionary systems. This technical report, therefore, concentrates on the technical aspects of data management.

ISO/IEC 9075 – *Information technology – Database languages – SQL*

This multipart standard is the formal specification of SQL, which is the basis for the database languages used by the popular RDBMS systems. Object-relational features are now included in the language and there are additional parts that cover Call-Level Interfaces, Persistent Stored Modules, the Management of External Data, Information and Definition Schemas, Routines and Types Using the Java Programming Language, and XML-Related Specifications. The latest edition, published in 2012, includes 'system versioned tables' to handle temporal data.

ISO/IEC 13249 – *Information technology – Database languages – SQL multimedia and application packages*

This multipart standard makes use of the user-defined types now available in SQL to specify the requirements for packages to handle, amongst others, full text, still images and spatial data.

ISO/IEC 10027 – *Information technology – Information resource dictionary system (IRDS) framework*

This standard provides a specification for recording models, including handling the version control of elements within those models. Unfortunately, as far as I am aware, no products were ever developed that complied with this standard.

ISO/IEC 11179 – *Information technology – Metadata registries (MDR)*

This multipart standard focuses on the registration of data elements and their meanings. It includes the following parts:

Part 1: Framework

Part 2: Classification

Part 3: Registry metamodel and basic attributes

Part 4: Formulation of data definition

Part 5: Naming principles

Part 6: Registration

The published complete edition is the second edition. However the third edition is currently under development. At the time of writing, the third edition of Part 3 (*Registry metamodel and basic attributes*) has recently been published and third editions of the remaining parts are under development. The third edition of Part 3 extends the registry metamodel to include concept systems so the capability of a registry that conforms to the third edition of ISO/IEC 11179 will be much enhanced.

ISO/IEC 19773 – *Information technology – Metadata registries (MDR) modules*

This standard defines a number of standard modules for registration in metadata registries, including postal data, phone number data and entity-person-group (EPG) data. The content of this standard will also be useful to anyone who is interested in standardising ways of handling international addresses or phone numbers, even if there is no intention of implementing a metadata registry.

ISO/IEC 19763 – *Information technology – Metamodel framework for interoperability (MFI)*

This multipart standard, most of which is still under development, focuses on the registration of models and the mappings between models to aid interoperability. Within the scope of this standard, interoperability is interpreted in its broadest sense and is defined as 'the capability to communicate, execute programs, or transfer data among various functional units in a manner that requires the user to have little or no knowledge of the unique characteristics of those units'.

To achieve this, the standard will cover ontologies, information models (including entity-relationship models, UML class diagrams and SQL schemas), process models and models of roles, goals and services. The parts currently planned are:

Part 1: Framework

Part 3: Metamodel for ontology registration

Part 5: Metamodel for process model registration

Part 6: Registry Summary

237

Part 7: Metamodel for service registration

Part 8: Metamodel for role and goal registration

Part 9: On Demand Model Selection for RGPS

Part 10: Core model and basic mapping

Part 12: Metamodel for information model registration

Part 13: Metamodel for forms registration

Your author is the editor of Part 12 (*Metamodel for the information model registration*) and the co-editor of Part 1 (*Framework*) and Part 10 (*Core model and basic mapping*).

ISO/IEC 24707 – *Information technology – Common logic*

This standard specifies a family of logic languages designed for use in the representation and interchange of information and data among disparate computer systems. At the time of writing, work is beginning on the development of a second edition.

ISO 8000 – *Data quality*

This multipart standard, most of which is still under development, focuses on data quality. The development is being carried out by the ISO technical committee that is responsible for automation systems and integration although its application will be far greater than this area. The impetus for the standard was to combat the poor quality of the data that was being exchanged between companies that needed to do business together.

APPENDIX K
BIBLIOGRAPHY

Adelman, S., Moss, L. and Majid, A. (2005) *Data Strategy*. Addison-Wesley.

Aiken, P. and Allen, M.D. (2004) *XML in Data Management*. Morgan Kaufman.

Barker, R. (1990) *CASE*METHOD: Entity Relationship Modelling*. Addison-Wesley.

Batley, S (2007) *Information Architecture for Information Professionals*. Chandos Publishing.

Brackett, M.H. (1994) *Data Sharing Using a Common Data Architecture*. Wiley.

Butler Group (2004) *Data Quality and Integrity: Essential Steps for Exploiting Business Information*. Butler Direct Limited.

Cameron, S.A. (2011) *Enterprise Content Management: A Business and Technical Guide*. BCS.

Cattell, R.G.C. and Barry, D.K. (eds). *The Object Data Standard: ODMG 3.3*. Morgan Kaufman.

Central Computer and Telecommunications Agency (1994a) *Corporate Data Modelling*. HMSO.

Central Computer and Telecommunications Agency (1994b) *Data Management*. HMSO.

Central Computer and Telecommunications Agency (1995) *Data Management Standards*. HMSO.

Checkland, P. (1981) *Systems Thinking, Systems Practice*. John Wiley & Sons.

Checkland, P. and Holwell, S. (1998) *Information, Systems and Information Systems: Making Sense of the Field*. John Wiley & Sons.

Checkland, P. and Poulter, J. (2006) *Learning for Action: A Short Definitive Guide to Soft Systems Methodology and its use for Practitioners, Teachers and Students*. John Wiley & Sons.

Chen, P.P.S. (1976) The Entity-Relationship Model: Toward a Unified View of Data. *ACM Transactions on Database Systems*, 1(1). 9–36.

Chisholm, M.D. (2010) *Definitions in Information Management: A Guide to the Fundamental Semantic Metadata*. Design Media Publishing.

Codd, E.F. (1970) A Relational Model of Data for Large Shared Data Banks. *Communications of the ACM*, 13(6). 377–87.

Connelly, T.M. and Begg, C.E. (2004) *Database Systems: A Practical Approach to Design, Implementation and Management (4th edition).* Addison Wesley.

Date, C.J. (2001) *The Database Relational Model: A Retrospective Review and Analysis.* Addison-Wesley.

Date, C.J. (2003) *An Introduction to Database Systems (8th edition).* Addison-Wesley.

Date, C.J. (2005) *Database in Depth: Relational Theory for Practitioners.* O'Reilly.

Date, C.J. (2006) *Date on Database: Writings 2000-2006.* Apress.

Date, C.J. and Darwen, H (1997) *A Guide to the SQI Standard (4th edition).* Addison-Wesley.

Date, C.J., Darwen, H. and Lorentzos, N.A. (2003) *Temporal Data and the Relational Model.* Morgan Kaufman.

Dick, K. (2000) *XML: A Manager's Guide.* Addison-Wesley.

English, L.P. (2002) Total Quality data Management (TQdM) Methodology for Information Quality Improvement. In Piattini, M.G., Calero, C. and Genero, M.F. (eds). *Information and Database Quality.* Kluwer Academic Publishers.

Genero, M.F. and Piattini, M.G. (2002) Conceptual Model Quality. In Piattini, M.G., Calero, C. and Genero, M.F. (eds). *Information and Database Quality.* Kluwer Academic Publishers.

Halpin, T. and Morgan, T. (2008) *Information Modeling and Relational Databases.* Morgan Kaufman.

Hay, D.C. (1996) *Data Model Patterns: Conventions of Thought.* Dorset House.

Hay, D.C. (2003) *Requirements Analysis: From Business Views to Architecture.* Prentice Hall.

Hay, D.C. (2011a) *Enterprise Model Patterns: The UML Version.* Technics Publications.

Hay, D.C. (2011b) *UML and Data Modelling: A Reconciliation.* Technics Publications.

Hillard, R. (2010) *Information-Driven Business: How to Manage Data and Information for Maximum Advantage.* John Wiley & Sons.

Howe, D (2001) *Data Analysis for Database Design (3rd edition).* Butterworth-Heinemann.

Inmon, W.H. and Nesavich. A. (2008) *Tapping into Unstructured Data: Integrating Unstructured Data and Textual Analytics into Business Intelligence.* Prentice Hall.

Inmon, W.H., O'Neil, B. and Fryman. L. (2008) *Business Metadata: Capturing Enterprise Knowledge.* Prentice Hall.

ISO/IEC 13249-2 (2003) *Information Technology – Database languages – SQL multimedia and application packages – Full-text.*

ISO/IEC 13249-3 (2011) *Information Technology – Database languages – SQL multimedia and application packages – Spatial.*

ISO/IEC 13249-5 (2003) *Information Technology – Database languages – SQL multimedia and application packages – Still image.*

ISO/IEC 2382-1 (1993) *Information Technology – Vocabulary – Part 1: Fundamental terms.*

ISO/IEC 9075 (2011) *Information Technology – Database languages – SQL.*

Krogstie, J., Halpin, T. and Siau, K. (2005) *Information Modeling Methods and Methodologies.* Idea Group Publishing.

Lambe, P (2007) *Organising Knowledge: Taxonomies, Knowledge and Organisational Effectiveness.* Chandos Publishing.

Lee, Y.L et al. (2006) *Journey to Data Quality.* The MIT Press.

Loshin, D. (2001) *Enterprise Knowledge Management: The Data Quality Approach.* Morgan Kaufman.

Maydanchik, A. (2007) *Data Quality Assessment.* Technics Publications.

McGilvray, D. (2008) *Executing Data Quality Projects: TEN STEPS to Quality Data and Trusted Information.* Morgan Kaufman.

Melton, J. (2003) *Advanced SQL:1999: Understanding Object-Relational and Other Advanced Features.* Morgan Kaufman.

Melton, J. and Simon, A.R. (2002) *SQL:1999: Understanding Relational Language Components.* Morgan Kaufman.

Morris, J. (2012) *Practical Data Migration (2nd edition).* BCS.

Mullins, C.S. (2002) *Database Administration: The Complete Guide to Practices and Procedures.* Addison-Wesley.

Olson, J.E. (2003) *Data Quality: The Accuracy Dimension.* Morgan Kaufman.

Pascal, F. (2000) *Practical Issues in Database Management: A Reference for the Thinking Practitioner.* Addison-Wesley.

PricewaterhouseCoopers (2004) *Global Data Management Survey.*

Redman, T.C. (2001) *Data Quality: The Field Guide.* Digital Press.

Reingruber, M. and Gregory, W.W. (1994) *The Data Modeling Handbook: A Best-Practice Approach to Building Quality Data Models.* Wiley-QED.

Ritchie, C. (2002) *Relational Database Principles (2nd edition).* Thomson.

Sadalage, P.J. and Fowler, M. (2013) *NoSQL Distilled: A Brief Guide to the Emerging World of Polyglot Persistence.* Addison-Wesley.

Simsion, G. (2007) *Data Modeling: Theory and Practice.* Technics Publications.

Simsion, G. and Witt, G. (2004) *Data Modeling Essentials (3rd edition).* Morgan Kaufman.

Sprague, R.A., Jnr. and McNurlin, B.C. (1993) *Information Systems Management and Practice (3rd edition).* Prentice Hall.

Stowell, F.A. (ed) (1995) *Information Systems Provision: The Contribution of Soft Systems Methodology.* McGraw-Hill.

Symons, C.R. and Tijsma, P. (1982) A Systematic and Practical Approach to the Definition of Data. *The Computer Journal,* 25(24).

Tozer, G. (1999) *Metadata Management for Information Control and Business Success.* Artech.

West, M. (2011) *Developing High Quality Data Models.* Morgan Kaufman.

Wilson, B. (1990) *Systems: Concepts, Methodologies and Applications (2nd edition).* John Wiley & Sons.

Wilson, B. (2001) *Soft Systems Methodology: Conceptual Model Building and Its Contribution.* John Wiley & Sons.

INDEX

1NF *see* first-normal form

2NF *see* second-normal form

3NF *see* third-normal form

a-priori algorithm, 145, 212–217

abbreviations, 84, 85, 201

access control

    authentication procedures, 99

    definition, xvii

    discretionary (DAC), xviii, 102

    mandatory (MAC), xix, 102–103

    purpose, 99

    for repositories, 127

    in SQL, 99–102

ACID properties, 106

aggregation, 150–151

Agricultural Metadata Element Set (AgMES), 89

Ajax (Asynchronous JavaScript and XML), 164–165

aliases, 81

alternate keys, 49

application software packages

    data management and, 131–132

    meaning, 131

association rules, 212–217

asynchronous replication, 139–140

attributes

    in conceptual data models, 23–24

    definition, xvii

    naming, 199, 203, 204–205

    in relational data models, 39

audit trails, 99, 104

authentication procedures, 99

backups, 107

Barker, R., 19, 173

BCNF *see* Boyce–Codd-normal form

behaviour, of objects, 149

Bell, D., 102

Bell–LaPadula Model, 102–103

Big Data, 165

BINARY LARGE OBJECT (BLOB) datatype, 159, 160

BLOB *see* BINARY LARGE OBJECT

BMP format, metadata in, 89

bottom-up integration, 134, 137, 139

Boyce–Codd normal form (BCNF), xvii, 49–50

business intelligence, 141

    data mining, 145–146

    data warehousing, 141–145

    online analytical processing, 144–145

    reporting tools, 144

Butler Group, 91, 95, 97

C++, 151

candidate keys, 49–50, 105

CAP principles, 165–166

CASE *see* Computer Aided Software Engineering

catalogs, 121–122

category entities, 179

CGI *see* Common Gateway Interface

CHARACTER LARGE OBJECT (CLOB) datatype, 159

Chen Entity-Relationship Model, 175–176

Chen, P., 175

class, of objects, 149

class terms, 85, 204

    restriction of, 86

CLOB *see* CHARACTER LARGE OBJECT

cluster analysis, 146

Codd, E., 39, 183

collection types, in SQL, 153

columns

    definition, xvii

    generally, 15, 19

    naming, 53, 200–201

Common Gateway Interface (CGI), 164

completeness, 93, 95

Computer Aided Software Engineering (CASE) tools, xvii, 122–123

conceptual completeness, 95

conceptual correctness, 95

conceptual data models

    attributes *see* attributes

    concepts, 22–39

    database physical design and, 52, 53

    definition, xvii

    entity subtypes *see* entity subtypes

    entity types *see* entity types

    example, 19, 20

    metadata model, 206–208

    naming standard, 196–200

    notations

        Chen Entity-Relationship Model, 175–176

        compared, 19, 181–182

        Ellis-Barker notation, 19, 173–175, 177

IDEF1X notation, 37, 177–179

Information Engineering notation, 176–177

UML notation, xxi, 19, 179–181

relational data analysis and, 51

relationships *see* relationships

roles, 51–52

conceptual organisation of data, 15

constraints

declaring, 21

entity subtypes and, 36

exclusivity and, 37

integrity, 105

key, 105

containment, 150–151

controlled vocabulary, 86

corporate data models

agreement, 78

attribute-trawling approach, 72–73

co-operative development, 78

core business primacy, 74

coverage, 74–75

definition, xvii

development, 72–74

enterprise awareness, 95

future-proofing, 75–78

generally, 69–70

joining project/area models, 73

nature, 70–72

principles, 74–78

top-down modelling, 73–74

correctness, 93, 95

cubes of data

operations on, 144–145

structure, 143–144

data

conceptual organisation, 15

definition, xvii, 5

enterprise-wide view, 9–10

granularity, 147

information and, 4–6

layers, 109–111

multimedia *see* multimedia data

problems with, 7–9

data administration

definition, xvii, 63–64

skills, 233–234

tasks, 82

data cache, 120

data clustering, 55, 120

data control language (DCL), 100–101

data definition language (DDL), 100, 151

data definitions

aliases, 81

in database systems, 13

development, 61

elements, 80–82

format, 81

names, 81

ownership, xviii, 81–82

significance statements, 81

stewardship, xviii, 82

synonyms, 81

valid operations, 81, 83

valid values, 81, 83

validation criteria, 81, 83

data dictionaries

CASE tools and, 121, 122–123

definition, xvii, 206

metadata models, 211

Data Dictionary System (DDS), 211

data governance, xvii, 67

data independence

logical, 13, 17

physical, 13, 14, 17

data integrity

entity integrity, 105

purpose, 104–105

quality and, 105

referential integrity, 105

using constraints, 105

data management

activities/deliverables, 60–63

benefits, 11, 64–65

as business issue, 10–11, 57–58, 62–63

definition, xvii, 57

education about, 60

effects of not having, 58–59

as information service, 62

international standards, 236–238

policy/strategy, xxv, 60–61

qualifications, xxv

relationship with information management, 63

responsibilities, 59–60

roles within, 63–64

software packages and, 131–132

support for system development, 61–62

data manipulation language (DML), 100

data marts, 142, 143

data mining

a-priori algorithm, 145, 212–217

cluster analysis, 146

definition, xviii, 145

neural networks, 146

statistical techniques, 145

data models

conceptual *see* conceptual data models

corporate *see* corporate data models

definition, xviii

development, 19, 61

hierarchical *see* hierarchical model of data

multidimensional, 143–148

network *see* network model of data

quality, 94–95, 193

relational *see* relational model of data

data naming

abbreviations, 84, 85, 201

class terms, 85, 204

in data definition, 81

example convention, 195–205

modifier terms, 85, 204

prime terms, 85, 204

problems with, 85–86

purpose, 84

thesauri, 86

data ownership, xviii, 81–82

data profiling, xviii, 96–97

data quality

as business issue, 97–98

causes of poor quality data, 92–93

constraints and, 105

data models, 94–95, 193

data profiling, xviii, 96–97

definition, xviii, 91

dimensions, 93–94

importance, 6–7

improving, 95–98

issues with poor quality data, 91–92

in repositories, 127

TEN STEPS process, 97

Total Quality data Management (TQdM), 96–97

data recovery, xviii, 106–108

data security

access control *see* access control

audit trails, 99, 104

authentication procedures, 99

Bell–LaPadula Model, 102–103

definition, xviii, 99

encryption, 104

multilevel security, xx, 103–104

policy, 99

data stewardship, xviii, 82

data warehouses

architecture, 141–142

definition, xviii

description, 141

multidimensional model of data, 143–148

OLAP and, 144–145

relational schemas, 146–148

see also data mining

database administration

database performance, 119–120

database physical design, 117–118

definition, xviii, 64

education/training, 118–119

responsibilities, 117–119

skills, 234–235

technical standard development, 115

database development process

database physical design, 19–22

information requirement analysis, 17–19

overview, 17–22

database logs, 107, 120

database management systems (DBMS)

definition, xviii

functions, 14–15, 55

generally, 13, 14

management, 118

security features, 99–100, 104

database object privileges, 101

database performance *see* performance

database physical design

conceptual data models and, 19–22, 52

first-cut design, 53–54

optimised design, 54–55

role of database administrator, 117–118

databases

advantages, 14

definition, xviii

description, 13

design for quality, 92–93

types of failure, 106–107

DATALINK datatype, 159, 160

datatypes

definition, xviii

generally, 54

structured types as, 155

Date, C., 135

DBMS *see* database management system

deadlocks, 120

denormalisation, 55, 120

dependent entities, 178

dice operation, 145

direct access, 12

directories, 121–122

discretionary access control (DAC), xviii, 102

disk mirroring, 107–108

distributed databases

availability, 135

bottom-up integration, 134, 137, 139

fragmentation/partitioning, 136–137

fundamental principle, 135

objectives, 135–136

rationale, 134–135

reliability, 135

replication management, 139–140

schemas, 135

top-down distribution, 134, 136–137

document stores, 166

Document Type Definition (DTD), 223

DoDAF, 65

domains

datatypes and, 54

definition, xviii–xix, 39

naming, 198, 202

drill-down (de-aggregation) operation, 145

DTD *see* Document Type Definition

Dublin Core, 88

duplication of data, 7–8

see also replication

edge tables, 230, 231

education/training

for database administrators, 118–119

for repository users, 127

Ellis, H., 173

Ellis-Barker notation, 19, 173–175, 177

embedded metadata, 89

encapsulation, 150

encryption, 104

encyclopaedias, 121, 122–123

English, L.P., 96

enterprise architecture

data management and, 65–66

definition, xix

frameworks, 65

enterprise awareness, 95

enterprise data models *see* corporate data models

enterprise resource planning (ERP) software, xix, 10, 58, 133

enterprise structure data, 110, 111

entities, xix, 22

entity integrity, 105

entity subtypes

as alternative to exclusive relationship, 37

in conceptual data models, 34–36

naming, 197

notations supporting, 177, 179

structured types and, 155

entity supertypes, 34–35

entity types

in conceptual data models, 22–23

definition, xix, 82, 84

in generic data models, 191

naming, 196–198, 202

subtypes *see* entity subtypes

supertypes, 34–35

EPISTLE (European Process Industry STEP Technical Liaison Executive), 192–193

ERP software *see* enterprise resource planning software

exclusive arcs, 36–37, 177, 179

eXtensible Markup Language *see* XML

extensible record stores, 166, 168

eXtensible Stylesheet Language (XSL), 224

extent, 151

external level schemas, 16–17

extraction, translation and loading (ETL) processes, 141

extranet, 161

file based data systems, 12

filegroups, 54

Finkelstein, C., 176

first-normal form (1NF), xix, 42–45

FOAF (friend of a friend), 169

foreign keys

constraints, 105

declaring, 21, 53–54, 155

definition, xix

in relational model of data, 45, 47

fragmentation, 136–137

Framework for Enterprise Architecture, 65–66

full replication, 139

Full-Text package, 160

function/procedure privileges, 100–101

galaxy schema, 147, 148

generalisation hierarchies, 179

generic data models, 191–194

global logical schemas, 135, 137, 139

granularity of data, 147

graph databases, 166

Gregory, W.W., 94–95

Hay, D., 173

hierarchical databases *see* hierarchical model of data

hierarchical model of data

limitations, 223

overview, 183–188

horizontal fragmentation, 137

HTML (HyperText Markup Language)

description, xix, 161

document format, 218–221

tags, 161, 218, 223

HTTP (HyperText Transfer Protocol), 161

hybrid fragmentation, 137, 138

hypercubes, 143

HyperText Markup Language *see* HTML

HyperText Transfer Protocol *see* HTTP

ICAM Definition Languages (IDEF), 177–178

IDEF *see* ICAM Definition Languages

IDEF1X notation, 37, 177–179

identifying relationships, 174–175, 178

inconsistency, 7–8, 9, 112

incremental backups, 107

independent entities, 178

indexes, 16, 55, 120

information

as business resource, 3–4, 10–11

data and, 4–6

definition, xix, 4, 5

importance of high quality, 6–7

sharing, xxv, 8, 11

Information Engineering notation, 176–177

information management

definition, xix

relationship with data management, 63

Information Management System (IMS), 183

information requirement analysis, 17–19

information resource management, xix

information systems, xix

inheritance

entity subtypes and, 35

in object oriented programming, 150

in object relational databases, 155–156

Integrated Database Management System (IDMS), 188

integrity *see* data integrity

internal level schemas, 16, 17

international standards, 236–238

Internet, the, 161

intranet, 161

Java, 151

JavaScript, 164, 218

JDBC (Java Database Connectivity), 164

JSON, 165, 166, 167

key-value stores, 166

keys

alternate, 49

candidate, 49–50, 105

foreign *see* foreign keys

in ODMG specification, 151

primary *see* primary keys

surrogate, 51, 191

knowledge bases, 126–127

knowledge discovery in databases (KDD), 145

LaPadula, L., 102

local logical schemas, 135, 136, 137, 139

locks, 120

logical data independence, 13, 17

logical level schemas, 16, 17

for distributed databases, 135, 136, 137, 139

McGilvray, D., 97

mandatory access control (MAC), xix, 102–103

many-to-many relationships, 32–33

mappings

logical/external level schemas, 17

logical/internal level schemas, 17

metadata model, 208–211

markup languages, 161

Martin, J., 176

master data

business processes and, 111

meaning, 111

problems, 112

master data management

definition, xx, 109

methods, 112–114

Master Data Management (MDM) Hub, 112–114

master-slave updating, 140

metadata

Agricultural Metadata Element Set (AgMES), 89

for describing document content, 88–89

for describing types of data, 87–88

Dublin Core, 88

embedded, 89

Learning Object Model, 89

meaning, xx, 109, 110

for multimedia data, 89

quality, 93, 94

storage, 121, 141

metadata models

for conceptual data models, 206–208

definition, 127, 206

for mappings, 208–211

for repositories, 123

for SQL logical schemas, 208

methods, 149

MODAF, 65

models see data models

modifier terms, 85, 204

multidimensional model of data

description, 143–144

querying, 144–146

relational DBMS and, 146–148

multilevel security, xx, 103–104

multimedia data

BLOB, 159, 160

CLOB, 159

DATALINK, 159, 160

definition, xx, 158

metadata, 89

packages, 160

storage, 158–160

multiple-part primary keys, 44–45, 46

mutually exclusive relationships

as alternative to subtypes, 37

notation, 36–37, 177, 179

n-ary relationships, 176

naming

SQL columns, 53, 200–201

SQL tables, 53, 200

see also data naming

native XML databases (NXDs), 163–164

network databases see network model of data

network model of data, 188–190

neural networks, 146

non-identifying relationships, 178–179

normal form

Boyce-Codd–normal form, xvii, 49–50

definition, xx

first-normal form, xix, 42–45

second-normal form, xxi, 45–46

third-normal form, xxi, 41, 46–48

normalisation, xx, 41–50, 139

NoSQL databases, 165–166

NULL, 21

NXDs see native XML databases

Object Data Management Group (ODMG) specification

attributes, 152

extent, 151

keys, 151

methods, 153

Object Definition Language (ODL), 151

Object Query Language (OQL), 151

relationships, 152–153

Object Definition Language (ODL), 151

object identifiers, 149, 151, 155

object orientation

aggregation, 150–151

behaviour, 149

class, 149

definition, xx, 149

encapsulation, 150

inheritance, 150

methods, 149

polymorphism, 150

state, 149

Object Query Language (OQL), 151

object relational databases

in SQL, 153–157

structured types, 153–157

object-oriented databases, 15, 151–153

objects, 149

occurrence data, quality, 93, 94

ODL see Object Definition Language

ODMG see Object Data Management Group

off-the-shelf packages, 131–134

OLAP see online analytical processing

Olson, J.E., 91, 92

OLTP see online transactional processing

one-to-many relationships, 27

one-to-one relationships, 31–32

online analytical processing (OLAP), xx, 144–145

online transactional processing (OLTP), xx, 144

ontologies, 167, 169

OQL see Object Query Language

ownership

data definitions, xviii, 81–82

data values, xviii, 82

packages

multimedia data, 160

off-the-shelf, 131–134

Pareto law, 132

partial replication, 139

partitioning, 136, 137

performance

causes of poor performance, 104, 119

design and, 118

improving, 17, 54–55, 119–120

PHP, 164, 218

physical data independence, 13, 14, 17, 55

physical database design see database physical design

physical file storage, 54

physical redundancy, 107–108

policies

data management, 60–61

data recovery, 106

data security, 99

polymorphism, 150

primary keys
    constraints, 105
    declaring, 21, 54
    definition, xx
    multiple-part, 44–45, 46
    in relational model of data, 41, 43–44, 49
primary names, 81, 195–196
prime terms, 85, 204
privileges, 100–101

qualifications, data management, xxv
Qualified Dublin Core, 88
query languages
    Object Query Language (OQL), 151
    XQuery, 224

RDBMS see Relational Database Management System
recursive relationships, 25
redundancy of data, 107–108
reference data, 109, 110, 111
referential integrity, 105
Reingruber, M., 94–95
relational data analysis, xx, 39–51
relational database management systems (RDBMS), xx
relational databases
    extracting data from XML, 230–232
    representing data as XML, 225–230
relational model of data
    attributes, 39
    definition, xxi
    description, 39, 183
    domains see domains
    foreign keys see foreign keys
    primary keys see primary keys
    relations see relations
    tuples, xxi, 39, 40, 41
relations
    composition, 39–40
    definition, xx
    normalisation, 41–50
    rules for, 40–41
relationships
    between relations, 45

in conceptual data models, 25–27
definition, xxi
identifying, 174–175, 178
many-to-many, 32–33
mutually exclusive, 36–37, 177, 179
naming, 199–200, 203–204
non-identifying, 178–179
notations, 181–182
one-to-many, 27
one-to-one, 31–32
recursive, 25
repeating groups, 41, 43
replication, 108, 137, 139–140
repositories
    architecture, 124
    as centralised information source, 123–124, 126–127
    definition, xxi, 206
    features, 124–126
    procurement, 125–126
    purpose, 121, 123–124
repository administration
    definition, xxi, 64
    responsibilities, 121–127
    skills, 235
representation terms see class terms
requirements, analysis, 17–19
Resource Description Framework (RDF), 167, 168–169
restricted terms, in naming, 201–204
roll-up (aggregation) operation, 145
rows, 15

schemas
    for data warehouses, 146–148
    definition, xxi, 13
    for distributed databases, 135, 136, 137, 139
    see also three-level schema architecture
scripting languages
    JavaScript, 164, 218
    PHP, 164, 218
scripts (SQL), 19, 21
second-normal form (2NF), xxi, 45–46
security see data security
semantic web, 167–169

sequential access, 12
SGML (Standard Generalised Markup Language), 161, 218
shredding, 230–231
significance statements, 81
'silo' mentality, 112
skills
    data administration, 233–234
    database administration, 234–235
    repository administration, 235
slice operation, 144–145
snowflake schema, 147
Spatial package, 160
specialisation hierarchies, 34
SQL
    columns see columns
    conceptual view of data, 15
    data control language, 100–101
    data definition language, 100
    data manipulation language, 100
    foreign keys, 21, 53–54, 155
    generally, xxi, 14
    multimedia data and, 159–160
    object relational databases and, 153–157
    primary keys, 21, 54
    privileges, 100–101
    scripts, 19, 21
    tables see tables
SQL/XML
    features, 164, 225
    mapping from relational database, 226
    shredding, 230–231
    XML datatype, 164, 225, 230
    XML publishing functions, 225–230
    XMLSERIALIZE function, 230
    XMLTABLE function, 230, 232
Standard Generalised Markup Language see SGML
Standard for Learning Object Metadata, 89
standards, international, 236–238
standby databases, 107
star schema, 146–147
state, of objects, 149
statistical techniques
    in data mining, 145
    see also a-priori algorithm

Still Image package, 160

structured data, xxi, 5, 158

structured query language *see* SQL

structured types, 153–157

   for multimedia data, 160

subtypes, entity *see* entity subtypes

supertypes, entity, 34–35

support threshold, 212–217

surrogate keys, 51, 191

synchronous replication, 139

synonyms, 81

syntactic completeness, 95

syntactic correctness, 95

'system high', 103

table privileges, 100, 101, 102

tables

   allocation, 54

   creation, 19, 21, 155–157

   definition, xxi, 15

   naming, 53, 200

   structured data types and, 155–157

tablespaces, 54

tags

   HTML, 161, 218, 223

   XML, 221, 223

taxonomies, 167

TEN STEPS process, 97

thesauri, 86

third-normal form (3NF), xxi, 41, 46–48

three-level schema architecture, 16–17

TIFF format, metadata in, 89

timeout intervals, 120

TOGAF, 65

top-down distribution, 134, 136–137

Total Information Quality Management (TIQM), 96

Total Quality data Management (TQdM), 96–97

transaction activity data, 110, 111

transaction audit data, 110

transaction logs, 107, 120

transaction structure data, 109, 110, 111

transactions

   ACID properties, 106

   failures, 106–107

   stored in data warehouse, 141

transitive dependency, 47

tuples, xxi, 39, 40, 41

UML (Unified Modelling Language)

   as alternative to data modelling, 19

   class model, 180

   overview, xxi, 19, 179–181

un-normalised form (UNF), 42

Unified Modelling Language *see* UML

Uniform Resource Indicator *see* URI

unstructured data, xxi, 5, 158

update-anywhere updating, 140

updating, in distributed databases, 140

URI (Uniform Resource Indicator), 161, 168–169

valid operations, 81, 83

valid values, 81, 83

validation criteria, 81, 83

versioning, 113–114

vertical fragmentation, 136–137

views, for access control, 100, 101–102

virtual tables *see* views

web browsers, 161, 162, 218

Web Ontology Language (OWL), 167, 169

web servers, 161, 162

West, M., 193

wide column stores, 166

world wide web, 161

   architecture, 162–163, 165

   semantic web, 167–169

three-tier architecture, 162–163, 165

   two-tier architecture, 162

XLink, 224

XML datatype

   from XML publishing functions, 228, 230

   uses, 164, 225

XML (eXtensible Markup Language)

   common element definitions, 223

   components, 223–224

   criteria for valid document, 222–223

   as data source for relational database, 163–164, 230–232

   definition, xxi

   description, 218, 221–222

   DTD (Document Type Definition), 223

   extracting from relational databases, 163–164, 225–230

   native XML databases (NXDs), 163–164

   SQL/XML *see* SQL/XML

   tags, 221, 223

   tree structure, 222

XML publishing functions, 227–230

XML Schema Definition (XSD), 223

XMLAGG function, 228, 230

XMLELEMENT function, 228

XMLFOREST function, 228, 230

XMLSERIALISE function, 230

XMLTABLE function, 230, 232

XPath, 224

XPointer, 224

XQuery, 163, 224, 230

XSD (XML Schema Definition), 223

XSL (eXtensible Stylesheet Language), 224

XSLT (XSL Transformations), 224

Zachman Framework, 65–66